Routledge Revivals

Jean D'Espagnet's
The Summary of Physics Restored
(Enchyridion Physicae Restitutae)

Jean D'Espagnet's
The Summary of Physics Restored
(Enchyridion Physicae Restitutae)

The 1651 Translation
with D'Espagnet's Arcanum
(1650)

Edited by
Thomas Willard

Routledge
Taylor & Francis Group

First published in 1999 by Garland Publishing, Inc.

This edition first published in 2018 by Routledge
2 Park Square, Milton Park, Abingdon, Oxon, OX14 4RN
and by Routledge
52 Vanderbilt Avenue, New York, NY 10017, USA

Routledge is an imprint of the Taylor & Francis Group, an informa business

Publisher's Note
The publisher has gone to great lengths to ensure the quality of this reprint but points out that some imperfections in the original copies may be apparent.

Disclaimer
The publisher has made every effort to trace copyright holders and welcomes correspondence from those they have been unable to contact.
A Library of Congress record exists under ISBN:

ISBN 13: 978-0-367-19118-4 (hbk)
ISBN 13: 978-0-367-19120-7 (pbk)
ISBN 13: 978-0-429-20055-7 (ebk)

Jean D'Espagnet's
The Summary of Physics Restored
(Enchyridion Physicae Restitutae)

ENGLISH RENAISSANCE HERMETICISM
VOLUME 7
GARLAND REFERENCE LIBRARY OF THE HUMANITIES
VOLUME 1109

Jean d'Espagnet's
The Summary of Physics Restored (Enchyridion Physicae Restitutae)

The 1651 Translation
with D'Espagnet's *Arcanum* (1650)

Edited by
Thomas Willard

Garland Publishing, Inc.
A member of the Taylor & Francis Group
New York and London
1999

Library of Congress Cataloging-in-Publication Data

Espagnet, Jean D', 1564– ca. 1637.
    [Enchyridion physicae restitutae. English]
    Jean D'Espagnet's the summary of physics restored : the 1651 transla-
tion with D'Espagnet's Arcanum (1650) / edited by Thomas Willard.
        p.   cm. — (English Renaissance hermeticism ; v. 7) (Garland ref-
erence library of the humanities ; vol. 1109)
    Includes bibliographical references and indexes.
    ISBN 0-8240-7542-0 (case : alk. paper)
    1. Hermeticism—Early works to 1800.   I. Willard, Thomas.
II. Title. III. Series. IV. Series. English Renaissance hermeticism ; 7.
BF1600.E8713   1999
135'.45—dc21   98-35046
                                                      CIP

Cover illustration depicts the frontispiece from *Arcanum* (1650). Courtesy of the
National Library of Medicine, Bethesda, Maryland.

Printed on acid-free, 250-year-life paper
Manufactured in the United States of America

CONTENTS

Contents

LIST OF ILLUSTRATIONS

Illustrations courtesy of the National Library of Medicine, Bethesda, Maryland.

GENERAL INTRODUCTION

The study of the nature, origin, dissemination, and influence of hermetic thought has been an important subject of Anglo-American and Continental scholarship for more than thirty years. At present, despite the recent deaths of pioneers like Frances Yates and D. P. Walker, it continues to attract the attention of scholars internationally and in a variety of fields: literature, history, philosophy, religion, art history and iconography, and the history of science and medicine. Evidence of this interest is abundant and has taken the form of an increasing number of scholarly articles, monographs, and collections of essays; the organization of international conferences; and the publication of several specialized journals devoted to this subject. However, it is generally acknowledged that research in hermeticism suffers from an acute lack of reliable primary texts, a deficiency which this series is intended to alleviate with respect to the English Renaissance and seventeenth century.

English Renaissance Hermeticism is a series of new, authoritative editions of rare hermetic and alchemical texts which, with few exceptions, have not been reprinted since their original publication in England in the sixteenth and seventeenth centuries. It includes treatises written originally in English, as well as early translations of works by Continental authorities—past and contemporary—that were widely read and influenced English Renaissance thought and art in important ways. In addition to prose treatises, the series will include at least one volume of previously unpublished alchemical poetry.

Authors and titles to appear in *English Renaissance Hermeticism* have been selected because of their intrinsic importance and also to demonstrate the wide range of alchemical and hermetic thought that flourished in the Renaissance, even as the era of the "New Science" was dawning. For example, the physical transmutation of metals, explanations of the preparation of the philosopher's stone, iatrochemistry, Paracelsian expositions, varieties of spiritual and mystical alchemy, Rosicrucianism and Cabalism are represented. A partial listing of authors includes Basil Valentine, Jean d'Espagnet, Roger Bacon, Oswald Croll, Nicholas Flamel, Robert Fludd, Eirenaeus Philalethes and Hermes Trismegistus. Thus the series will include works that are among the least accessible and most important for interdisciplinary research, and are intended to comprise a core collection of texts which are vital as background to the study of Renaissance literature, intellectual history, science, and philosophy.

Primary place in this series will be given to treatises on *hermeticism* rather than *hermetism.* According to a scholar recently concerned with defining varieties of Renaissance occultism, the latter narrowly designates religious and philosophical writings attributed to Hermes Trismegistus and their interpretation throughout history. *Hermeticism,* more eclectic and broader in scope, refers to an "amorphous body of notions and attitudes deriving not merely from Hermes but also from the mystical side of Plato and his Neoplatonic successors and from such other esoteric systems as the numerology of Pythagoras and the Jewish cabala."[1] It is this syncretic body of knowledge, belief, and speculation that provides a basis for the theory and practice of magic, astrology, and, especially, alchemy with which most of these Renaissance writers are concerned.

Finally, volumes appearing in the *English Renaissance Hermeticism* series will have several features in common: all will be edited by scholars active in the field of hermetic studies; all will have new, reset texts carefully transcribed and verified against original editions (facsimile reproduction will be used only for title pages and illustrations). Texts will be edited conservatively,

---

[1]See Wayne Shumaker, "Literary Hermeticism: Some Test Cases," in *Hermeticism and the Renaissance: Intellectual History and the Occult in Early Modern Europe,* ed. Ingrid Merkel and Allen G. Debus (Washington: Folger Shakespeare Library, 1988), 293–94.

preserving old spelling (except for ordinary normalizations) and punctuation. All volumes will feature critical introductions and full scholarly notes, bibliographies, and indices.

Stanton J. Linden
General Editor

INTRODUCTION

On 17 June 1623, the Paris publisher Nicholas Buon received the imprimatur for a handsome quarto containing two tracts by an "anonymous author."[1] Buon dedicated the book to Prince Henry of Bourbon, saying:

> Here are two little tracts which promise great things—the first the reestablishment of natural science, the other the revelation of the secret of the philosophers' stone—and because they have fallen into my hands without the name of their author I have decided to dedicate them most humbly to you, so that they have the blessing of being approved by your admirable judgment.[2]

The book was a revelation, Buon told readers, as clear and complete as they could wish. The first tract restored the wisdom of the ancients, the sum of natural knowledge known as *physis*. The second illuminated the secret of later ages, the *lapis philosophorum*. The *Enchiridion PhysicæRestitulæ* (Handbook of Recovered Science) and *Arcanum HermeticæPhilosophiæOpus* (Secret Work of Hermetic Philosophy) gained a reputation for unusual clarity in a famously obscure subject. Books on alchemy had been the rage in Paris for the past decade, made popular by the legend of Nicholas Flamel,[3] but self-promoting *souffleurs*

---

[1]From the title page of *Enchiridion Physicæ Restitutæ . . . Tractatus alter scriptus Arcanum HermeticæPhilosophiæOpus* (Paris, 1623); reproduced in figure 1. The separate titles are hereafter abbreviated *EPR* and *AHP*. Section references (§) are to numbered aphorisms, common to all editions; page references are accompanied by parenthetical references to specific editions. For further details see the "Chronological Listing of Books Containing Works by Jean D'Espagnet," following this introduction.

[2]*Enchiridion*, sig. a2r-v. Translations are mine unless noted otherwise.

[3]See Laurinda Dixon's introduction to *Nicholas Flamel: His Exposition*, English Re-

(puffers) seemed to blow smoke in everyone's eyes. Here was a book that cleared up some of the mystery in a manner attractive to the seventeenth-century French mind. The main mystery was the author's identity.

His identity was established a quarter-century later when Jean Bachou translated the tracts into French. Bachou revealed that the mottoes on the separate title pages were anagrams:

> I discovered that each of these mottoes, and especially the lat-
> ter, is an anagram of Joannes D'Espagnet, believed to be the
> true name of the author whose book I wanted to understand.
> I concluded that M. D'Espagnet, President of the Parliament
> of Bordeaux, could in fact be the author of this work, which
> must give him immortal glory for having reestablished the phi-
> losophy of the ancients in its purity. Those who knew him,
> and his capacity, have given assurances of this.[4]

Buon may have known as much in 1623, for his bookshop "at the sign of Sir Claude and the wild man in the Rue Jacob" had published another book by D'Espagnet seven years earlier. However, it served the author's purpose to hide behind anagrams, just as it would later seem prudent for a Parisian woman to take the pseudonym Pauline Réage; for the alchemy in the *Arcanum* proved as vulnerable to public outcry in the early seventeenth century as the eroticism in her *Histoire d'O* (Story of O) would prove in the mid-twentieth century.[5] In some respects he is still hidden. "Espagnet's history is nearly as great an Arcanum as that of which he has attempted the solution," George Ferguson quipped in his bibliography of alchemy.[6] Very little is said about his life in most accounts, and the evidence about the public official from Bordeaux has little to do with the legend that has

---

naissance Hermeticism, no. 2 (New York, 1994).

[4]*La philosophie naturelle restablie en sa purété*, trans. Jean Bachou (Paris, 1651), sigs. a7v–a8r.

[5]See John de St. Jorre, "The Unmasking of O," *New Yorker* (1 Aug. 1994), 42–50.

[6]*Bibliotheca Chemica: A Catalogue of the Alchemical, Chemical and Pharmaceutical Books in the Collection of the Late James Young of Kelly and Durris*, 2 vols. (Glasgow, 1906), 1:249. Hermann Kopp's outrageously confused account of D'Espagnet's tracts is typical of errors that can creep into the work even of careful scholars; see *Die Alchimie in Älterer und Neuerer Zeit*, 2 vols. (Heidelberg, 1886), 2:341.

grown up about the author of the *Arcanum*.[7] I shall therefore tell his story first, then show how he placed his tracts in the alchemical tradition, how his English translators handled them, and how his reputation grew. After that I shall discuss the tracts themselves and this edition of their English translations.

The Hermetic Magistrate

Jean D'Espagnet grew up in a large house on the Rue Hâ in Bordeaux.[8] His father, Arnauld D'Espagnet, was a successful physician from St. Émilion, across the Garonne River from Bordeaux and a few miles farther inland. His mother, Jeanne Mestadier, was the widow of a mechanical engineer from Bazas, also in the Garonne district. As their only son, Jean inherited the family house and passed it on to his only son. (No daughters are mentioned.) The house was rebuilt in the eighteenth century and was eventually replaced. Some carved stones from an old building, now in the Musée d'Aquitaine, are reputed to bear D'Espagnet's cabalistic designs. The stones speak to his reputation in Bordeaux and suggest something about his origins.

The name Jean D'Espagnet (sometimes Jean d'Espagne) means "John of Spain" and indicates that his ancestors came from Spain. The motto affixed to the *Arcanum*, "Penes Nos Unda Tagi," not only conceals the name "Ioann D'Espagnetus" but reveals a connection with the one of the four great rivers of Spain: "I come from the moving waters of the Tagus." The

---

[7]Like Allen Debus, I have found the national biographies more useful than the scientific biographies; see *The French Paracelsians* (Cambridge, 1991), 209–10, and compare the evidence collected in G. Brunet, "Jean d'Espagnet," *Nouvelle biographie générale*, 15 (1858), 402–3, as corrected in J. Maxwell, *Un magistrat hermétiste* (Bordeaux, 1896), and supplemented in J. Domergue, "Jean d'Espagnet," *Dictionnaire de biographie Française*, 12 (1970): 1491, with the sketchy data offered subesquently in H.L.L. Busard, "Jean Despagnet," *Dictionary of Scientific Biography*, 4 (1971): 74–75. Also see the biographical data on D'Espagnet and his son in Cornélius de Waard, Mme. Paul Tanery, and René Pintard, eds., *Correspondance du P. Marin Mersenne, Religieux Minime*, 10 vols + index (Paris, 1945–72), 5:577–78 and 7:56, and Bernard Husson, ed., *Anthologie de l'alchimie* (Paris, 1971), 141–42.

[8]Some family members now use "Despagnet" or "Espagnet," but I use the form the author favored, "D'Espagnet."

Tagus was an auspicious place of origin for an alchemist, long renowned for its golden sands; Ovid wrote of "Tagus floating in his melted gold" after Phaeton let the sun's chariot veer too close to earth.[9] The river flowed past Toledo on its way from the central highlands to the sea at Lisbon, and Toledo was famed for cabalists and magicians like Virgil of Toledo. Perhaps D'Espagnet was descended from converted Jews, or *conversos*, who were driven out of Spain by the Inquisition. The French astrologer Michel de Nostradame (1503–1566) came from a similar background on his father's side, as did the essayist Michel de Montaigne (1533–1592) on his mother's. The new Christians were noted for their learning. Medicine was a common profession, followed by Nostradamus. Law was another, and the young Jean D'Espagnet turned to the law.

D'Espagnet was appointed a counselor, or court lawyer, in an act notarized in the Parliament of Bordeaux on 23 July 1590. He was certified, on his mother's oath, to be "approximately twenty-six years of age." A successful public servant, he was made President of the Parliament on 11 November 1601 (a position reserved by statute for men over forty years of age) and Counselor of State on 16 October 1602. In 1611, he became President of the Chamber of Edict of Nérac, and Jean de Baudier (or Bavolier) succeeded him as President of the Parliament. However, Baudier died after a month in office, and D'Espagnet resumed the duties for another four years, retiring on 10 December 1615. Awarded the title of Honorary President (*Président à mortier*) on 8 April 1620, he continued his legal practice as late as 1637. However, he considered himself retired from "*publick employments*," as he noted in the preface to the *Enchyridion* in 1623, and only then began to write in earnest.

D'Espagnet married Charlotte de Mangeau ca. 1694, and the couple had one son. Étienne D'Espagnet was born ca. 1596, became a parliamentary counselor in 1617, was married at the

---

[9]*Metamorphoses* 2.251; John Dryden's translation. The gold in the Tagus was roughly comparable to "all the tea in China" a few centuries later; see Juvenal, *Satires* 3.54–55, adapted in Montaigne's essay "On Presumption" (*Essais*, 2.17) and identified in *Les essais de Michel, Seigneur de Montaigne*, ed. Marie le Jars de Gournay (Paris, 1635), 503.

family house on the Rue Hâ in 1629, and had a son in 1634. On the basis of these public records, we may assume that Jean D'Espagnet was born no later than 1564 and died no earlier than 1637.[10]

We learn more about D'Espagnet from books published in his lifetime. In the last of these to appear in print, the ingenious Marie le Jars de Gournay addressed a verse epistle "*A Monsieur le President d'Espaignet, Conseiller d'Estat.*" In rhymed alexandrines, she recalled a journey from Paris to Bordeaux in the winter of 1594– 95. She travelled with D'Espagnet and his new wife, the former Charlotte Mangeau:

> Our friendship started when I went to see
> Montaigne's tomb, his daughter and family,
> Travelling with you, as you first led your wife
> Into the country of your ancient birthplace.[11]

Mademoiselle de Gournay (1566–1645) had written a fan letter to Montaigne that impressed him so highly he showed up at her door the next day, proposing that she become his adopted daughter (*fille d'aillance*) after the custom of the day. Gournay helped Montaigne's widow prepare the posthumous edition of the *Essais*, published in 1595. Her epistle to D'Espagnet has been called her "self-portrait." However, the main thing that she reveals about herself, and playfully asks D'Espagnet "to approve or censure," is her passion for alchemy:

> Alchemy is mine, but not its train of follies:
> To squander, deceive, believe unquestioningly;
> To expect a sea of gold, trumpet it endlessly.

---

[10]He is not to be confused with the Hugenot preacher Jean D'Espagnet (1591–1659), who wrote an *Essay des merveilles de dieu* (London, 1657); the author is identified as "Ministre de la parole de Dieu en l'Eglise Françoise de Westminster" (sig. A6r).

[11]The poem, first published in *L'Ombre de la Damoiselle de Gournay* (Paris, 1626), 1144, is reprinted in Mario Schiff, *La fille d'alliance de Montaigne, Marie de Gournay* (Paris, 1910), 107–13. Gournay's poem helps date D'Espagnet's marriage. The trip to Bordeaux is described in Marjorie Henry Ilsley, *A Daughter of the Renaissance: Marie le Jars de Gournay, Her Life and Works* (The Hague, 1963), 76-82. The poem is also discussed in F. Sécret, "Littérature et alchimie," *Bibliothèque dHumanisme et Renaissance* 35 (1973): 528–29; I owe this last reference to Didier Kahn.

I have claimed nothing, have spent very little,
Expect and owe less, hope without belief.

Her attitude toward alchemy becomes a metaphor for her approach to life generally, as she chooses between secrecy and candor, selfishness and liberality. The poem was written "nearly twenty years" after the journey, was not published until 1626, and was revised in editions of 1634 and 1641. A note on the line "Alchemy is mine, but not its train of follies" in the 1641 edition states: "This was so during the first impression of this book, but no longer." In the same year, Gournay published an essay about alchemy as a noble art, practiced by kings of France and men of quality. She confesses that she took it up nearly fifty years before and pursued it passionately for eight years:

> The first year, then, that I labored on this art cost me a certain amount, not greatly excessive and not from my inheritance, for my discoveries and labors. It was natural to spend more during this first year than in the others because I was ignorant of the conduct of this work. During the seven years following, or a little longer, I performed several operations, at a cost of eighty to one hundred sous altogether.[12]

From the poem and essay, we may suppose that D'Espagnet aroused Gournay's interest in alchemy during their two-week journey from Paris to Bordeaux, or that she aroused his. He was talking about alchemy even as a young man.

About the time Gournay wrote her epistle to D'Espagnet, he was busy with two commendatory poems for a book by Pierre de Lancre (ca.1555–ca.1631), a fellow senator of Bordeaux. The longer poem, written in Latin elegiacs, told the chilling tale of a witch hunt:

By Jean D'Espagnet,
President of the Senate of Aquitaine
and Counselor of his most dear and sacred Majesty's Chamber,
The Sorcerers' Contest
Wherein two magistrates of this senate, P. de Lancre

---

[12]*Les Advis ou les preseus de la Demoiselle de Gournay* (Paris, 1641), 509; quoted in Sécret, 528.

and D'Espagnet, chosen for an expedition into Cantabria,
rooted out the
sorcerers and set the truth strictly in order.

Recently leaving the curved coast of Spain,
Half running, half destroyed,
Witches returning to the perilous gates
Of their Queen Proserpine.
We helped them thither, the weak, wicked crowd
Poured out of Charon's cup,
Now fated by black stones picked from the urn,
Condemned to death.
I took joy that the cross redeemed me fully
From hosts of exposed demons,
From crafty lars, from witches at the crossroads,
Set to sweet rest.[13]

The poem continues in the same vein for another hundred and
one couplets and then concludes with a final reference to the
black stones and the speedy enforcement of the royal laws.

Both men were charged with the mission, as Lancre explained:

> The King, having been informed that his country of Labourd
> was heavily infected by sorcerers, commissioned a judge and
> a magistrate of the Parliamentary Court of Bordeaux, in the
> month of May in the year 1609, to investigate the crime of
> sorcery in the said region of Labourd and the surrounding
> area. The commission was given to Judge D'Espagnet, the
> King's Counsellor in his Council of State, and me.[14]

However, Lancre took a far more active role in the investigation than D'Espagnet did. We can hear the bureaucratic foot-
dragging on the senior member's part. D'Espagnet remained
in Nérac on business for several months after the letters patent
were issued on 17 January 1609, and even after a royal letter
urged the counselors to make haste; when they left in May, he

---

[13]Pierre de Lancre, *Tableau de l'inconstance des mauvais anges et demons* (Paris,
1612), sig. aa2r.
[14]Lancre, *Tableau de l'inconstance*, sig. ei1

insisted on getting back for the feast of St. Martin, in November; and before he reached the destination, the Labourd region in the Pyrenees, he accepted a comission to survey the waterways and islands between France and Spain. Lancre had to study the literature on witchcraft, which he mastered so quickly that he found a witch in Nérac before leaving for the Labourd region. He had to conduct the trials himself, without speaking a word of Basque, and had to rely heavily on the testimony of children. In a period of four months, he examined some five hundred sorcerers under torture and had most of them executed. Though critical of the Spanish Inquisition, which swept through the area in 1610, he was no less efficient. He claimed he could spot the devil's mark on anyone. Moreover, he wrote like an angel. His account of the Black Sabbath, illustrated on a fold-out plate, became a standard reference because it was clearer than any other.[15]

Espagnet also contributed a poem in French:[16]

Sonnet
of the same M. D'Espagnet to the honorable
de Lancre

So constantly you treat inconstancy,
    Lancre, you make us see the many changes
    Of demons, bizarre hosts of the universe,
In a second tableau that you paint for France.
But why? Do you not see how inconstant
    Those shadows are that hover at the edge
    Of the underworld, before this perverse people
On whom your judgments made just vengeance?
And now you assure, in a contrary way,
    That immortality follows their death.
    Your pen has given them immortal life,
And so another evil has been born,
    Thousands of witches, from the ashes, who
    For such a life would welcome even death.

---

[15]Jules Michelet admired the clarity of Lancre's style; see *La Sorciere*, ed. Lucien Refort (Paris, 1957), 2: 33-41 (book 2, chap. 4).

[16]Lancre, *Tableau*, sig. aaa2r.

Lancre's book was his second. He had ventured into print five years earlier with a treatise on universal inconstancy, a fashionable topic in an age of future shock; Montaigne's essay "On the Inconstancy of Our Actions" is a well known example.[17] D'Espagnet's sonnet seems ambiguous. It praises Lancre's efficiency and his style, but hints that Lancre has given immortal fame to the infamous. Even the Latin poem is ambiguous when we consider that D'Espagnet takes his references from Classical culture, rather than Lancre's work, and when we note that Lancre himself quotes poets as factual authorities. Roland Villeneuve, who has devoted a book to Lancre's campaign against witchcraft, remarks that D'Espagnet "ironizes agreeably" in the poem, accepting no responsibility for the "massacres."[18] Margaret McGowan, who has written at length on Lancre's rhetoric, notes that Lancre's changes in the revised edition are mostly stylistic and concludes: "His fertile imagination has conjured up a powerful world which gains authority from fevered accumulation of words and from the sheer weight of evidence produced."[19] Whereas Montaigne was skeptical of charges against witches,[20] Lancre thought skepticism dangerous and relied on intuition where reason could not go. D'Espagnet seems closer to Montaigne, not speaking out against the trials but perhaps entertaining doubts. Lancre's readers usually notice D'Espagnet's lack of interest in the trials and his conventional, non-commital praise of Lancre's performance.[21]

---

[17]Pierre de Lancre, *Traité de l'inconstance universelle* (Paris, 1607; 2nd ed. Paris, 1610). See Isa Dardano Basso, *L'ancora e gli specchi: lettura del* Tableau de l'inconstance et instabilité de toutes choses *di Pierre de Lancre* (Roma, 1979). Also see Montaigne, *Essais*, 2.1.

[18]Roland Villeneuve, *Le fléau des sorciers: La diablèrie basque au XVIIe siècle* (Paris, 1983), 77.

[19]Margaret McGowan, "Pierre de Lancre's *Tableau de l'Inconstance des Mauvais Anges et Demons*: The Sabbat Sensationalized," *The Damned Art: Essays in the Literature of Witchcraft*, ed. Sydney Anglo (London, 1977), 196. Carlo Ginzburg takes a kinder view of Lancre's learning, which in some ways anticipates modern anthropology; see *Ecstasies: Deciphering the Witches' Sabbath*, trans. Raymond Rosenthal (New York, 1991), 136–39.

[20]See Montaigne's essay "On the Lame," *Essais*, 3.11.

[21]McGowan, 198, n. 4; Nicole Jacques-Chaquin, ed. *Pierre de Lancre: Tableau de l'inconstance des mauvais anges et demons* (Paris, 1982), 39, n. 17.

D'Espagnet presided over the Chamber of Edict in Nérac
for three years. He so impressed the Mareschal of Ornano, Lieu-
tenant General of the government in Guienne, that he was offered
the furniture from a room where a former king of France once
stayed. D'Espagnet asked only to have the manuscript he found
in the king's cabinet. He took it to be an unfinished treatise that
the king wrote for his son, and he undertook to prepare it for
the press. The work was published in 1616 by Buon, who would
later publish the anonymous tracts on alchemy. The title page
told the story of D'Espagnet's discovery:[22]

THE ROSARY
OF WARS COMPOSED
BY THE LATE KING LOUIS
XI under this title:
For
his son Charles, the Dauphin,
Published from the manuscript found at
the Castle of Nérac in the cabinet of the King
by the Esteemed President D'Espagnet, Counselor
of the King in his Privy and State Councils.
And afterward a Treatise
OF THE INSTRUCTION
OF THE YOUNG PRINCE,
Written by the same President D'Espagnet
FOR THE KING.

In fact, the book had been published ca. 1489, in a rare edition of
which only two copies are known to exist; it had been reprinted
in 1522. Manuscipt copies at the Bibliothèque Nationale contain the real author's name in an anagram: Pierre Choînet or
perhaps Étienne Porchier.[23] D'Espagnet recognized the literary
and historical merit. He preserved the old language and spelling,

---

[22]*Rozier des guerres* (Paris, 1616).
[23]Paul Needham, *Early Printed Books: Major Acquisitions of The Pierpoint Morgan
Library, 1924-1974* (New York, 1974), item 37.

and completed the old king's design:

> Having recognized that the design of King Louis XI, in his
> *Rozier*, was to shape the youth of his son the Dauphin, af-
> terwards his successor, and that he had nevertheless only
> touched on his principal points, I felt obliged in publishing this
> manuscript to add this supplement as a piece of his design.[24]

D'Espagnet dedicated his supplement to Louis XIII, who
succeeded Henry IV in 1610. Religious tensions had increased
under the new king, who did less to guarantee the freedoms
promised in the Edict of Nantes, and one may detect the gentlest
possible censure in D'Espagnet's words of advice.[25] He spoke of
his public service in the past perfect tense and showed that he
had his mind on other things. The alchemist Raymond Lull had
also written a *Rosary*, he noted.[26]

Buon published Lancre's revised exposé of witchcraft in 1616,
the same year as the *Rosary of Wars*. In 1617, Buon published
a book of princes, also prepared by Lancre.[27] The careers of
Lancre and D'Espagnet had run closely parallel thus far, but
diverged in the next decade. In 1622, Lancre finished a second book on sorcery, again published by Buon and attacking
the "incredulity" of those who doubted its threat to the social
order.[28] He warned Frenchmen to shun demonic messages wher-
ever they appeared, whether in Virgil or in modern-day wizards.
He was quoted, inevitably, as an authority on the dangers of
sorcery. Some intellectuals thought this was all terribly *passé*.
The learned young Gabriel Naudé, a member of the scientific
circle that included René Descartes and Marin Mersenne, wrote
a lengthy defense of "great men who have been falsely suspected
of magic." Naudé said he undertook the project after coming
across a tract of 1624 that echoed Lancre's warnings word for

---

[24]*Rozier des guerres*, sig. F5v.

[25]For a good overview of the upheavals in religion and thought, see Stephen Toulmin,
Cosmopolois: The Hidden Agenda of Modernity (New York, 1990), chap. 2.

[26]*Rozier des Gverres*, sigs. A4v and E4v. D'Espagnet apparently refers to the *Rosarium Philosophorum*, usually attributed to Arnold of Villanova.

[27]Pierre de Lancre, *Livre des princes* (Paris, 1617).

[28]Pierre de Lancre, *L'incredulité et mescreance du sortilege plainement convaincue*
(Paris, 1622).

word.[29] Lancre replied with a third book on sorcery, offering further ways to spot witches and get rid of them.[30] He died soon after, forever associated with the witch hunts of an earlier day. Meanwhile, D'Espagnet was making friends in the scientific circle where Lancre was spurned.

From his early (and apparently abiding) interest in alchemy, D'Espagnet went on to study other sciences. He and his son collected mathematical manuscripts, and his son became a friend of Pierre de Fermat (1601-65), the great mathematician. Through Fermat, the elder D'Espagnet was in touch with Marin Mersenne, the scientific reformer. Another correspondent of Mersenne's identifies D'Espagnet as the author of *Enchyridion*.[31]

When Bachou made his French translation of D'Espagnet's *Enchiridion*, about a decade after the author's death, he ranked D'Espagnet with the progressive thinkers of Europe who had challenged the Aristotelian orthodoxy—with Telesio and Campanella in Italy, with Francis Bacon and Robert Fludd in England, and with Ramus and Descartes in France.[32] These may seem strange allies in retrospect, especially Bacon and Fludd, advocates of the New Science and the ancient theology. Reform took many guises in the seventeenth century. Bachou revealed the identity concealed in the anagrams, and we are now in a position to guess why they were well concealed.

The imprimatur for the *Enchiridion* and *Arcanum* was issued in June 1623, during what Frances Yates has called "The Rosicrucian Scare in France."[33] The pamphlets denouncing those Protestant Paracelsians, the Rosicrucians, took a page, at the least, out of Lancre's voluminous works. They claimed that the Rosicrucians were wizards and reported that several had been condemned as sorcerers. One told of a Rosicrucian gathering in

---

[29]Gabriel Naudé, *Apologie pour touts les grands personnages qui ont esté faussement soupçonnez de magie* (Paris, 1625), sig. A5r–v. Other references to Lancre appear in the chapter on Virgil; see esp. 607–8.

[30]Pierre de Lancre, *Du sortilege* (n.p., 1627).

[31]Waard, Tanery, and Pintard, eds., *Correspondance du P. Marin Mersenne*, 1:xviii; 5:573–78.

[32]*La philosophie naturelle*, trans. Bachou, sig. A7r.

[33]Frances A. Yates, *The Rosicrucian Enlightenment* (London, 1972), chap. 8.

Lyons, using such standard accusations from witch trials as the ability to move about invisibly. Even the scholarly Naudé wrote on the Rosicrucian phenomenon. In such a climate, there was a big market for books on magic and considerable danger of being called a magician. It had been scarcely a decade since Lancre's account of magicians burned alongside witches had been a best-seller. It was only prudent for an alchemist to proceed with caution, concealing either his affinities or his name.

D'Espagnet left no doubt about his affinities. Among the ancients, he turned most often to Virgil and especially to the descent into the underworld, in the sixth book of the *Aeneid*, that gave Virgil the reputation as a necromancer. Among the alchemists, he showed special interest in Lull, whom Naudé had listed as a source for the Rosicrucians. He did not mention Paracelsus, but voiced special admiration for Michael Sendivogius, whose theories derived from Paracelsus and whose work was closely studied in early Paracelsian circles.[34] D'Espagnet described Sendivogius as "a noble Polonian not more famous for his learning then subtilty of wit [not named] whose name notwithstanding a double Anagram hath betraied."[35] Sendivogius had concealed his name in two anagrams, of which the better known is *Divi Leschi Genus Amo* (I love the order of the lamb of God). It seems no surprise to find that D'Espagnet's first motto, *Spes Mea in Agno* (my faith is in the lamb), echoes the motto of Sendivogius. The work of Sendivogius was popular in France. The first half of his *New Light of Alchemy* was translated into French five years after it first appeared in Latin; the second half was also translated and was printed with a tract attributed to Flamel.[36] D'Espagnet's work soon joined this lofty company.

---

[34]See Thomas Willard, "The Twelve Keys of Orthelius," *Hermetic Journal* 42 (Winter 1988): 14–24. Also see Rafal T. Prinke, "Michael Sendivogius and Christian Rosenkreutz: The Unexpected Possibilities," *Hermetic Journal* n.s. 2 (1990): 72-98.

[35]*Arcanum*, trans. Elias Ashmole (London, 1650), 11; Ashmole's brackets.

[36]*Cosmopolite ou nouvelle lumiere de la physique naturelle*, trans. M. de Bosnay (Paris, 1609); *Traicté de souphre*, trans. F. Guiraud, and bound with *Thresor de philosophie ou original du dessir desiré d. N. Flamel* (Paris, 1628). The catalogue of the William Andrews Clark library lists an English translation of Bachou's translation: *A Philosophical Account of Nature in General, and of the Generation of the Three Principles of Nature. . . . Translated from the French by John Digby* (London, 1722).

Between 1638 and 1647, D'Espagnet's alchemical tracts appeared in smaller reprint editions. These editions were prepared by "I.C. Chymierastes," presumably an alchemist with the initials "I.C." (or "J.C.") who considered himself "one who took part in the chimaera," that is to say, the concealed identity. There may be a further pun on *chymia* (chemistry) or *chemiatria* (medical chemistry). The editor expanded one aphorism in the *Arcanum*, adding details to the last formula. He wrote a note on a second aphorism, concerning the timing of the alchemical work, and drew up an astrological chart by way of illustration.[37] He also wrote an afterward on Hermes Trismegistus, the supposed inventor of the art of alchemy.[38] His work went into third and fourth "editions" (or printings). When the Latin texts were next reprinted, in the *Bibliotheca Chemica Contracta* (1653), they appeared with works by two of D'Espagnet's favorite alchemists: the poet Joannes Aurelius Augurellus, who wrote *Chrysopoeia* (goldmaking), and Sendivogius, the "noble Polonian" who hid his identity in anagrams. Bachou announced plans to turn the *Enchiridion* into French verse, in heroic couplets; the translation is otherwise unknown.[39]

English Translations

By the time that Bachou's translation reached French readers, in the spring of 1651, D'Espagnet's work was already available in English. A German translation of the *Arcanum* had appeared

---

Alan Prichard correctly identifies this as a translation of Sendivogius' work; see item 432.3 in *Alchemy: A Bibliography of English Language Writings* (London, 1980). Digby appears to follow *Les œuvres de Cosmopolite, divisez en trois parties*, trans. Antoine Duval (Paris, 1669–71).

[37]See Appendix II and figure 10.

[38]See Appendix I.

[39]*L'Oeuvre secret de la philosophie d' Hermès precédé de la philosophie naturelle restitué*, trans. Lefebvre-Desagues, (Paris, 1972), 23. Numerous prose transcriptions of both works exist in manuscript collections. Some are in Latin (e.g., Narbonne MS 18[5]), some in French (e.g., Rome, Bibliotheca della'Accademia dei Lincei MSS. Verginelli-Rota 40-41, some even in Italian (e.g., Glasgow University MS. Ferguson 56). I owe these references to Adam McLean.

in Amsterdam in 1647, the same year as the last reissue of Chymierastes' edition. Then, in March of 1650, Elias Ashmole came across the *Enchiridion* and *Arcanum* in the "amended" Latin edition of 1638-42.[40] Ashmole had just finished translating the "chemical collections" of Arthur Dee, and was impressed by parallels in the *Arcanum.*[41] *"Finding it a piece of very* Eminent Learning *and* Regard," he said, "*I adventured to translate it likewise and perswaded the* Printer *to joyn them into one* Book."[42] He made the translation in less than a month, for it was in the bookshops by April 12, the date recorded by the stationer George Thomason on the title page of his personal copy.[43] Ashmole described the *Arcanum* as "*The Work of a concealed Author,*" but he worked out the anagram in a manuscript note as "Johann Despagnetus."[44]

An English translation of the *Enchiridion* appeared in 1651 with the variant spelling *Enchyridion.*[45] It had no introduction, and did not name the translator, but there is good reason to think that it was prepared by John Everard (1575–ca.1650). Most famous for his translation of the *Corpus Hermeticum,*[46] Everard was a collector and translator of alchemical manuscripts. Several of these manuscripts came into the possession of Elias Ashmole, who described him as "a laborious searcher into this mysterious learning."[47] Nominally Anglican, he was impris-

[40]See figure 6.

[41]See figures 4 and 5.

[42]*Arcanum*, trans. Elias Ashmole (London, 1650), sig. A8v. See Appendix III and Charles Webster, "Elias Ashmole," *Dictionary of Scientific Biography*, 1 (1970): 316–18. Dee's *Fasciculus Chemicus* has been edited for the English Renaissance Hermeticism series by Lyndy Abraham.

[43]British Library shelfmark E.1325(1). Available in the Thomason Tracts collection from University Microfilms, reel 176.

[44]MS. Ashmolean 1374, fol. 86; cited in C.H. Josten, *Elias Ashmole (1617-1692): His Autobiographical and Historical Notes, His Correspondence, and Other Contemporary Sources Relating to his Life and Work*, 5 vols. (Oxford, 1966), 2:524n7. Josten prints the forty-one names on Ashmole's distribution list, which does not include Dee's (2:513-21).

[45]See figure 3.

[46]*The Divine Pymander of Hermes Mercurius Trismegistus*, trans. Dr. [John] Everard (London, 1650); 2nd ed.(London, 1657).

[47]Josten 2:733 and n6.

oned for heresy under James I, and so frequently that the king said he should be called "never-out." Under Charles I, he was fined repeatedly for unorthodox views: Anabaptist, Antinomian, Familist.[48] The first hint that Everard made the translation comes from Samuel Hartlib, a reformer in all things and the father-in- law of a hopeful alchemist. Hartlib heard that the "Enchiridion Physicae of Despagne" was an important source on the alchemical mystery.[49] In 1651, he noted that Everard had translated the *Enchyridion*.[50] A quarter-century later, the great occult publisher William Cooper noted in his *Catalogue of Chymicall Books* that the *Enchyridion* was "Trans. by Dr. Joh. Everard."[51]

D'Espagnet's work was readily available to readers in the Enlightenment, in the Latin anthologies of Nathan Aubigné de la Fosse (1653, 1673) and Jean-Jacques Manget (1702), and the German anthology of Friedrich Roth-Scholz (1728– 32).[52] A few aphorisms of the English Arcanum were included in Francis Barrett's *Lives of the Alchymistical Philosophers* (1814).[53] The entire *Arcanum* was revised a century ago by W. Wynn Westcott as volume one of his ambitious Collectanea Hermetica series "because since its first publication in 1623, in the Latin language, no alchymic tract has been more widely read, and no other has been so often reprinted." Westcott's revision might be called a bowdlerization, for he thought that "the language was more forcible and plain than our present delicate manners would appreciate." He thus changed "Moon" back to "Luna" and omitted some detail about the lunar work:

first of all (being ravished with love) she climbs up unto the

---

[48]Christopher Hill, *The World Turned Upside Down* (London, 1972), 149.

[49]Samuel Hartlib, "Ephemerides," Sheffield University MS, 1648, T–V7. I have used the typewritten transcript prepared by G.H. Turnbull.

[50]"Ephemerides," 1651, A–B4.

[51]William Cooper, *The Catalogue of Chymicall Books* (London, 1675), sig. B2r; Cooper did not make the attribution in his earlier catalogue of 1673, but did so in the later edition of 1688.

[52]*Deutsches Theatrum Chemicum*, ed. Friedrich Roth-Scholz, 3 vols. (Nürnberg, 1728-32), 3:823–912.

[53]Alan Pritchard, *Alchemy*, items 50.1 and 445.2.

male untill she hath wrested from him the utmost delights of Venus, and fruitful seed: nor doth she desist from her embraces, till that being great with childe, she slips away gently.[54]

Westcott was a founder of the Hermetic Order of the Golden Dawn and deposited a copy of his edition in the library of the order's London lodge. One industrious reader restored Ashmole's original words. The reader was most likely a lodge member, and R.A. Gilbert, who now owns the copy, likes to think that it was W.B. Yeats.[55]

Immortal Glory

When Bachou identified "M. d'Espagnet, President of the Senate of Bordeaux" as the author of the *Enchyridion*, he added that D'Espagnet deserved *vne gloire immortelle* for having reestablished the philosophy of the ancients. Opinion certainly ran high, at home and abroad. Pierre Borel noted the claim for D'Espagnet, "President of the Burgundians," in the first bibliography of alchemy to appear in any modern language, though he was not sure that D'Espagnet wrote both tracts.[56] Charles Sorel, claiming to be the "premier historian of France" though better known to posterity for his comedies, discussed D'Espagnet alongside Ramus and Descartes in a book "on the perfection of mankind." He cited the *Enchiridion* in Bachou's translation and confirmed Bachou's estimation:

---

[54]*Arcanum*, trans. Ashmole (1650), 22; *Arcanum*, ed. [W. Wynn Westcott] (London, 1891), 7, 9. A recent reissue (1988) follows Westcott's edition; it omits the preface but preserves obvious spelling errors like "sendete" for "sendeth" in the same aphorism.

[55]R.A. Gilbert, "The Quest of the Golden Dawn: A Cautionary Tale," *Cauda Pavonis*, 8, no. 1 (Spring 1989): 5–6. I am grateful to Mr. Gilbert for sending a photocopy of the annotated text.

[56]Pierre Borel, *Bibliotheca Chimica; seu, Catalogus Librorum Philosophicorum Hermeticorum* (Paris, 1654), 13–14 and 86. Borel's claim that the *Enchiridion* was the work of an imperial chevalier (*eques imperialis*) may have owed something to D'Espagnet's hand in publishing the *Rozier des guerres*. Roth-Scholz reported the remark and added that it was not easy to believe; *Deutsches Theatrum Chemicum*, 3: 822–23.

One could say that this is the first book to have appeared in France that offers a natural philosophy completely contrary to Aristotle's, although the author pretends he is simply reestablishing the ancient philosophy. If anything, there are too many things of his own invention.[57]

Sorel noticed D'Espagnet's design "to make the new philosophy speak to chemical concerns" and conceded that the general prejudice about the philosophers' stone as a mere chimera would weigh against the book "were it not for the fine manner of explication which has given it a [favorable] reputation."[58] Before the century was out, Descartes' biographer, Pierre Bayle, wrote a glowing entry on D'Espagnet for his great historical dictionary. D'Espagnet was "one of the learned men of the seventeenth century," Bayle wrote. "He sampled the new philosophy, and his works show its public progress."[59]

In England, the popular alchemical writer Thomas Vaughan told his readers: "As for *Authors*, I wish thee to trust no *moderns*, but *Michael Sendivow*, and that other of *Physica Restituta*, especially his *first Aphoristicall part*."[60] Vaughan included a marginal reference to the *Enchiridion* in the same volume.[61] Samuel Butler, who modelled his character of "An Hermetical Philosopher" on Vaughan, remarked that Vaughan was "very impartial to himself; for in forbidding his Disciples to read any modern Books, but only Sendivogius and *Enchyridion PhysicæRestitutæ*, he does Justice on his own Works, and very ingeniously shows us how they are best to be understood."[62] Jonathan Swift, who read Butler carefully and learned from him, associated Vaughan with those who would read nothing but Sendi-

---

[57]Charles Sorel, *De la perfection de l'homme* (Paris, 1655), 249. Sorel had written a book *Des talismans* (Paris, 1636), inspired by the occultist Jacques Gaffarel.

[58] *De la perfection*, 250.

[59]Pierre Bayle, *Dictionaire historique et critique*, 4 vols. (Rotterdam, 1697), 2:407. Bayle's careful attention to each of D'Espagnet's works is the real mark of his admiration; he notes the sources and influence of D'Espagnet's non-alchemical work (408).

[60]*Anima Magica Abscondita* (London, 1650), 55.

[61]*Anima Magica Abscondita* (London, 1650), 55.

[62]Samuel Butler, *Characters and Passages from Note-Books*, ed. A.R. Waller (Cambridge, 1908), 99.

vogius and other moderns. Swift had the hack author of *A Tale of a Tub* complain of Homer that "he seems to have read but very superficially, either *Sendivogius, Behman,* or *Anthroposophia Theomagica*," the last being a tract by Vaughan.[63]

The American alchemist who wrote as Eirenaeus Philalethes also had kind words for D'Espagnet's book. In a dream vision, he received a copy from Nature herself:

> THen I lift up mine eyes, and behold I saw *Nature* as a Queen gloriously adorned, sitting upon her Throne, and in her hand a fair Book, which was called *Philosophy Restored to its Primitive Purity*; whom with low submission I did obeysance to, and she graciously took notice of me, and gave me this Book to eat it up, which I did, and straight-way she had another of the same in her hand: Then was my Understanding so enlightned, that I did fully apprehend all things which I saw and heard.[64]

The dreamer eats the *Enchiridion,* as the prophet eats the sacred scroll (Ezekiel 3:1-3; Revelation 10:8-10). He is at once enlightened: *"my Intellectuals seemed as though the Candle of the Lord had been kindled in them "* (Proverbs 20:27). A voice assures him that he is lucky indeed:

> Then said the Voice, *Thou art happy in that thou hast seen her, more happy in that she gave thee that Book, which few in an Age attain to; most happy in that thou couldest and didst eat it, which every one that hath it cannot do: She therefore whom thou seekest for, is gone into her retired Solitudes, and as a Legacy hath left thee two great Treasures, the Treasure of Riches, and the Treasure of Long Life.*[65]

As he wanders through the dream palace, the dreamer enters a room where alchemists walk about a talk and read by the light of "Fox-fire and Glow-worm-Tails." He tries to read D'Espagnet, but in vain: "I took out of my Pocket a small Book to see if I could read in it, it was called *Enchiridion PhysicæRestitutæ,*

[63]Jonathan Swift, *A Tale of a Tub,* (London, 1704), 116; §5. *"Behman,"* corrected to *"Behmen"* in later editions, refers to the German mystic Jacob Boehme.

[64]Eirenaeus Philalethes, *Ripley Reviv'd* (London, 1678), 103.

[65]*Ripley Reviv'd,* 104–5.

with an *Arcanum* at the end of it, and I could not read one word in it."[66]

An old alchemist, ruddy faced and bleary eyed, acosts the dreamer and praises the book, saying that it agrees with Sendivogius. He then reads a lot of nonsense from it, "such Processes that I had never heard of." The dreamer later finds that he has been trying to read by "the Light of Fancy, and not of Nature." One scholar suggests the old alchemist represents Vaughan, who also thought D'Espagnet and Sendivogius said the same thing.[67] But the old puffer is uttering a commonplace, which D'Espagnet himself encouraged. In another treatise, Eirenaeus praised Sendivogius and D'Espagnet, along with Flamel and Ripley, as the most useful of authors.[68] The point seems to be that one can read a book wrongly or rightly, depending on whether one is enlightened by fancy or nature.

English-speaking scientists also took interest in D'Espagnet. Writing from Paris in 1659, the future secretary of the Royal Society, Henry Oldenburg, told his friend Robert Boyle of "a nameless Encheridion physicae restitutae, wch I doe not dislike, supposed to be made of one Mr d'Espagnet of Tolose."[69] John Locke, who would become the Society's most famous philosopher, owned a copy of the *Enchiridion*.[70] Meanwhile, a secret society in Restoration England, modelled on the Rosicrucian manifestoes, required probationers to make a "serious study of the Bible and the Book called Ench: Phil: Restituta."[71]

---

[66] *Ripley Reviv'd*, 123.

[67] William R. Newman, *Gehennical Fire: The Lives of George Starkey, an American Alchemist in the Scientific Revolution* (Cambridge, MA, 1994), 222–27.

[68] *The Metamorphosis of Metals*, chap. 2, in it The Hermetic Museum, ed. A.E. Waite (London, 1893), 2:234.

[69] A. Rupert Hall and Marie Boas Hall, eds., *The Correspondence of Henry Oldenburg*, 13 vols. (Madison and London, 1965–86), 1:215.

[70] John Harrison and Peter Laslett, eds., *The Library of John Locke* (Oxford, 1965), under "Alchemia."

[71] British Library MS. Sloane 3667, fols. 29v–30r; discussed in Robert M. Schuler, "Some Spiritual Alchemies of Seventeenth-Century England," *Journal of the History of Ideas* 41 (1980): 295–96, and Ron Heisler, "Introduction to the Hermetic Adepti," *Hermetic Journal* 35 (Spring 1987): 34–41 (40). Schuler notes that Sendivogius was the nominal founder (303).

D'Espagnet's fame grew in the northern European states. The Danish alchemist Olaf Borch (1626–90) met D'Espagnet's son, who was about sixty years old and a senator of Tolouse:

> a fine man, erudite, a chemist, and one addicted to Lullius, who, in his opinion, had laid down the whole chemical science and in whose writings nothing but chemistry was to be found. I asked in private whether his father was not the adept who made his superior book public. I was left in suspense as to whether the father revealed anything to the son, considering the silence required by this study, or whether the son knew nothing for certain. Be that as it may, the father need have had no obligation to say anything to the curious that his golden book did not make public.[72]

Borch was left more than a little confused and concluded by paraphrasing D'Espagnet's epigram on his *librum aureum.* Meanwhile, the learned German profesor, Daniel Georg Morhof (1639–91), praised the *Arcanum* as elegantly written, easily understood, and clearly an important source for the mysterious Eirenaeus Philalethes.[73] Morhof's friend Johann Ludwig Hannemann (1640–1724), a professor of natural philosophy at Cologne, wrote a poem in Morhof's praise,[74] and later addressed Morhof's doubts about alchemy in a book-length commentary on the *Arcanum.* Whereas Morhof had followed Borel in doubting that D'Espagnet wrote both tracts, Hannemann relied on the account of Borch (as we know from his reference to Tolouse) and regarded D'Espagnet as the author of both: "a most excellent philosopher, of great industry and acute intelligence." Hannemann warned that he was not an adept himself; he had not penetrated the sanctuary of nature, but worked out the allegory with reference to works like the *Kabala Denudata* of Christian Knorr von Rosen-

---

[72]Olaus Borrichius, *Conspectus Scriptorum Chemicorum Illustrorum* (Havniae, 1697), 36–37. Borch mentions the connection between alchemy and Rosicrucianism a few pages earlier (32). Borch did not mention D'Espagnet in his earlier *De Ortu, et Progressu Chemicae, Dissertatio* (Hafinae, 1668).

[73]Daniel Georg Morhof, *De Metallorum Transmutatione,* in *Dissertationes Academicæ & Epistolicæ* (Hamburg, 1699), 293.

[74]In Morhoff, *Dissertationes,* 137.

roth, who had himself translated the *Enchiridion* into German.[75] Hannemann assured readers that D'Espagnet was sincere and candid and would not lead them astray.[76] Hannemann later wrote a commentary on the *Enchiridion* as well.[77] Hannemann's commentaries are cited in the *Deutsches Theatrum Chemicum*, where they promote D'Espagnet's reputation as a writer who could shed light on Eirenaeus Philalethes, if not on the *mysterium magnum* itself. The *Deutsches Theatrum Chemicum* was an improved translation of the *Arcanum*, making D'Espagnet available to Goethe's generation.

During the occult revival in the late nineteenth century, D'Espagnet was put forward as an exemplar of "the mystic side of alchemy."[78] He was an important source for Ethan Allen Hitchcock, the American general who claimed "that *Man* is the *Subject* of Alchemy" and quoted at length from Ashmole's translation of the *Arcanum*.[79] Hitchcock's English counterpart, the ingenious Mary Anne Atwood, makes no reference to D'Espagnet, but draws indirectly on his work through her beloved Thomas Vaughan. Her concern with the personal element of transformation is suggested in *The Chemical Wedding*, a novel based loosely on her life story, where the image of Beya and Gabritus joined in love is crucial to the plot.[80] Arthur Edward Waite, who pursued the Hitchcock-Atwood theory of a spiritual tradition in alchemy, made frequent recourse to D'Espagnet, none perhaps more interesting than a note in his "supplement" to Martin Ruland's *Lexicon of Alchemy*:

---

[75]Christian Knorr von Rosenroth, *Kabala Denudata*, 2 vols. (Sulzbach, 1677). Knorr's translation of D'Espagnet's *Handbuch der ... Naturkunst* (i.e., *Enchyridion*) is bound with his translation of Sir Thomas Browne's *Pseudodoxia Epidemica* (Frankfurt, 1680). Joachim Telle brought this to my attention.

[76]Johann Ludwig Hannemann, *Instructissima Pharus* (Kiloni [Cologne], 1712), sigs. 3r–4r, 190. A commendatory note from a German in Philadelphia, Pennsylvania, shows that D'Espagnet's reputation had reached the New World.

[77]Johann Ludwig Hannemann, *Synopsis PhiloshophiæNaturalis Sanctioris Illustrata id est, Commentarius in PhysicæRestitutæEnchiridion* (Tübingen, 1718).

[78]A.E. Waite, *The Secret Tradition in Alchemy* (London, 1926), 338–41.

[79]Ethan Allen Hitchcock, *Remarks upon Alchemy and the Alchemists* (Boston, 1857), 36; quotations cover 113-15 and 167-75.

[80]Lindsay Clarke, *The Chemical Wedding* (London, 1989), 320–45.

ALCHEMY — Authorities therein: Among later writings on the Hermetic science, there is a French Catechism of Alchemy which, as it is founded directly on a unique MS. of Paracelsus, is of very high authority. It says that to obtain a knowledge of the mysteries of the art, it is necessary to be acquainted with all the works of Hermes, which should be first studied, and their lessons put to heart. The disciple should then proceed in the following order with his reading: 1. The Passage of the Red Sea. 2. The Entrance into the Land of Promise. 3. Paracelsus, especially his *Manual*. 4. Raymond Lully, particularly his *Vade Mecum*, *Lignum Vitae*, Testament, and *Codicil*. 5. The *Turba Philosophorum*. 6. Denis Zachaire. 7. Trevisan. 8. Roger Bacon. 9. D'Espagnet.[81]

D'Espagnet is the final authority, as Paracelsus is the first; they both have claims in physical as well as spiritual alchemy.[82]

In the twentieth century, Hitchcock's theories were brought into psychology by Herbert Silberer, a member of Freud's Vienna circle. Although Silberer did not cite D'Espagnet, he drew upon Hitchcock and cited the Swiss psychologist C.G. Jung.[83] Jung went on to become the alchemist of the modern psyche and made frequent use of D'Espagnet.[84] He was principally concerned with the symbolism in the *Arcanum*, especially when it was drawn from classical mythology: Diana and Venus, Hercules and Jove. He also drew attention to an anonymous French alchemist whose work is translated in the *Theatrum Chemicum*. Some have identified the alchemist as D'Espagnet, and while they are probably mistaken, the work is sufficiently interesting to warrant an appendix (IV).

---

[81]A *Lexicon of Alchemy* (London, 1893), 339. This entry is from the "supplement" based heavily on the *Dictionnaire Mytho-Hermétique* of Antoine-Joseph Pernety (Paris, 1807). Compare the list of authorities in Pernety's entry on "Alchymie" (17–19), which also ends with D'Espagnet.

[82]See Arthur Waite, ed., *Lives of the Alchymistical Philosophers* (London, 1888), 19–21, 170. Waite notes Hitchcock's claims about D'Espagnet, but also notes D'Espagnet's claims as a physical alchemist.

[83]Herbert Silberer, *Problems of Mysticism and Its Symbolism*, trans. Smith Ely Jelliffe (New York, 1917).

[84]Jung discussed *AHP*, §42, 46, 48, 73, and 137 in *Psychology and Alchemy*, trans. R.F.C. Hull, 2nd ed. (Princeton, 1968) and *Mysterium Coniunctionis*, trans. R.F.C. Hull, 2nd ed. (Princeton, 1970).

D'Espagnet's name shows up regularly in books by "serious" alchemists. He was an important source for Julius Evola, who in turn is a useful commentator.[85] He was also a source for Eugène Canseliet, the disciple of the mysterious Fulcanelli, who used the rare first edition of D'Espagnet's tracts.[86] His name also appears in occult fiction. The protagonist of Michel Butor's *Portrait of the the Artist as a Young Ape* respectfully studies "le Président d'Espagnet."[87] Umberto Eco takes an epigraph from D'Espagnet to place the golden fleece, and his novel *Foucault's Pendulum*, squarely in alchemical tradition.[88] And the narrator of Evan S. Connell's novel *The Alchymist's Journal* cites D'Espagnet on Jupiter and Saturn, or tin and lead. "Splendid!," he says. "We strike our brow with admiration."[89]

Organization of the Texts

Although offered as numbered aphorisms, in the manner of Francis Bacon's *Novum Organum* (1620), D'Espagnet's tracts are carefully organized. The longer *Enchyridion PhysicæRestitutæ* (Handbook of Recovered Science) establishes the physical basis of alchemical transmutation. The accompanying *Arcanum HermeticæPhilosophiæOpus* (Secret Work of Hermetic Philosophy) describes the alchemical work itself. The first tract follows the course of creation, beginning and ending with God; the second follows the alchemist's quest from dream to realization. For D'Espagnet, the arrangement of information is an essential part of the information itself, especially since many books of alchemy are deliberately disordered to conceal information from the "vul-

[85]Julius Evola, *The Hermetic Tradition*, trans. E.E. Rehmus (Rochester, VT, 1995).

[86]Eugène Canseliet, *Deux logis alchimique* (Paris, 1979), 281–82.

[87]Michel Butor, *Portrait de l'artiste en jeune singe* (Paris, 1967), 45.

[88]Umberto Eco, *Foucault's Pendulum*, trans. William Weaver (New York, 1989), 353; see *Arcanum*, §138. Eco said he bought two thousand books, one-fifth of them rare, as he worked on the novel; Marshall Blonsky, "A Literary High-Wire Act," *New York Times Magazine* (10 Dec. 1989): 78.

[89]Evan S. Connell, *The Alchymist's Journal* (San Francisco, 1991), 86; see *AHP*, §78. Connell also paraphrases *EPR*, §1 (168).

gar" reader.

In "The Author's Epistle" to the *Enchiridion*, D'Espagnet explains how he came to write the tract. Having retired from public life, he turned to study and considered the "Errours of the Ancients." After debating whether to write and how much to reveal, he decided to err on the generous side. He begins the tract by discussing God (§1–5), Nature (§6–12), the first matter (§13–18), and the creation of the world (§19–21). He comments on each day of creation (§22–38). Then he considers the reciprocal relations of matter and spirit or light (§39–49). He discusses the elements in general (§50–58), then devotes separate aphorisms to earth (§59–63), water (§64-73), air (§74–89), and fire (§81–89), including under this last the sun and light (§90–93). He treats the sympathy and antipathy of the elements (§94–98) and the four qualities: "hot & cold, moist and drie" (§99–117). Here he establishes the image of the double wheel of opposites, generating and corrupting all living things.

D'Espagnet returns to the four elements in their combinations (§118–34). He observes that the elements interact by three "operations" in nature: "by Sublimation, Demission or Refusion, & by Decoction" (§135–42). He explores the relations of the macrocosm and microcosm, and of things above and below (§143–50). He discusses the *tria prima* of sulphur, mercury, and salt (§151–52), the doctrine of atomism (§153), and the three kingdoms of minerals, vegetables, animals (§154–59), all contained in the microcosm (§160–61). He next treats the relations of the body, soul, and spirit (§162–65), form and being (§166–71), and other such combinations (§172–86). He concludes that "life is an harmonicall act" and explores the harmonies of matter and spirit (§187–93). He maintains that fire and light are spiritual, not material, deriving ultimately from God (§194–201). He thinks of air as the ideal medium and bond (§202–6), and he discusses the bonds of actives and passives, ideas and senses (§207–13). He considers the radical moisture in all things (§214–25) and the radicals in nature (§226–31). Finally, he turns to the creation at large and to topics like celestial motion (§232–39) and the reaches of space. In an unusual statement for his time, he describes space as almost infinite (§240–44). In conclusion, he observes that God is perfected in the will and understanding of man, and says he has tried to expand this understanding (§245).

The tract has a circular quality. It begins and ends with God, moves through the creation to man, the microcosm, who is a reflection of the created world, or macrocosm, and who seeks God through the macrocosm. Indeed, the treatise has clockwork precision:

God
(§1–5, 245)
XII

Cosmos	Nature
(§232–44)	(§6–12)
XI	I
Radical moisture	First matter
(§213–31)	(§13–18)
X	II
Light of nature	Creation of the world
(§193–212)	(§19–38)
IX	III
Multiplication	Elements and
and re-creation	substances
(§172–92)	(§39–134)
VIII	IV
Threefold	Three wheels of
nature of things	natural operations
(§162–71)	(§135–45)
VII	V

Man, the microcosm
(§146–61)
VI

In the preface to the *Arcanum*, D'Espagnet addresses the "Students of Hermetick Philosophy," warning them about false alchemists and protesting that he has told the truth out of respect for the art and its true seekers. He begins the work proper with a series of caveats to such students (§1–15). They must be pure of heart and ready to devote all their energy to the art.

They are best advised to find "a faithfull Guide and Teacher," but can learn the rudiments from books if they choose wisely. D'Espagnet then discusses the Sun and Moon, i.e., gold and silver (§16–32). Because alchemy is perforce the art of transmuting metals, the student must necessarily begin and end with these materials, and must pay special attention to the laws of marriage, i.e., the principles of union. Next, D'Espagnet discusses mercury (§33–51): how the philosophers' mercury is prepared and what it is called. He is now ready to discuss the practice of alchemy (§52–82).

D'Espagnet describes the stages or "Keys" of the art and the colors and signs associated with each stage. At the end of this account, he likens the alchemical work to a wheel, or a wheel within a wheel, and describes "the Circulation of the Elements" during the process of transformation (§83–91). He turns his attention to the necessary equipment for the fire (§92–108), the vessel (§109–15), and the furnace (§116–18). He has now given the student all it takes to complete "the first work" of alchemy or "White Worke," and he gives a summary formula with time requirements (§119). He next takes the student through the second or red work, which entails production of the philosophers' sulphur and elixir (§120–36). The treatise closes with further advice on timing (§137) and a final warning to seekers of the golden fleece: "Speak little, Meditate much, and Judge aright" (§138).

The tract thus has an introduction (§1–15), a conclusion (§137–38), and three partitions: the material (§16–51), the first work (§52 119), and the second work (§120–36). Whereas the *Enchyridion* has a circular motion from God and back to God, the *Arcanum* moves from ignorance to knowledge, from discovery of the true matter to completion of the great work.

Note on this Edition

This edition reproduces Everard's translation of the *Enchyridion* and Ashmole's translation of the *Arcanum* with complete fidelity to the seventeenth-century editions. The original spelling, capitalization, italics, and punctuation have been retained, even the occasional interchange of i for j and u for v. Regularizations include ß=ss and ū=um.

Corrections in the text have been kept to a minimum; they are made only when something is clearly wrong and are indicated in the Textual Notes. I have kept the typographical practice consistent only to the extent that I have placed a period after every aphorism number and at the end of every aphorism, even when it is missing in the original. In the *Enchyridion*, the period appears after the aphorism numbers in the first 120 aphorisms, but is omitted thereafter; the fourth aphorism is not numbered at all.

I have found no significant variants among different copies of the 1650 *Arcanum* and the 1651 *Enchyridion*. Neither the 1650 nor the 1651 text is any credit to the printer's art; both include inverted fonts, broken fonts, wrong fonts, and missing spacers. Hyphenation at line end is lackadasical. Occasionally the wrong word is given, or a word is repeated where the context and the original Latin text clearly call for its antonym. Many sentences lack end punctuation. One recalls Benjamin Franklin's distrust of the "great Guzzlers of Beer" in London printing houses a century later. Rather than build a monument to such error, I have corrected it where I can find warrant. Some poorly inked characters— hyphens, commas, and the like—show up in one copy but not in another. Some misspelled words are spelled correctly in the catchword, and some missing words are provided there. Given choices like these, I have silently followed the better one.

The original edition of 1623 has marginal notes throughout. Because several identify sources, I take them to be the author's.

Because most have been left out of later editions and translations, I have chosen to place them in the commentary. I have
recorded the Latin marginalia in the capitals used in 1623, with
my translations in brackets.

Acknowledgments

I have based the text of this edition on copies of D'Espagnet's
works in the National Library of Medicine, in Bethesda, Maryland. The library's History of Medicine section includes extensive holdings in Paracelsian and alchemical texts, meticulously
catalogued and now accessible in that most Hermetic of spaces,
the Internet. The library staff offered pleasant working condi-
tions, and photographed the pages reproduced in this edition.

I checked my transcriptions against copies at the Folger
Shakespeare Library, in Washington, D.C. Stanton and Lucy
Linden checked the transcriptions against copies at the British
Library, Dr. Williams' Library, and the Wellcome Institute, all
in London; and copies at University Library, Glasgow. I am
grateful to them for their attention to the details.

Correspondents around the world have provided crucial information. I thank James Carscallen of Toronto, Allen Debus of
Chicago, R.A. Gilbert of Bristol, Didier Kahn of Paris, Adam
McLean of Edinburgh, Joachim Telle of Heidelberg, and anyone
else I have neglected to mention. At Garland, Phyllis Korper
has overseen the English Renaissance Hermeticism series from
its conception; Gary Kuris also took an early interest in the
project.

My labors here, as elsewhere, are dedicated to my wife, Mar-
ilyn, who is a spiritual as well as a pharmaceutical chemist.

ENCHIRIDION
PHYSICÆ
RESTITVTÆ,

IN QVO VERVS NATVRÆ CONCENTVS
exponitur, plurimíque antiquæ Philosophiæ errores
per canones & certas demonstrationes dilucidè aperiuntur.

Tractatus alter inscriptus
ARCANVM HERMETICÆ
PHILOSOPHIÆ OPVS:

In quo occulta Naturæ & Artis circa lapidis Philosophorum materiam & operandi modum canonicè &
ordinatè fiunt manifesta.

Vtrumque opus eiusdem authoris anonymi
SPES MEA EST IN AGNO

PARISIIS,
Apud NICOLAVM BVON, in via Iacobæa sub signo D. Claudij, & Hominis Sylueſtris.

M. DC. XXIII. = *1643*
Cum Priuilegio Regis.

Figure 1.   Title-page from the first edition of *Enchyridion* and
Arcanum (1623).

ARCANVM
HERMETICÆ
PHILOSOPHIÆ
OPVS.

In quo occulta Naturæ & Artis circá Lapidis Philosophorum materiam &
operandi modum canonicè &
ordinatè fiunt manifesta.

Opus eiusdem authoris ANONYMI.

PENES NOS VNDA TAGI.

PARISIIS,
Apud NICOLAVM BVON, sub signo
D. Claudij, & Hominis Syluestris.
MDC. XXIII.

Cum priuilegio Regis.

Figure 2. Separate title-page for *Arcanum* (1623).

Bibliography

I. Chronological Listing of Books Containing

Works by Jean D'Espagnet[1]

Lancre, Pierre de. *Tableau de l'inconstance des mavvais anges et demons, ou il est amplement traicté des sorciers et de la sorcelerie.* Paris, 1612. [Includes Espagnet's commendatory poems, "Pancrativm Sortilegorvm" and "Sonnet." Both poems appear in the revised editions of 1612 and 1613.]

Louis XI (attrib.). *Le rozier des gverres composé par le fev Roy Lo[u]is XI. de ce nom: Povr Monseignevr le Dauphin Charles son fils. Mis en lumiere sur le Manuscrit trouué au Chasteau de Nerac dans le cabinet du Roy par le Sieur President D'Espagnet, Conseiller du Roy en ses Conseils d'Estat & Priué. Et en suite un traitté de l'institvtion dv ievne prince, fait par le dit Sieur President D'Espagnet. Av Roy.* Paris, 1616. [Facsimile. Collection Zanzibar. Paris, 1994.]

Enchiridion PhysicæRestitutæ, in quo verus naturæconcentus exponitur, plurimique antiquæPhilosophiæerrores per canones & certas demonstrationes dilucide aperiuntur. Tractatus alter inscriptus Arcanum HermeticæPhilosophiæOpus, in quo occulta Naturæ& Artis circa lapidis Philosophorum materiam & operandi modum canonice & ordinate fiunt manifesta. Utrumque opus ejusdem authoris anonymi Spes mea est in Agno. Paris, 1623.

*Enchiridion PhysicæRestitutæ. . . . Tractatus alter inscriptus Arcanum HermeticæPhilosophiæOpus. 3rd ed. Paris: N. de Sercy, 1642. [British Library copy has a separate title page for *AHP*, dated 1638; the 1650 translation is based on this edition.]

---

[1]An asterisk indicates a book I have not personally examined.

*Enchiridion Physicæ Restitutæ. . . . Tractatus alter inscriptus Arcanum Hermeticæ Philosophiæ Opus. [Wellcome Institute copy has a separate title page for *AHP* dated 1647.]

Enchiridion Physicæ Restitutæ. . . . Tractatus alter inscriptus Arcanum Hermeticæ Philosophiæ Opus . . . Utrumque opus ejusdem Authoris anonymi. 4th ed. emendata & aucta. Rothomagi [Rouen], 1647.

*Das Geheimnüße der Hermetischen Philosophey. Im welchem die Verborgenheit der Natur vnd der Kunst ... geoffenbahret wird. Amsterdam, 1647.

Dee, Arthur. *Fasciculus Chemicus; or, Chymical collections, Expressing the Ingress, Progress, and Egress, of the Secret Hermetick science, out of the choisest and most famous authors... Whereunto is added, the Arcanum; or, Grand secret of Hermetick Philosophy.* Both made English by James Hasolle [anagram of Elias Ashmole]. London, 1650. [Includes *Arcanum; or, The grand secret of Hermetick philosophy... The work of a concealed author... The 3rd ed. amended and enlarged.* Reprined without *AHP* in the English Renaissance Hermeticism series; see Abraham under Secondary Sources.]

Enchyridion Physicæ Restitutæ; or, The Summary of Physicks Recovered. Wherein the true Harmony of Nature is explained, and many Errours of the Ancient Philosophers, by Canons and certain Deomnstrations are clearly evidence and evinced. [Trans. John Everard.] London, 1651.

La philosophie naturelle restablie en sa purcté . . . avcc lc traicté dc l'ouvrage secret de la philosophie d'Hermez, qui enseigne la matiere, & la façon de faire la pierre philosophale. Trans. Jean Bachou. Paris, 1651.

Bibliotheca Chemica Contracta. Ed. Nathan Aubigné de la Fosse. 4 parts in 1 volume. Geneva, 1653. [Includes *EPR* and *AHP* as parts 3 and 4.] Reprinted Bologna, 1673.

*Des vortrefflichen Engelländers Thomæ Brown, der Artzney Dr Pseudodoxia Epidemica, Das ist: Untersuchung derrer Irrhümer so bey dem gemeinen Mann und sonst hin und wieder im Schwange gehen.

Trans. Christian Peganius (pseudonym of Christian Knorr von Rosenroth). Franckfurt and Leipzig, 1680. [Includes *Curiser Tractätlein eines Handbuchs der wieder zu recht gebrachten Naturkunft darinn der Grund der gantzen Chymischen Wissenschaft enthalten.*]

*Das geheime Werck der hermetischen Philosophie, worinnen die natrlichen und künstlichen Geheimnüße der Matiere des philosophischen Steins, wie auch die Art und Weise zu arbeiten . . . offenbahret sind. Leipzig, 1685.

Bibliotheca Chemica Curiosa. Ed. Jo. Jacob Mangetus. 2 vols. Geneva, 1702. [Vol. 2 includes *Enchyridion PhysicaeRestitutae. . . . Tractatus alter scriptus Arcanum HermeticaePhilosophiaeOpus.*]

Deutsches Theatrum Chemicum. Ed. Friedrich Roth-Scholtz. 3 vols. Nürnberg, 1728–32. [Vol. 3 includes *Das geheime Werck der hermetischen Philosophie, worinnen die natrlichen und künstlichen Geheimnüße der Matiere des philosophischen Steins, wie auch die Art und Weise zu arbeiten . . . offenbahret sind.*]

An English Translation of the Hermetic Arcanum of Penes Nos Unda Tagi. 1623. With a preface and notes by "Sapere Aude" (initiatic motto of W. Wynn Westcott). Collectanea Hermetica, no. 1. London, 1893. [Reprinted without introduction. Edmonds, WA, 1988.]

L'Oeuvre secret de la philosophie d'Hermès précedé de La philosophie naturelle restituté. Trans. and ed. J. Lefebvre-Desagues. Bibliotheca Hermetica. Paris, 1972. [Reprint. Éditions Retz. Paris, 1977.]

II. Alchemical Anthologies

The Hermetic Museum Restored and Enlarged. Frankfurt, 1678. English trans. [by W.A. Ayton?]. Ed. A.E. Waite. 2 vols. London, 1893.
    The Golden Tract. 1:9–50.
    Nicholas Flamell, *A Short Tract, or Philosophical Summary.* 1:141–47.
    The Glory of the World. 1:165–242.
    The Book of Lambspring. 1:271–305.
    Thomas Norton, *The Ordinal of Alchemy.* 2:1–67.
    Michael Sendivogius, *The New Chemical Light.* 2:79–158.
    [Eirenaus Philalethes], *An Open Entrance.* 2:159–98.
    Michael Maier, *A Subtle Allegory concerning the Secrets of Alchemy.* 2:199–223.
    [Eirenaeus] Philalethes. *The Metamorphosis of Metals.* 2:223–45.

Theatrum Chemicum. Ed. Lazarus Zetzner and heirs. Vols. 1-6. 2nd edition. Strasbourg, 1659–61. [Facsimile. 6 vols. + introduction by Maurizio Barracano. Torino, 1981.]
    Gerard Dorn, *Speculativa Philosophia.* 1:238–76.
    Gerard Dorn, *Physica Genesis.* 1: 331–61.
    Gerard Dorn, *Physica Trithemii.* 1:362–99.
    Bernardus Trevisanus, *De Alchemica Liber.* 1:683–709.
    Aristoteles (attrib.), *De Perfecto Magisterio.* 3:76–127.
    Joannis Aurelius Augurellius, *Chrysopoeia.* 3:197–244.
    Raymond Lull, *Clavicula.* 3:295–303.
    Nicholas Barnaud, *Liber Secreti Maximi Totius.* 3:774–83.
    Nicholas Barnaud, *QuadrigæAuriferæ.* 3:790–849.
    Raymund Lull, *Theorica.* 4:1–134.
    Raymund Lull, *Practica.* 4:135–70.
    Raymund Lull, *Compendium.* 4:171–95.
    Gaston Dulco, *De Recta et Vera Progignendi Lapidis Philosophici.* 4:388–4129.
    Bernardus Penotus, *Canones seu Regulæ Decem, de Lapide Philosophico.* 4:414–16.
    [Michael Sendivogius], *De Lapide Philosophorum.* 4:417–56.
    Beatus, *AureliæOccultæPhilosophorum.* 4:462–512.

Hermes Trismegistus (attrib.), *Tractatus Aureus.* 4:592–705.
Turba Philosophorum. 5:1–52.
Kalid, *Liber Trium Verborum.* 5:186–90.
Senior, *De Chemia.* 5:191–239.
Guilielmus Mennens, *Aurei Velleris.* 5:240–422.
Philosophus Anonymous, *Instructio de Arbore Solari.* 6:163–93.
Tabula Smagardina. 6:715.

III. Other Primary Sources

Aristotle. *The Complete Works of Aristotle.* Ed. Jonathan Barnes. 2 vols. Princeton, 1984. (References are to Bekker numbers, given in the margins.)

——————————. *Aristoteles Latinus.* 7 vols, continuing. Leiden, 1953–

Ashmole, Elias. *Theatrum Chemicum Britannicum.* London, 1652.

Bacon, Francis. *The Tvvoo Bookes of Francis Bacon of the Proficience and Aduancement of Learning, Divine and Hvmane.* London, 1605.

Bayle, Pierre. *Dictionaire historique et critique.* 4 vols. Rotterdam, 1697.

Borel, Pierre. *Bibliotheca Chimica; seu, Catalogus Librorum Philosophicorum Hermeticorum.* Paris, 1654.

Borrichius, Olaus. *Conspectus Scriptorum Chemicorum Illustriorum.* Havinæ [Copenhagen], 1697.

——————————. *De Ortu, et Progresus Chemicæ, Dissertatio.* Hafinae [Copenhagen], 1668.

Butler, Samuel. *Characters and Passages from Note-Books.* Ed. A.R. Waller. Cambridge, 1908.

Cooper, William. *The Catalogue of Chymicall Books.* London, 1675. [See Linden under Secondary Sources.]

The Egyptian Book of the Dead: The Papyrus of Ani. Trans. E.A.

Wallis-Budge. London, 1895.

Ficino, Marsilio. *Opera Omnia.* 2 vols., continuous pagination. Basel, 1587. [Commentary on *Pymander* and *Æsclepius*, with translations, 1836–71.]

Fludd, Robert. *Utriusque Cosmi Historia.* 2nd ed. Frankfurt, 1624.

Geber. *The Works of Geber, Englished by Richard Russell, 1678.* Ed. E.J. Holmyard. London, 1928.

Gournay, Marie le Jars de. *Les advis ou les preseus de la Demoiselle de Gournay.* Paris, 1641.

——————. *L'ombre de la Demoiselle de Gournay.* Paris, 1626.

Hannemann, Johann Ludovic. *Instructissima Pharus in Oceano Philosophorum Ostendens Viam Veram & Tutam. Ad ophir auriferum, i.e. Commentarivs Hermetico spagyricvs in Arcanum PhilosophiæHermeticæ, authoris qui latet sub ænigmate Penes nos unda Tagi. Cum responsione & resolutione CVIII. questionum olim ab Excell. Morhofio autori propositarum.* Kiloni [Cologne], 1712.

——————. *Synopsis PhilosophiæNaturalis Sanctioris Illustrata id est, Commentarius in PhysicæRestitutæEnchiridion.* Tübingen, 1718.

Hartlib, Samuel. "Ephemerides." University of Sheffield Library.

Hermes Trismegistus (attrib.). *The Divine Pymander of Hermes Mercurius Trismegistus. Translated by that learned Dr. Everard.* Preface by J[ohn] F[rench]. 2nd ed., expanded. London, 1657. [First published 1650.]

Hippocrates (attrib.). *Del regime salutare.* Trans. Alberto Lodispoto. Roma, 1960.

Knorr, Christian, Freiherr von Rosenroth. *Kabala Denudata.* 2 vols. Sulzbach, 1677.

Lancre, Pierre de. *Du sortilege.* N.p., 1627.

_____. *L'incredulité et mescreance du sortilege plainement convaincue.* Paris, 1622.

_____. *Livres des princes.* Paris, 1617.

_____. *Traité de l'inconstance universelle.* Paris, 1607. [2nd ed. Paris, 1610.]

Maier, Michael. *Arcana Arcanissima, hoc est, Hieroglyphica Ægypto-Græca.* London, 1614.

_____. *Atalanta Fugiens.* Trans. Joscelyn Godwin. Grand Rapids, MI, 1989.

_____. *Symbola AureæMensæDuodecim Nationum.* Frankfurt, 1617.

_____. *Viatorum.* Oppenheim, 1618.

Montaigne, Michel. *Les essais de Michel, Seigneur de Montaigne. Edition nouvelle. Exactement corrigee selon le vray exemplaire. Enrichie a la marge du nom des autheurs citez, et de la version de leurs passages, mise à la fin de chaque chapitre. Auec que la vie de l'Autheur.* Ed. Marie le Jars de Gournay. Paris, 1635.

Morhof, Daniel Georg. *Dissertationes Academicæ& Epistolicæquius rariora quaedam argumenta erudite.* Hamburg, 1699. [Includes *De Metallorum Transmutatione.*]

Morienus. *A Testament of Alchemy, Being the Revelations of Morienus, Ancient Adept and Hermit of Jerusalem to Khalid ibn Uazid ibn Mu'awiyya, King of the Arabs of the Divine Secrets of the Magisterium and Accomplishment of the Alchemical Art.* Trans. Lee Stavenhagen. Hanover, NH, 1974.

Naudé, Gabriel. *Apologie pour touts les grands personnages que one esté faussement soupçonné de magie.* Paris, 1625.

Oracles Chaldaïques. Ed. and trans. Édouard des Places, S.J. Paris, 1971.

Bibliography

Pernety, Antoine-Joseph. *Dictionnaire Mytho-Hermétique.* Paris, 1807. [Freely adapted in the supplement to Ruland.]

Philalethes, Eirenaeus. *Ripley Reviv'd.* London, 1678.

Plato. *The Collected Dialogues of Plato, Including the Letters.* Ed. Edith Hamilton and Huntington Cairns. New York, 1961. [References are to Stephanus numbers, given in the margins.]

Rosarium Philosophorum. Francoforti, 1550. [Facsimile reprint with a German trans. by Lutz Claren and Joachim Huber and annotations by Joachim Telle. 2 vols. Weinheim, 1992.]

Ruland, Martin. *A Lexicon of Alchemy.* English trans. [by Julius Kohn?]. Ed. Arthur E. Waite. London, 1893.

Sendivogius, Michael. *Dialogue Mercurii Alchymisticæet Naturæ... Auctore eo, Qui Divi Leschi Genus Amat.* Kiloni [Cologne], 1607.

——————. *Cosmopolite ou nouvelle lumiere de la physique naturelle. Traduit nouvellement de Latin en Franois* [by M. de Bosnay]. Paris, 1609.

——————. *A Philosophical Account of Nature in General, and of the Generation of the Three Principles of Nature: Viz., Mercury, Sulphur, and Salt, out of the Four Elements. Translated from the French by John Digby.* London, 1722.

——————. *Traicté du souphre.* Trans. F. Guiraud. Paris, 1628. [Bound with a reprint of the *Nouvelle lumiere* and with *Thresor de philosophie ou original du desir desiré de N[icholas] Flamel.*]

Sorel, Charles. *De la perfection de l'homme.* Paris, 1655.

——————. *Des talismans.* Paris, 1636.

Swift, Jonathan. *A Tale of a Tub.* London, 1704.

Vaughan, Thomas. *Anthroposophia Theomagica* and *Anima Magica Abscondita.* London, 1650.

_____. "To the Reader." *Henry Nollius: Hermetical Physick.* [Trans. Henry Vaughan.] London, 1657.

_____. ed. *The Fame and Confession of the Fraternity of R:C:.* London, 1652.

IV. Secondary Sources

Abraham, Lyndy, ed. *Arthur Dee: Fasciculus Chemicus.* English Renaissance Hermeticism, no. 6. New York, 1997.

Basso, Isa Dardano. *L'ancora e gli specchi: lettura del* Tableau de l'inconstance et instabilité de toutes choses *di Pierre de Lancre.* Roma, 1979.

Boas, George. "Nature." *Dictionary of the History of Ideas.* Ed. Philip P. Wiener. 5 vols. New York, 1968–74. 3: 346–51.

Brunet, G. "Jean d'Espagnet," *Nouvelle biographie générale,* 5(1858): 402–3.

Busard, H.L.L. "Jean Despagnet," *Dictionary of Scientific Biography,* 4 (1971): 74–75.

Butor, Michel. *Portrait de l'artiste en jeune singe.* Paris, 1967.

Canseliet, Eugène. *Deux logis alchimiques: en marge de la science et de l'histoire.* Paris, 1979.

Clarke, Lindsay. *The Chemical Wedding.* London, 1989.

Connell, Evan S. *The Alchymist's Journal.* San Francisco, 1991.

Copenhaver, Brian P., ed. and trans. *Hermetica: The Greek Corpus Hermeticum and the Latin Asclepius in a New Translation.* Cambridge, 1992.

Craven, J.B. *Count Michael Maier, Doctor of Philosophy and of Medicine, Alchemist, Rosicrucian, Mystic, 1568-1622: Life and Writings.*

1

Kirkwall, 1910.

Curtius, E.R. *European Literature and the Latin Middle Ages.* Trans. Willard Trask. New York, 1953.

Damigeron (attrib.). *De Virtutibus Lapidum: The Virtues of Stones.* Ed. Joel Radcliffe. Trans. Patricia Tahil. Seattle, 1989.

Debus, Allen G. "Afterword: Alchemy and the History of Science." *Cauda Pavonis* 10, no. 1 (Spring 1991): 13–14.

——————. *The French Paracelsians: The Chemical Challenge to Medical and Scientific Tradition in Early Modern France.* Cambridge, 1991.

——————. "The Paracelsian Aerial Nitre." *Isis* 55 (1964): 43–61.

Dixon, Laurinda, ed. *Nicholas Flamel: His Exposition.* English Renaissance Hermeticism, no. 2. New York, 1994.

Domergue, J. "Jean d'Espagnet." *Dictionnaire de biographie Française,* 12 (1970): 1491.

Eco, Umberto. *Foucault's Pendulum.* Trans. William Weaver. New Yori, 1989.

Economou, George D. *The Goddess Natura in Medieval Literature.* Cambridge, MA, 1971.

Evola, Julius. *The Hermetic Tradition: Symbols and Teachings of the Royal Art.* Trans. E.E. Rehmus. Rochester, VT, 1995.

Faivre, Antoine. *The Golden Fleece and Alchemy.* English trans. Albany, 1993.

Ferguson, George. *Bibliotheca Chemica: A Catalogue of the Alchemical, Chemical and Pharmaceutical Books in the Collection of the Late James Young of Kelly and Durris.* 2 vols. Glasgow, 1906.

Foucault, Michel. *The Order of Things.* English trans. [by Alan Sheridan]. New York, 1970.

Fowden, Garth. *The Egyptian Hermes: A Historical Approach to the Late Pagan Mind.* 2nd ed. Princeton, 1993.

Gilbert, R.A. "The Quest of the Golden Dawn: A Cautionary Tale." *Cauda Pavonis* 8, no. 1 (Spring 1989): 5–6.

Ginzburg, Carlo. *Ecstasies: Deciphering the Witches' Sabbath.* Trans. Raymond Rosenthal. New York, 1991.

Godwin, Joscelyn. *Robert Fludd: Hermetic Philosopher and Surveyor of Two Worlds.* London, 1979.

Hall, A. Rupert, and Marie Boas Hall, eds. *The Correspondence of Henry Oldenburg.* 13 vols. Madison, WI, and London, 1965–86.

Harrison, John, and Peter Laslett. *The Library of John Locke.* Oxford, 1965.

Henninger, S.K. *Touches of Sweet Harmony: Pythagorean Cosmology and Renaissance Poetics.* San Marino, CA, 1974.

Heisler, Ron. "Introduction to the Hermetic Adepti." *Hermetic Journal* 35 (Spring 1987): 34–41.

Hill, Christopher. *The World Turned Upside Down.* London, 1972.

Hitchcock, Ethan Allen. *Remarks upon Alchemy and Alchemists.* Boston, 1857.

Husson, Bernard, ed. *Anthologie de l'alchimie.* Paris, 1971.

Ilsley, Marjorie Henry. *A Daughter of the Renaissance: Marie le Jars de Gournay, Her Life and Work.* The Hague, 1963.

Jacques-Chaquin, Nicole, ed. *Pierre de Lancre: Tableau de l'inconstnaces des mauvais anges et demons.* Collection Palimpseste. Paris, 1982.

Josten, C.H., ed. *Elias Ashmole (1617-1692): His Autobiographical and Historical Notes, His Correspondence, and Other Contemporary Sources Relating to his Life and Work.* 5 vols. Oxford, 1966.

Jung, C.G. *Aion: Researches into the Phenomenology of the Self.* Trans. R.F.C. Hull. 2nd ed. Princeton, 1968.

_____. *Mysterium Coniunctionis.* Trans. R.F.C. Hull. 2nd ed. Princeton, 1970.

_____. *Psychology and Alchemy.* Trans. R.F.C. Hull. 2nd ed. Princeton, 1968.

_____. . *The Psychology of the Transferrence.* Trans. R.F.C. Hull. Princeton, 1969.

Kopp, Hermann. *Die Alchimie in Älterer und Neuerer Zeit.* 2 vols. Heidelberg, 1886.

Koyré, Alexandre. *From the Closed World to the Infinite Universe.* Baltimore, 1957.

Linden, Stanton J. *William Cooper's A Catalogue of Chymicall Books, 1773-88: A Verified Edition.* Garland reference library of the humanities, no. 670. New York, 1987.

Maier, C.A. *Soul and Body: Essays on the Theories of C.G. Jung.* San Francisco, 1986.

Matton, Sylvain. *"De l'arbre de vie ou de l'arbre solaire* par Jean Vauquelin des Yveteaux." *Chrysopœia* 1 (1987): 209-84.

Maxwell, J. *Un magistrat hermétiste.* Bordeaux, 1896.

McGowan, Margaret. "Pierre de Lancre's *Tableau de l'Inconstance des Mauvais Anges et Demons*: The Sabbat Sensationalised." *The Damned Art: Essays in the Literature of Witchcraft.* Ed. Sydney Anglo. London, 1977. 182–201.

Merchant, Carolyn. *The Death of Nature.* San Francisco, 1979.

Michelet, Jules. *La sorciere.* Ed. Lucien Refort. 2 vols. Paris, 1957.

Needham, Paul. *Early Printed Books: Major Acquisitions of the Pierpoint Morgan Library, 1924-1974.* New York, 1974.

Bibliography

Newman, William R. *Gehennical Fire: The Lives of George Starkey, an American Alchemist in the Scientific Revolution.* Cambridge, MA, 1994.

Oxford English Dictionary. Compact edition. 2 vols. Oxford, 1971. Reprint of *A New English Dictionary on Historical Principles.* 13 vols. Oxford, 1933.

Pagel, Walter. *The Smiling Spleen: Paracelsianism in Storm and Stress.* Basel, 1984.

Pereira, Michela. *The Alchemical Corpus Attributed to Raymond Lull.* Warburg Institute Surveys and Texts, no. 18. London, 1989.

Prinke, Rafal T. "Michael Sendivogius and Christian Rosenkreutz: The Unexpected Possibilities." *Hermetic Journal* n.s. 2 (1990): 72–98.

Pritchard, Alan. *Alchemy: A Bibliography of English-Language Writings.* London, 1980.

Schiff, Mario. *La fille d'aillance de Montaigne, Marie de Gournay.* Paris, 1910.

Scholem, Gershom, ed. *Zohar: The Book of Splendor.* New York, 1963.

Schuler, Robert M. "Some Spiritual Alchemies of the 17th Century." *Journal of the History of Ideas* 41 (1980): 293–318.

Scott, Walter, ed. and trans. *Hermetica: The Ancient Greek and Latin Writings which Contain Religious or Philosophic Teachings Ascribed to Hermes Trismegistus.* 4 vols. Oxford, 1924-36.

Sécret, F. "Littérature et alchimie." *Bibliothèque d'Humanisme et Renaissance* 35 (1973): 499–531.

Silberer, Herbert. *Problems of Mysticism and Its Symbolism.* Trans. Smith Ely Jelliffe. New York, 1917.

Szydlo, Zbigniew. "The Alchemy of Michael Sendivogius: His Central Nitre Theory." *Ambix* 40, no. 3 (Nov. 1993): 129–46.

Toulmin, Stephen. *Cosmopolis: The Hidden Agenda of Modernity.* New York, 1990.

Villeneuve, Roland. *Le fléau des sorciers: La diablerie basque au XVIIe siècle.* Paris, 1983.

Waard, Cornélius de, Mme. Paul Tanery, and René Pintard, eds. *Correspondance du P. Marin Mersenne, Religieux Minime.* 10 vols + index. Paris, 1945–72.

Waite, A.E. *Lives of the Alchymistical Philosophers, Based on Materials Collected in 1815, and Supplemented by Recent Researches.* London, 1888.

——————. *The Secret Tradition in Alchemy.* London, 1926.

Webster, Charles. "Elias Ashmole." *Dictionary of Scientific Biography,* 1 (1970): 316–18.

——————. *The Great Instauration.* London, 1975.

Wheelwright, Philip, ed. *The Presocratics.* New York, 1966.

Willard, Thomas. "The Twelve Keys of Orthelius." *Hermetic Journal* 42 (Winter 1988): 14–24.

Yates, Frances A. *Giordano Bruno and the Hermetic Tradition.* Chicago, 1964.

——————. *The Rosicrucian Enlightenment.* London, 1972.

Sigla

AHP: Jean D'Espagnet, *Arcanum HermeticæPhilosophiæ*

EPR: Jean D'Espagnet, *Enchyridion PhysicæRestitutæ*

HM: *The Hermetic Museum*, English translation, ed. A.E. Waite (London, 1893)

NLM: National Library of Medicine

OED: *Oxford English Dictionary* (1st edition)

Rosarium: *Rosarium Philosophorum* (Frankfurt, 1550)

Rulandus: Martinus Rulandus, *A Lexicon of Alchemy*, English translation, ed. A.E. Waite (London, 1893). Includes Waite's *Supplement to the Alchemical Lexicon of Martinus Rulandus*

Symbola: Michael Maier, *Symbola Auræ Mensæ* (Frankfurt, 1617)

TC: *Theatrum Chemicum* (6 vols., Strasbourg, 1659-61)

Unless otherwise noted, references to *AHP* and *EPR* are to the English translations of 1650 and 1651, respectively. References to other editions are followed by the dates in parentheses; see the "Chronological Listing of Books Containing Works by Jean D'Espagnet."

Enchyridion
PHYSICÆ
RESTITUTÆ;
OR,
The Summary of Physicks
Recovered.

Wherein the true Harmony of NA-
TURE is explained, and many
Errours of the Ancient PHI-
LOSOPHERS, by Canons
and certain Demonstration
are clearly evidenced
and evinced.

LONDON,
Printed by W. Bentley, and are to be
sold by W. Sheares at the Bible, and
Robert Tutchein at the Phœnix, in
the New-Rents in S. Pauls
Church-Yard. 1651.

Figure 3.   Title-page from the English translation of *Enchyridion* (1651).

Enchyridion
PHYSICÆ
RESTITUTÆ;

OR,

The Summary of Physicks
Recovered.

Wherein the true Harmony of NA-
TURE is explained, and many
Errours of the Ancient *PHI-
LOSOPHERS,* by Canons
and Certain Demonstrations,
are clearly evidenced
and evinced.

LONDON,

Printed by *W. Bentley,* and are to be
sold by *W. Sheares* at the *Bible,* and
Robert Tutchein at the *Phenix,* in
the New-Rents in S. *Pauls*
Church-Yard. 1651.

The Authours Epistle.

TO THE

HONOURERS

OF

Natural Light.

1]   *AFter I had lately with-drawn my self from publick employments, & reprieved my Soul from the dangerous attendants
of a COURTIER'S life, and had now ancor'd my thoughts in
a blest retirement, I alwayes had resounding the Echo of that
poetical passage in mine ears:*

Here is the Freedom the Soul gains,
Enfranchiz'd from her golden Chains.

*Now began I to feel those thoughts of Natural Philosophie, al-
wayes fostered by me, though till now, as it were ill attended,
to give a fresh and sprightly Spring in my Soul. I could not but
upon their return, give them a wonted and merited Wellcome,
that I might by the gain of this inward and Natural Light, repair
my voluntarie ressignment of that outward and deceitfull splendour: Besides, by this course, I had hopes to wipe off a publick
guilt, for now did I apprehend the charge of a desertour of publick employments, and of the Laws of my Countrie likely to fall
upon me, therefore lest this might issue a deep censure, I fled to
that Sanctuarie, the Studie of the Occult, and almost unsearch-
able Laws and Customes of Nature in the Universe, the common*

Countrey of all, hoping a securitie in this studie, and a protection from this Policie. For certainly civil Constitutions will not decree any remarkable Amercement upon him, who laying down the burden of those Troubles, doth retire himself to the general service of the World.

2] *Now was my Soul rowling within it self thought concerning the Sovereigntie, Lawes, Order, Government, Harmonie, Effects, Causes, yea, the unconceivable Riches of Nature; now indeed was I lost in admiration of these, which astonishment, though it be an evidence of ignorance, yet it is also an incentive to knowledge, for it causeth the Soul to soar above, by which it is enkindled with a burning desire to know what it is, as yet ignorant of, though affected to.*

3] *My Soul being thus enflamed, brought several philosophical Constitutions to a severe Test, and upon the touch, assented not to their Veritie, because Nature did seem to dart some weak and waining Light, as it were breaking forth upon the confine and border of a scarcely discerned Truth, till at length, the Light began so to rise, as to break through the encompassing Fogs, and to break into my Soul, whereby it was not onely made more resplendent, but also more confident, not onely to view the ground, but also to dig for the Treasure.*

4] *The first Errours of the Ancients, and which are the worst and radicall Errours that came into my thoughts, were those concerning the Principles of Nature, concerning the first Matter and that Universal Form, from which all things flow, concerning the Number of the Elements, their Qualities, their Opposition, Scituation, Reciprocation; when I had seriously turned these within my thoughts, I layed hold of an Opinion different from the Current; neither was the authoritie of ancient Philosophers, nor their ingenious, but unsatisfactorie reasonings, able to divert my mind from that perpetual devotion, in which it stood to the light of Nature. So now what I first admired, I now affected, yea, that Love, which hath no weapons but fierie rayes, strook my soul into a flame, to enter into the most secret and sacred rooms of Nature.*

5] *But I was long in a suspensive Dispute with my self, whether it were my dutie to communicate to you,* the Students

6

of Philosophie, *those secrets I have found, suspicious lest it might prove a disgust to you, a danger to my self; for I found Experience the best Counsellour to give me warning to be wise by the folly of others, and to learn to stand by their falls; for I alwayes was musing how many had wrackt their credit by scribling, how our modern Wits are close in their commendations, but lavish enough in their detraction of other mens labours, how attempting their souls are in fancying and fostering follies, how obstinate in the retaining a conceived Truth; yea, I considered it was not onely a project of difficultie, but also of danger, to pull up a received and an acknowledged Opinion, and to implant a new and divers.*

6]   *But in this Conflict, (Ye most ingenious Assertours of Natural Light) the victorie fell upon the love of you, and of Truth, so that I was determined, that since those had been the Motives to the Disquisition of these Truths, they should also be the Incentives to their publication. Yet let me have this Boon granted, that if you will be competent or just Judges, let not the swoln names of* Plato, Aristotle, *and of any other prime Philosophers, be summoned as convicting witnesses; or empannell'd as a condemning Jury, but lay aside their nominal, though seemingly real authority, and bind not your souls to a continued credulity of their positions; but preserve your Souls free to your selves.*

7]   *In the reading of the learned Monuments of former Ages, let not the popular fancy of their general Applause, bewitch you into a blind Belief of all their Notions. Far be it from me to stain their Credit, or detract from their Learning, who alwayes had exhibited by me almost a Divine Adoration, there is no earthly glory competible to theirs: they were the Men that first took infant Philosophie into their arms, and nourished it up to so incredible a strength and stature, that those lofty souls seemed to have cut off from succeeding Ages, the hope of an Addition to their Labours, and to an advancement of Learning.*

8]   *Yet as for the deep search of the winding creeks of Nature, and for the exquisite knowledge of her concealed Mysteries, the growing Age of Philosophie, even in its own judgement, did not comprehend them, these were brought forth by the fertile Brains of future Times, they brought to light Obscurities, they polish'd roug-hewn principles, they propt up perplexities. So did Knowledge get its accomplishment by Age, and Truth its perfection by Time, which demonstrates the vigour of our present years, and that the number of things we know, is far less than of those of which we are ignorant.*

9] *Philosophy is not like a Garment, as that age should wear it or worse it, and they that pretend a gray head to their errours, by this seek not so much to patronize it, as to discredit it.*

10] *Forbear I beseech you, by an unadvised censure, to condemn me without plea, if I shall seem to unsettle the boundaries of Philosophy, be not angry, and accuse me as sacrilegious, but consider whether I do not aym at their settlement rather than otherwise? whether I do not rather confirm than weaken her priviledges? whether I do not rather honour than impayr her Royalty? upon which grounds I hope She will, as by way of requital, not deny me her assistance, as a buckler against the delusions of Sophisters, and a breast-plate against the environed darts of either Envy or Ignorance. These Beasts will bark, the first pining at anothers good, the second raging in its own clouds, both break into the cultivated Gardens of Knowledge, and the delightfull paradise of Philosophy, and either snip or blast the endeavours of a more fortunate Genius. These to no purpose strive to stop my course by their frights, I am seated above their highest reach; as long as I can see the Deity of Truth, under her patronage I walk, I work secure. Onely be you pleased to accept these sprinklings of my retirement, with the same soul it is presented, if any thing seem in it to disrellish, deal so gently as that you may seem rather not to comply, than wholly to refuse. I shall in the interim reach my end, if my pains shall cause you to fall upon greater attempts with better success.*

In Physicam Restitutam Epigramma

En Physicæ jubar exoriens, quam forte sinistrâ
    Barbaries Stygiis merserat atra vadis.
Sic formæ & dotis Physicæ sibi damna rependi
    Aspicit, ut plures speret habere procos.
O stupor! ô miro quem non percellit amore!
    Non Venus è patrio gratior orta mari.
Nec se restituti putat his haec aurea scriptis,
    Sed nasci è cerebro parturiente Jovis.

An Epigram for the Recovered Knowledge of Nature

Behold the rising light of Nature, whom
Barbarians cruelly sank in Stygian gloom.
Her beauty and lost dowry are returned,
So she may hope for many suitors earned.
Oh, wondrous silence! Who is not deep in love?
Not even Venus from the sea could move
Us so, nor could this golden book instead,
As she who sprang from Jove's birth-giving head.

9

Enchyridion Physicæ
Restitutæ.

OR,

A Summary of the Physicks

Recovered.

THE FIRST RULE.

GOd is an Eternal Being, an infinite Oneness, the radical Principle of all things, whose Essence is an incomprehensible Light; his Power, Omnipotency; whose beck is an absolute act. He that dives deeper, is swallowed up in a trance and silence, and is lost in the abyss of unfathomed glory.

2. Most of the Ancients conceived the world from eternity to have been figured in its Archetype, and Original, which is God, who is all Light: before the Creation of the Universe he was a book rowld up in himself, giving light onely to himself; but, as it were, travailing with the birth of the world, he unfolded himself, and that work which lay hid in the womb of his own mind, was manifested by extending it to view, and so brought forth the *Idæl-world,* as it were in the transcript of that divine Original, into an actual and material world. This is hinted by *Trismegist,* when he says, *That God changed his form, and that all things were in a sudden revealed and brought to light.* For the world is nothing else but the disclosed image of an occult Deity. This beginning of the world the Ancients seem to have denoted in the birth of their *Pallas,* out of the brain of their *Jupiter,* by the Mid-wiffery of *Vulcan,* that is, by the help of divine fire or light.

3. The eternal Parent of all things, not less wise in governing, than powerfull in creating, did so orderly dispose the whole

organical frame of the world, that the highest are so intermixt with the lowest, and the lowest interchangeably and inconfusedly with the highest, and have an Analogical likeness, so that the extreams of the whole work by a secret bond, have a fast coherence between themselves through insensible *mediums,* and all things do freely combine in an obedience to their Supream Ruler, and to the benefit of the inferiour Nature, onely being subject to a dissolution at the will of him who gave them their constitution. Wherefore it is well said of *Hermes, That whatsoever is below, hath an assimulation to somewhat above.*

4. He that transfers the sovereign order of the Universe to any Nature diverse from the Nature of God, denies a God. For it cannot be just to conceive any other uncreated Deity of Nature, as the Cause of the production or conservation of the several Individuals of this large frame of the world, besides that spirit of the divine Worker, which lay upon those first waters, and brought forth the seeds of all things, confusedly rowld in the first Chaos, from their power into act, and wheeling them by a perpetual alternation, doth mannage them Geometrically by composition and resolution.

5. He that knows not the soul of the world to be that Spirit, the Creatour and Governour of the World, by its continued infusion, of its breathing upon the works of nature, and by its enlarged diffusion through all things, giving to all things a set, but secret motion according to their kind: he is wholly an *Ignaro* of the laws of the Universe, for he that created, cannot but assume the power of ruling what is created, and it must be acknowledged, that all things have their creation, generation and conservation by the same Spirit.

6. Notwithstanding this, he that shall grant Nature the honour of being the second universal Cause attending on the first, and as it were an instrument moved by it, and of giving, according to a material order, an immediate motion to every thing in the world, will not speak what disagrees with the opinion of Philosophers or Divines, who call that *Natura naturans: i.* Nature giving nature: this, *Natura naturata,* Nature made nature.

7. He that is verst in the secrets of Nature, will acknowledge this second Nature the attendant of the first, to be the spirit of

11

the Universe, or the quickening virtue of that light created in the beginning, and contracted into the body of the Sun, and endowed with an hidden faecundity. *Zoroaster* and *Heraclit* called this *The Spirit of Fire, the invisible Fire, the Soul of the world.*

8. The order of Nature is nothing else than a large Rowl of the eternal Laws, which being Enacted by the highest Sovereign, and Recorded and written in various leaves to innumerable people of a various nature, by the auspicious power of which Laws, the frame of the Universe doth accomplish its motions, life and death always attending on the margins of the last Volume, and the other spaces being taken up by alternal motions.

9. The world is as it were a Smiths-work made orbicular, the links of the chain enclasping it, each the other, are the parts of the world, Nature as it were deputed to sit in the middle, always present, and ever working, continually repairs the changes and motions of all things.

10. The whole world, as it hath its constitution from a three-fold Nature, so hath it its distinction into a three-fold Region, *viz.* The *Super-celestial,* the *Celestial,* the *Sub-celestial.* The *Super-celestial* is that which is otherwise termed the *Intelligible,* it is altogether spiritual and immortal, having the nearest approach to the Divine Majesty. The *Celestial* is seated in the middle, which having alloted to her the portion of the most perfect bodies, and being replenished with spirits, doth pour out by the conveyance of spiritual channels, numberless efficacies and vital breathings, not enduring a corruption, onely having attained its period subject to change. Lastly, the *Sub-celestial,* or Elementary Region, hath its assignment in the lowest portion of the world. This being wholly of a corporeal nature, doth enjoy spiritual gifts and benefits, (the chief of which is in life) by loan onely, and upon request, being as it were to repay Heaven for it. In the bosom of this Region there is no generation without corruption, no birth without death.

11. It is enacted and setled by the Laws of the Creation, that the lowest things should immediately be subservient to the middle, the middle to those above, these to the Supream Rulers beck. This is the Symmetry, the order of the whole Universe.

12. It is the excepted priviledge alone of the Creatour, as he

created all things according as he pleased out of nothing, so to reduce what he hath created into nothing: for whatsoever being or substance hath an impress from him, cannot deny subjection to him, but is prohibited by Natures law, to return to a *Non-Entity*. Therefore *Trismegist* did truly assert, *That nothing in the world doth die, but pass into a change*, for mixt bodies have their composition from the Elements, which by natures rotation are again resolved into the Elements.

> *Hence is this sequel, that by Natures cost*
> *All's cloth'd with what's its own, nothing is lost.*

13. The Philosophers did believe a first matter to be of an elder birth to the Elements, but this as it was but scarce apprehended by them, so was it as briefly, and as it were in the clouds, and obscurely handled by them, they made it void of qualities and accidents, yet the first subject of them without quantity, yet by which all things have their dimensions, endowed with simplicity, yet capable of contraries, without the reach of sensible knowledge, yet the basis of sensibles, drawn out through all places, yet unperceiveable; covetous of all forms, tenacious of none, the root of all bodies, yet not sensible but conceiveable, onely by an act of the intellect: lastly, nothing in act, all things in aptitude. So have they laid a fancy for the foundation of nature.

14. *Aristotle* more wary, though he believed the eternity of the world, yet hinted a certain first and universal matter. In the discussion of this he used sobriety and ambiguity, alwayes avoiding its creeks and perplexities, so that he opined it better to conceive one inseparable matter of all things, which yet hath a respective difference, from which, the first bodies with the rest, which are under sense, have their subsistence; that this is the first principle of them, and not to be separated from them, but always joyned with a repugnancie, always subject to contraries, from which the Elements are produced.

15. The Philosopher had been righter, if he had asserted that first matter free from the conflict of Contraries, and disengaged from that pretended repugnancy, since there is no contrariety inherent in the very Elements, but what is the result of

13

the intention of their qualities, as we are informed by the daily experience of fire and water, in which, whatsoever opposition there is, ariseth from the heightening of their qualities. But in the proper and true Elements, which couple in the generation of mixt bodies, those qualities which are in a remiss degree in them, are not repugnant each to other: for their temperature doth not admit a contrariety.

16. *Thales, Heraclitus,* and *Hesiodus* accounted water the first matter of all things, to whose opinion the Writer of the holy *Genesis* seems to consent: This they call an *Abyss* and *Water,* by which I guess they understood not our ordinary water, but a kind of slime, or moist and dark vapour, roaving here and there, and driven in an uncertain motion without any certain order.

17. I am not at present able to lay down any positive determination concerning the first Principle of things, since it being created in the dark, could never by mans invention be brought to light, therefore whatsoever the troup of Philosophers and Divines do opine, whether these things are so or no, the Authour of Nature alone knows, therefore pardon is to be allowed to him that in dark Doctrines hits what is most likely.

18. Some of the *Rabbines* agreeing, conceived an ancient, but obscure and inexpressible principle, the matter of all improperly called *Hyle,* which is more properly termed not so much a body, as a large shadow, not a thing, but a dusky image of a thing, or the smoaky appearance of an Entity, a most dark night, a covert of clouds, actually all nothing, potentially all things which cannot be found but in fancie, and understood in a dream. Our imagination cannot exhibit to us this doubtfull principle, this depth of darkness, no more than our talk can through the ears imprint the knowledge of the Sun into a man that was born blind.

19. The same men had an opinion that God brought forth and created the nearest approching matter of the Elements and the World, to wit, that dark, formless, and indigested Abyss out of that farthest Principle: the Scripture calls this Mass sometimes *Earth void and emptie,* sometimes *Waters,* although actually it were neither, yet potentially and by way of assignment, it was both: we may give a probable guess that it was not unlike to

a dark smoak or vapour, in which was closed a stupifying spirit of cold and darkness.

20. The division of the higher waters from the lower, expressed in *Genesis,* seems to be done by the severing the subtile from the thick, and as it were a thin spirit from that smoaky body; there was needfull therefore of that lightsom spirit proceeding from the Word of God. For light, which is a fiery spirit, by separating things of a diverse nature, did drive down the thicker darkness from the nearest and highest Region, and uniting the matter of one and the same kind, being of a thin and a more spiritual substance, inflamed it as an unquencheable oyl, to burn before the Throne of the Divine Majesty. This is the *Empyræan Heaven,* seated between the Intellectual and Material heaven, as the Horizon and Finitor of each, receiving spiritual endowments from that above, and deriving them down to the inferiour adjoyning middle heaven.

21. Reason required that this dark Abyss, or next matter of the World, should be watry and moist, that it be the better subject to be attenuated, and that by this flux of the matter by attenuation, the whole frame of the Heavens and of the rest of the Fabrick, might issue forth and might be laid out in a continuous body. For it is the property of moisture to flow, and the continuity of every body is the effect of the moisture of it. For moisture is the glue and joyncture of Elements and bodies. But fire acting upon moisture by heat, doth rarifie, for heat is the instrument of fire, by which it doth act two opposite works by one and the same labour, separating the moist nature from the earthy, & by rarifying that, condenseth this: So that by the separation of the things of a diverse, proceeds a congregation of things of the same nature. By this first principle of Chymistry, the uncreated spirit, the artifex of the world, did distinguish the confused natures of things.

22. The Architectonique Spirit of the world began the work of Creation from two universal principles; the one formal, the other material, for otherwise what is the meaning of the words of the Prophet, *Gen.* 1. *God created the Heaven and the Earth?* & c. unless that in the beginning of the information of the matter, he distinguished it into two chief principles, a formal and a

material Heaven and Earth; by the word *Earth,* is to be understood that dark, and as yet unshaped mass of the waters and Abyss, as is apparent by the subsequent words, (*The Earth was void and without form, and darkness was upon the face of the depth,* &c.) which the Creatour did shut in and comprise within the highest, to wit, the *Empyrean Heaven,* which is Natures first formal, though farthest principle.

23. For the Spirit of God, which is the brightness of the Deity, being poured out upon the Waters, that is, upon the moist and large surface of the depths, in the very moment of creation, light presently broke up, which in the twinkling of the eye, surprized the highest and more subtile part of the matter, and encompassed it as it were with a fringe, and border of light, as that lightening is which is darted from the East to the West, or like a flame which fires the smoak. So was the birth of the first day, but the lower portion of darkness devoid of light, continued night, and so the darkness had its division into day and night.

24. Concerning that first Heaven, that formal Principle, it is not declared to have been void, empty, and wrapt in darkness, which is a sufficient evidence, that that Heaven which was first spread out, was forthwith severed by the light from the subjacent dark Mass, by reason of the nearness of the Glory and Majesty of God, and the presence of that lightsom Spirit flowing from it.

25. There was therefore in the beginning two Principles of all things created, one full of light, and bordering upon the spiritual Nature, the other wholly corporeal and dark; the first, that it might be the Principle of motion, light, and heat; the second, of a drowsie, dark, and cold being: the first active and masculine, the other the passive and feminine Principle. On the part of the former comes a motion in the Elementary world to Generation, from whence proceeds life; from the other part comes the motion to corruption, the principle of death. So that is the double fringe or border of the lower world.

26. But because Love is extensive, and acts without from it self, the Divine Nature impatient of its solitude, and taken with its own beauty in the light already created, as in a Mirrour, and earnestly desirous to enlarge it, and to multiply his image, commanded that light to be extended and propagated. Then

the light, the fiery spirit issuing from the Divine understanding, and rowling it self in a Circulation, began to work upon the nearest darkness, and having prevailed upon it, and sunk it down towards the Centre, and there sprung forth the second day, and there was seen the second mansion of light, or the second Heaven, comprizing all the airy Region, in whose higher Region are so many Torches kindled and scattered: In the lower are seated the seven wandering Stars according to their order, that they might, as so many Presidents and Rulers, give orders by their light, motion and influence to the subjacent Nature.

27. And least any thing should be defective in this great work, already drawn out in the mind of God, the same Spirit by his glittering and fiery sword beat off the banded darkness, and that shade that lay under him, and thrust it down into the Centre of the Abyss, so the lowest part of the Heavens was enlightened, which we rightly term *Air,* or the *lowest Heavens:* Then was the third day. But the darkness which at first did overcast the whole face of the Abyss, being thrust down by the supervening light into the lowest Region, was so thickened by reason of the straitness of the room, and the binding force of the Cold, that it passed into a huge mass of a watry Nature, the Kernel and Centre of the whole workmanship, as it were a dale and heap of darkness, being poiz'd in the middest of the waters, and bound up of the dregs and thick matter of the Abyss, into a firm and dark body of earth. After this, upon the driving of the Spirit, the waters fled from the surface of the earth, casting themselves about the borders of it, and there appeared drie land, that it might produce almost an infinite number of several sorts of Plants, and receive as guests so many kinds of creatures, especially Man the lord of all, and provide to them food, and to man a plentifull sufficiency of all conveniencies. The Earth therefore and the Water made one Globe, by reason of whose thickness, the shadow, the image of the dark Abyss, doth continually beset the whole Region of the Air bordering upon it, and opposite to the Sun, for it shuns and flies the assayling light, and so in the assault is upon a continual retreat.

28. That Light, which upon the conquest and destruction of the darkness, had seized upon and spread it self upon the parts of

the Abyss, it seemed best to the great Creatour to contract into that most resplendent and illustrious for quantity and quality, for bigness and beauty, that Globe of the Sun, that as the Light was more narrowly pent, so it might be more efficaciously powerfull, and might dart its beams with more vigour, as also that the created Light, the nearest approaching nature to the divine glory, proceeding from an uncreated unity, might through its unity be poured upon the creatures.

29. From this glorious lamp of the world do all the other bodies borrow light; for that dark shade which we sensibly perceive in the Globe of the Moon, by reason of the neighbouring earth, and the extension of her shadow, we may credibly guess the like to be in the other globous bodies, though not perceivable by reason of their distance. Indeed the prime and most principal nature of sensibles, the fountain of light, ought to be one, from which these things below might receive the breath of life. Whence is that true saying of the Philosopher, *The Sun and man beget man.*

30. It was not an improbable affection of some of the Philosophers, *That the soul of the World was in the Sun, and the Sun in the Centre of the whole.* For the consideration of equity and nature seem to require, that the body of the Sun should have an equal distance from the fountain and rise of created Light, to wit, the *Empyrean Heaven,* and from the dark Centre the Earth, which are the extreams of the whole Fabrick, whereby this lamp of the world, as a middle Nature and Joyner of both Extreams, might have its scite in the middle, that it may the more commodiously receive the rich treasuries of all powers from the chief Spring, and upon a like distance convey them to things below.

31. Before the Contraction of this light into the body of the Sun, the earth spent an idle time in its solitude, looking for a male, that being impregnated by his copulation, it might brigh forth all sorts of creatures, for as yet it had been delivered onely of abortives and Embryoes, to wit, of Vegetables onely. For the weak and faint heat of that scattered light, could not get the conquest of that moist and cold matter, nor put forth its virtue in any higher actings.

32. From the light therefore the Elements, as well as the first

matter, had their information, and so attained a joynt nature of light, and by kindred a fast friendship betwixt themselves, not according to the vulgar opinion, an hatred and quarrel; they embrace each the other with a common bond of friendship, that they may joyn themselves to the making up of several mixed bodies, according to their several kinds. But the light of the Sun being of a far greater power than this former, is the Form of all forms, or the Universal form which doth convey all natural forms in the work of generation, into the disposed matter and seed of things. For every particular nature hath within it a spark of light, whose beams do in a secret manner attend with an active & motive power.

33. It was necessary that the entire portion of the first matter, allotted to this lower Region, as well as the Elements who did flow from it, should be seasoned from the beginning with a light tincture of that first Light, whereby they might be the better fitted to receive that greater and more powerfull light in the information of mixt bodies. So fire with fire, water with water, light with light being *homogeneous* bodies, have a perfect union.

34. From the sight & efficacy of the Sun, we may inferre that he is in the stead of an heart to the Universe, for from him is life derived to all parts, for light is the Chariot of life, yea the fountain and next cause, and the souls of creatures are the beams of that heavenly light, which do breath life into them, exempting onely the soul of man, which is a ray of the *Super-celestial* and uncreated Light.

35. God hath imprinted in the Sun a threefold image of his Divinity, the first in his unity, for Nature cannot away with a multiplicity of Suns, no more than the Deity can with a plurality of Gods, that so one may be the spring of all. Secondly, in its Trinity, or his threefold office. For the Sun, as Gods Vicegerent, doth dispense all the benefits of Nature by light, motion, and heat: from hence is life, which is the supream and most accomplisht act of Nature in this world, beyond which cannot go, unless backward. But from Light and Motion issues heat, as the third in the Trinity proceeds from the first and the second Person. Lastly God, who is the Eternal Light, Infinite, Incomprehensible, could express and demonstrate himself to the world

onely by light. Let none therefore wonder, why the Eternal Sun did beautifie that most excellent draught of himself, which was his own making, that heavenly Sun with so great endowments, for in him hath he pitcht his pavilion.

36. The Sun is a transparent Mirrour of the Divine Glory, which being seated above the sense & strength of material creatures, did frame this glass, by whose resplendency the beams of his Eternal Light might be communicated by reflection to all his works, and so should by this reflection be rendered discernable. For it is beyond the capacity of any mortal to have any immediate view of that Divine Light. This is the Royal eye of the Divinity which doth conferre by his presence, life, and liberty to his suppliants.

37. The last work of this Great Worker, and as it were the corollary and shutting of all, man enters a Summary of the Worlds Fabrick, a small draught of the Divine Nature. The Creatour deferred his making to a part of the sixth Light, and the last of all his working, that the rich Furniture of Nature, and all endowments of things both above and below, might bring their confluence to the humane nature as to another *Pandora.* Thus the things of the world being ordered, man wanted onely to be annexed as the perfection of all; whereby nature, being now strengthened by a various light, might bring into his perfect temperature more refined Elements, and that there might be the best Clay for the forming of so exquisite a Vessel. Yea, the lower Globe and the inhabitants of it did require such a Governour, lest otherwise they might refuse his Rule.

38. Upon the sixth day from the Creation, the third day of the Suns rising, did man rise out of the Earth: by the time of his production, and the number of the days is shadowed forth a great mysterie. For as upon the fourth day of the Creation the whole light of the heaven was gathered into the single bodie of the Sun, and on the third day from the making of the Sun, which was the sixth day from the beginning of the Creation, the Clay of the Earth received the breath of life, and was formed into a living man the image of God: So on the fourth Millenary day from the beginning of the world the uncreated Sun, *viz.* the Divine Nature, infinite and never before comprehended within

any bounds, was willing to be comprized, and in a manner shut into the cage of an humane bodie. Upon the third day or millenarie (for a thousand years with God are but as one day) after the first rising of that Sun, and about the end of the sixth day, to wit, of the millenarie from the Creation, shall fall out the glorious Resurrection of the Humane Nature in the second coming of that supream Judge, which was also præsignified to us by his blessed Resurrection on the third day. So did the Prophet in his *Genesis* roul up the secret age and destine of the world.

39. Although the Almightie, according to his pleasure, created the World, yet could have brought it out of darkness into light (if his will had so been) in a moment, and by a beck: for he said, and it was so. Yet the order of Creation of principles, and successively of the natures according to their times, was set in the mind of God, which order, rather than the work it self of Creation, that sacred Philosopher seems to describe in his Genesis.

40. There seems to have been in the beginning a threefold way of the information of the first matter. For in what portion of the matter there was an irrational lightsom form, and without proportion above the rest, as in the Empyrean heaven, where the light first seized upon the matter, then the form having as it were an infinite virtue, did swallow up its matter, and translated it into a nature almost spiritual and free from any accident.

41. But where the virtues of the form and matter did meet in an equal poyz and a just equallitie, according to which, the ætherial heaven, and the celestial bodies are informed, there the action of the light, whose force in acting is of greatest power, did proceed so far, that it did reserue its matter from all original blemishes, as also from the loathsom infection of corruption after a wonderfull sort, by illumination and attenuation, and this is to be accounted as a truly perfect information.

42. The third way of informing the matter is, in which a weaker form remains, as it often happens, though after divers ways in this our Elementarie region, in which the appetite of the matter, which is an evidence of weakness and imperfection, luxuriating, and lavishly springing in its basis and root, cannot be sufficiently satisfied, by the reason of its remotion and distance

from its former principle, neither can this weakness be cured. Hence the matter not being fully informed according to its desire, languisheth under the desire of a new form, which having attained, it doth bring to it, as to its husband, the dowrie, a large wardrobe of corruption and faults. This sullen, perverse wrangling and inconstant matter, doth always burn for new beds, greedily wooing all forms which it longs for if absent, hates, if present.

43. By which it is evident, that the leaven of alteration and corruption, and at length the fatal venom of death do happen, not from the repugnancie of qualities, but from an infected Matrix, and from the menstruous poyson of a dark matter, and this causeth it to fall out both in elements and in the mixt bodies of this lower region: because the form weakened and insufficient by its defilement and imperfection, and being not of a just poiz and assize, could not purge it out in its first and radical union. This is confirmed by holy Writ, in which we may observe our first Parent was not created according to his matter immortal, but that he might be guarded from the tincture and corruption of the matter, and therefore God set in Paradise a Tree abounding with the fruit of Life, which he might make use of as his assertour & guardian from the frailty of his matter, and the bondage of death, from the presence and use of this he was sequestrated after his fatal fall, and final sentence.

44. Two there were therefore first principles of Nature, before which were none, after which all, to wit the first matter, and its universal form, by the copulation of which issued the Elements as second principles, which are nothing else but the first matter diversly informed; out of the mixture of this is made the second matter, which is the nearest subject of accidents, and doth receive the various turns of Generation and Corruption. These are the degrees, this the order of the Principles of Nature.

45. Those who annex to the Matter and Form, a third Principle, viz. Privation, do blast Nature with a Calumnie, far from whose purpose it is to admit a Principle that shall go counter to her intention, but her end in Generation being to obtain a Form, to which Privation is adverse, certainly this cannot be part of Natures aim: They had spoken more to the purpose, if

they had made Love a principle of Nature, for the matter being widowed in its form, covets eagerly the embracing of a new. But Privation is the meer absence of a form, upon which ground the honourable title of being a principle of Nature, is no way due to it, but rather to Love, which is a mediatour betwixt that which desires, and that which is desired, betwixt what is beautifull, and what is deformed, betwixt matter and form.

46. Corruption is far nearer than Privation to the principle of Generation, since that is a motion disposing the matter to generation by successive degrees of alteration; but Privation acts nothing, is of no work in generation, but Corruption doth both promote and prepare the matter, that it may be put in a capacity of receiving the form, and as it were a mediatrix, doth act Pander-like, that the matter may the more easily get a satisfaction for its lust, and by his help may the sooner obtain the copulation of a form: Corruption therefore is the instrumental and necessary cause of Generation. But Privation is nothing else but a meer vacancy of an active and formal principle; *and darkness was upon the face of the depths,* to wit, of the uninformed and dark matter.

47. The harmony of the Universe consists in the diverse and gradual information of the matter. For from the poized mixture of the first matter and its form, flows both the difference of the Elements, and of the Region of the world, which is briefly, but truly set out by *Hermes,* when he said, *That whatsoever is below, hath an assimulation with somewhat above.* For things above and below, were made of the same matter and form, differencing onely in respect of their mixture, scite and perfection, in which the distinction of the parts of the world, and the latitude of all Natures, are handled.

48. We must believe that the first matter, after it had received information from the light, and was distinguished by it into several things, did go wholly out of it self, and was transmitted into the Elements, and that which was compounded by them, and was wholly exhausted in the consummation of the work of the Universe, so that those things which were closed in her, being brought forth, and exposed to view, she began wholly to lie hid in them, and we must acknowledge it is not to be found

in a separation from them.

49. Nature hath left us a shadow of that ancient confused Mass, or first matter in drie water, not wetting, which rising out of those impostumes of the earth or Lakes, doth spring forth big with a manifold seed, being also volatile by reason of its lightness through its heat, from which being coupled with its male, he that can take out and separate, and joyn again ingeniously the intrinsecal Elements, he may well boast that he hath gained the most precious secret of Art and Nature; yea, a *Compendium* or brief of the Heavenly Essence.

50. He that searcheth for the simple elements of bodies, separated from all mixture, takes a labour in vain, for they are unknown to the most piercing judgements of men, for our common elements are not the simple element, yea, they are inseparably mixed one with another. The Earth, Water, and Air, may be more truly called the Parts that perfect and compleat the Universe, rather than Elements, yet they may be rightly termed the Matrix's of them.

51. The bodies of Earth, Water, and Air, which are sensibly distinguished by the sphears, are different from the elements which Nature maketh use of in the work of Generation, and which make up mixt bodies, for these in their mixture in respect of their thinness, are not discernable, but are barr'd from the senses, until they conjoyn in a condensed matter and body.

> *There never hath a creature been,*
> *Whose principles were to be seen:*

But these things which fill up the inferiour Globe of the Universe, as too thick, impure, and indigested, are debarred from the right of perfect generation, for they are rather the shadows and figures of elements, than true Elements.

52. Those Elements which forming Nature makes use of in her mixtions, and in making bodies, although they are not to be found out before mixtion, yet in the finished work, and in the compleatly mixed body, because their parts have a correspondence proportionable with the parts of the world, and have a kind of Analogie with them, we may call them by the same names, the more solid parts, Earth; the moister, Water; the

more spiritual, Air; the inborn heat, Natures fire; the hidden and essential virtues, a man may safely term Heavenly and Astral Natures, or the Quint-Essence, and so every mixed body may by this Analogie triumph in the title of *Micro-cosme.*

53. He that did appoint the first Elements for the generation of bodies, alone knows how out of them to make all particulars, and to resolve them, being made, into them again.

54. Let not them therefore refuse the Light, who working about the Elements of Nature, either in the production of some body from them, or the resolution of some into them, create their own trouble, since these Elements are onely subject to the dominion of Nature, and delivered to her onely from their beginning, altogether unknown to all our art, and not compassible by our endeavours.

55. The Element of Nature may be termed the most simple portion of the first Matter, distinguished by its peculiar difference and qualities, constituting a part of the essence in the material composition of mixt bodies.

56. By the Elements of Nature, are denoted the material principles, of which some have a greater purity and perfection than others, according to the greater Power and Virtue of that form that gives the compleatment. They are for the most part distinguished according to their rarity or density, so that those that are more thin, and approach nearer to a spiritual substance, are therefore the more pure and light, and so are the more fit for motion and action.

57. Upon this ground it was that reverend Antiquity did feign, that the whole Empire of the world was divided between the three Brothers, the Sons of *Saturn* as coheirs, because it acknowledged onely three Elementary Natures, or rather three parts of the Universe. For by *Jupiter,* the Omnipotent, who shared heaven as his portion, armed with his treble-darted Thunder-bolt, superiour to the rest of the brothers, what did those professours of mysteries understand, but that the Heavens, being the Region of heavenly bodies, do assume a priviledge of Sovereignty over these inferiour beings. But they placed *Juno,* wife to *Jupiter,* to præside over the lowest Region of the Heaven, or our Air, because this Region troubled with vapours, being

25

moist and cold is as it were in a manner defiled and impure, and nearest approaching to a female temperament, as also because it is subjected to the orders of the higher Regions, receive their effects, and communicates them to us, twisting it self with more condensed natures, and stooping them to the bent of Heaven. But because male and female differ onely in sex, not in kind, therefore would they not have the Air, or the lower Heaven to be distinct in its essence and kind, as another Element from the higher Heaven, but onely diversified in place and by accidents. To *Neptune* the God of the Sea, they attributed a dominion over the waters. By *Pluto,* the lord of the lower parts, abounding in wealth, they denoted the Globe of the Earth replenished with riches, with the desire of which the minds of men being inflamed, are bitterly tormented. So that those wise men admitted of three parts of the Universe, or if you please, of three Elements, because under the Nature of Heaven they comprized the name of Fire, and therefore did they draw *Jupiter* armed with his Thunder.

58. We are Schollars to experience in this, that all the bodies of mixt beings, have their analysis and resolution into drie and moist, and that all the excrements of creatures, are terminated by the same differences; from whence it is clearly evident, that their bodies are made up onely of two sensible Elements, in which notwithstanding the other are virtually and effectually. But Air, or the Element of the lower Heaven, is not the object of our sense, because in respect of us it is a kind of spiritual being. The fire of Nature, because it is the formal principle, cannot be wrought to any separation or comprehesion by any destruction by way of resolution, nor by any art or artifice of man. For the nature of Forms is not subjected to the censure of the Senses, because of its spiritual being.

59. The Earth is the thickest body of the Universe, therefore is it accounted the heaviest and the centre of it, we must assert its nature contrary to the received opinion, to be accidentally drie, because it doth retain most of the close and dark nature of the first matter, but a shade and darkness are the coverts of cold, from whence they flie the light, and are diametrically opposite to it, but the Earth, in respect of its extream density, is the mother of shade and darkness, hardly passable by light and

heat, therefore roughly knit by an hightened cold. And for this reason black choller is to be esteemed the coldest humour of all, because it is under the power of the Earth, the Earth under *Saturne,* who is accounted the Authour of a cold and melancholick temperature. Further, those things that are ingendered in the bowels of the Earth, of the substance of the Earth, as Marble and Stones are of a cold nature, although we must otherwise conceive of metals, because they are rather of an airy nature, and have in them sparkles of the Fire of Nature, and a spirit of Sulphur congealing their moist and cold matter. Yet *Mercurie* surpassing the rest in moisture and cold, is beholding to the Earth for his coldness, and to the Water for his moisture. It is otherwise with those things that are produced in the Sea, as in *Amber* and *Coral,* and many other things that have their beings from the Sea and fresh Waters, which as it is apparent, are of a hot temper, so that we have this instruction both from reason and experience, that the greatest coldness is to be attributed to the Earth, not to the Water.

60. But driness doth agree to the Earth accidentally onely, and in a remiss degree; for it was created in the middest of the Waters, and the order of beings required, that in respect of its gravity, being sunk in the Waters, it should never separate from them; but the Creatour using his Prerogative, having removed the Waters, gave to it an open surface, that so there might be room made both for the creation of mixed Beings, and for their habitation. The Earth therefore was enfranchiz'd from its natural yoke of bondage and subjection to the Waters, not by any order of Nature, but by a priviledge of favour, that so having its face wipt, it might lift up a dry visage to the view of the Heavens, and might partake of the welcome light of the world.

61. Every cold and drie is averse from the faculty of Generation, unless it be helped out by some eternal helps; therefore it was the will of the Supream Authour of Nature, to heat the cold womb of the Earth with an heavenly fire, and adjoyned to the drie globe of the Earth the moist nature of Water, that so by the mixture of two generative causes, moist, and hot, the sterility of the Earth might be helped, and that by the mediation of the concourse and mixture of all the Elements, the Earth might

27

be made a natural Vessel for fruitfull Generation. Therefore all Elements, and all qualities are in the Earth.

62. The body of the Earth was rightly created by the great God of a spongeous nature, that so there might be a recaptacle for Air, Showers, and heavenly Influences, and also that the moist vapours being expelled by the force of inward heat, from the Centre to the Superficies, through the porous passages of the Earth, might by a mean putrefaction corrupt the seeds of things, and so prepare for generation; these being thus disposed, receive that enlivening and heavenly heat. For Nature hath sunk in the depths a magnetick love, by the actings of which they draw down, and suck out the efficacy and virtue of things above, which do increase the strength of the information, and hasten the sweetness of vital Air.

63. The heat that comes from the inwards of the Earth, is moist and impure, and doth corrupt by reason of the tainted mixture of Earth and Water; But the most pure and heavenly doth generate by excitation, dilation, and furthering the inbred heat to life, even that inbred heat which is hidden in the seeds of things, and as Natures secret closed in their centre. But because both these heats are of the same kind, they have a joynt and amicable operation in the act of generation, and are inseparably united, until they are brought forth to life and large vegetation.

64. Water is of a middle nature, betwixt what is thick and what is of a thin nature, betwixt the Earth and the Air; Natures *menstruum,* a volatile body, flying and not enduring fire, drawn forth by a moderate heat into a vapour, assuming multiplyed shapes, more unstable than *Proteus.*

65. The moist Element is *Mercurie,* which sometimes assuming the nature of a bodie, sometimes of a spirit, doth attract to himself by his revolutions, the virtues of superiour and inferiour Beings, and as it were receiving their instructions, doth trade in commerce as their agent or factor, amongst the remotest natures of the Universe, neither will he leave his trafficquing till all the Elements of the corruptible Nature receive their fixation and purgation by fire, and there issue upon it an Universal Sabbath.

66. Water, being the nearest in nature to the first matter, doth easily receive her impress. The Chaos, the ancient Parent

of all things, was a kind of subtile and dark vapour, a kind of a moist dark substance, like a thin smoak, from whose most subtile part the Heavens are drawn forth into order, which a three-fold difference divides into a three-fold province; to wit, the Supream, which is the noblest, the middle which assumes the second place of dignity and honour, the lowest is inferiour to the other two both in scite and honour. The thicker substance of the matter went to the making of that watry heap, which is a middle nature. The thickest part, which is as it were the dregs of the whole Mass sate down to the bottom, and was setled for the globe of the Earth. The extremities of this artifice, to wit, the Heaven and the Earth, did recede more from the first state of their matter, and from their ancient shape; the Heaven in regard of its great rarity and levity, the Earth in respect of its great density and gravity. But the Water, which was a mean betwixt them, continued a nature more like the first formless Abyss from whence it proceeds, so that with ease it turns it self by rarefaction into smoak or vapour, which is the image of the ancient *Hyle*, or first Matter.

67. Moisture is more proper to Water than Coldness, because Water is of a greater rarity, and more lightsom than Earth, but those things which communicate most of light, are farthest off from cold; the more rarity there is in any thing, the nearer vicinity there is to light. Water retained the symbole of moisture from the first matter the Abyss, as the Earth coldness. For the Architect Spirit of the World divided the more thick parts into those two nearly-allied Natures.

68. Coldness wooes Driness, and invests it self with it where it is vigorously predominant by the constriction of moist beings, and by the desiccation of them, as is evident in Snow, Ice, and Hayl. For it is the work of Nature to bind and drie the Water, than which nothing is more humid by the proper instrument of Cold; yea, the principal and common subject of Heat and Cold, is humidity, by both which it is so strongly assailed, till it be conquered: from whence it falls out, that in *Autumn* so many drie leaves fall at the first cold, that the stalks of feeble Plants upon the strength of Winter, in the height of Drought, are void of moisture, and drie away: The cold penetrating doth so scorch,

and makes so furious an assault upon the vital humours: hence proceeds flaggy and withered age, at length death comes and cuts down all with his well-set sickle, and sweeps you into his general Granary. How then can any one conceive Cold to be friendly to Moisture, and to be its inherent property? Since Nature suffers not the Elements to act against each other, lest they should destroy and oppose each the others power, but an intense Cold quickly would bring under a remiss and weak moisture, and would swallow it up all by a violent constriction: so that by this means one of the Elements being lost, there would necessarily follow an imperfection in the work of the rest, and a deficiency in the generation of all things. It is therefore not suitable to the Law of Nature, to invest Water with the property of being cold in the highest degree.

69. Out of these solider Natures of Earth and Water, doth Nature extract her Elements, by which she compacts Vessels and corporeal Organs: for out of the commixture of both is made a clay, which is the next matter of things in generation: for it is in stead of the Chaos, in which virtually and confusedly are all Elements. Out of this clay was the first Father of mankind created, and after all Generation issued from it. In the Generation of creatures, is a clay made of the seed and the *menstruum,* from whence proceeds the living Creature. In the production of Vegetables, the seeds do first fall into a subtile clay by putrefaction, and then are wrought up to a vegetable body. In the generation of Mettals, there comes forth a clay from the perfect mixture of Sulphur and Mercury, and their resolution in a fat Water, by which means the mettallick bodies are indurated by a long decoction. In the Philosophical resolving of mettals, and in the creation of that Philosophical Secret, first is brought forth a clay out of the seed of both parents purged and mixed.

70. Water is the base and root of all moistures, yea, it is moisture it self: from which all moist things receive their denomination, therefore Water may be rightly defined the Fountain of the moist Element, or the Spring of moisture, whose property it is to wet by its liquour. But those things are termed humid, which do in themselves according to a less or greater degree, contain a moisture, or a watry liquor. Moisture is receivable

of all qualities, so bloud and yellow choller are humours, endued with their own heat, although they have their foundation in the Element of Water. *Aqua-fortis* and the like are empowered with a burning and a fiery nature. The burning Water, and many other essences which are extracted from oyls and water, do abound in heat, although the root of them, which is Water, be cold, because Nature doth first imprint in a moist element various resemblances and signatures of its powers, and doth in it en-root and infuse its principal and choice qualities. Moisture is the first subject of Nature, upon which her prime care is bestowed, her first charge layed out, by whose liquour it doth dilute and mingle various colours, and indelible tinctures: To it first do the spiritual qualities communicate themselves, in it first do they take up their being and actings.

71. The lower Waters being divided into two, do occupy a double seat, for one part of them brimming the Earth, doth lean on it as it were as its proper Base, and with the Earth makes but one Globe: the other part flying upward, doth range up and down the Region of the neighbour Air, and there making to it self many masqued fancies of bodies, and various figures of several phantasms doth reave hither and thither, over-hanging the lower Region.

72. Always there is a great part of the Waters that keep above, and being driven to and fro by the Caroach of the Wind, doth post over divers parts of the Air, which was in this manner ordered from the Day of the Creation, by the enacting of the Wisdom of GOD, that so the uncumbered and plain face of the Earth, might be unmasked and fited for the generation of things. For the Channels of the Sea and Rivers were not sufficient to receive the whole Waters, but if all should break the confining Bars of the Heavens, and come rumbling down, it would not onely cover the plain face of the Earth, but it may be, overtop the highest Mountains. Such an enloosening of the Cataracts of Heaven, we may guess, did occasion the old Cataclysm or Deluge.

73. Water is not onely sublimated into a vapour by heat alone, neither is it onely bound up in a cloud by cold, but to both the virtues of the Sun and the Stars do contribute their

aids, not onely by multiplying the vigours of the Elements, but also by a kind of Magnetick virtue, attracting and retaining a moisture much or less, according to their different position, and the diverse figure of Heaven: from whence we observe the various ordering of years and times; for indeed that Mass of Waters is not kept in, so poized onely by the solidation of Cold or the Air, but by the powerfull order and regiment of superiour bodies.

74. Lest there might seem to Divine justice a want of judgements for the execution of his wrath, he made that Ocean which is poized over our heads, to be volatile or flying, and withal brought into his Armoury those fiery darts, his Thunder-bolts, that so the presumptuous sinners that cannot be won by love, might be wrought about by fear.

75. They are much out of the way, who do attribute to Air moisture in the highest degree, upon this ground, because it is easily kept in within the bounds of another, but hardly within its own; for this is the property of light and liquid bodies, not of moist, and so doth better agree with fire and Heaven, which natures are more rarified, than with Water and Air: for bodies that are rarified, because they of their own will flow every where, cannot be comprized within their own bounds, and therefore stand in need of another. Onely firm and solid bodies are kept in within their own compass and superficies, which cannot be done by those things that are of a subtile nature, because by reason of their thinness they melt and are fluid, and so less consistent: From whence this follows that the Air is a body of greater rarity, but not of greater humidity.

76. The Air from it self hath no quality intense and in the highest degree, but sometimes hath them upon loan elsewhere. The nature of Air is a middle nature betwixt things below and above, and so doth with ease assume the qualities of those that border upon it, from whence it happens that its inferiour Region, according to the diversity of times, hath a variety of temper, which inconstancy is occasioned by the changes of the neighbouring and thicker bodies of Water and Earth, whose state is easily altered by heat and cold.

77. The whole Air is the Heaven, the floor of the World, Natures sieve, through which the virtues and influences of other

bodies are transmitted: a middle nature it is that knits all the scattered natures of the Universe together: a most thin smoak, kindled by the fire of Heaven, into a light, as it were an immortal flame: the subject of light, and shade of day and night, impatient of vacuity: the principal transparent: the easiest receiver of almost all qualities and effects, yet the constant retainer of none: a borderer upon the spiritual nature, therefore in the Tracts concerning the Mysteries of Philosophers, it is called by the name of a *Spirit.*

78. The lower Region of the Air is like unto the neck or higher part of an *Alembick,* for through it the Vapours climbing up, and being brought to the top, receive their condensation from Cold, and being resolved into water, fall down by reason of their own weight. So Nature through continued distillations by sublimation of the Water, by cohobation, or by often drawing off the liquour being often poured on, the body doth rectifie and abound it. In these operations of Nature, the Earth is the Vessel receiving. Therefore the Region of the Air that is nearer to us, being bounded by the Region of Clouds, as by a vaulted Chamber, is of a greater thickness and impurity than those Regions above.

79. The middle Region of the Air is not that, in which is the gathering of the Clouds, from whence are Lightenings and Thunders, which is onely the higher part of the lower Region, and the border of it: but that which is above the Clouds is to be stiled *The Middle Region,* whither the watry Being, by reason of its gravity, cannot reach, yet whither sulphureous exhalations, disburthened of the load of their Vapours, do climb up, and there by a motion, either of their own, or anothers, being kindled, burn. Such are the flaming Meteors of divers sorts, which are viewed in the middle Region, whence we may guess, that it abounds with a hot and moist, though not a watry, yet a fat Being, which is the food of fire. In this Region is much peace and a good temperature, because it is not hurryed with the tempests of any wind, and onely the lighter excrements of the inferiour Nature sucked up hither.

80. The higher Region near the Moon is all airy, not fiery, as it hath been taken up, though falsely, in the Schools. There

is the peaceable habitation of the purest Air, and as it borders upon the Heavenly Region, so it approacheth it in nature, for it is not defiled with the least smut of the lower Abyss. There is a temperature in the highest, a purity but little inferiour to that of the neighbouring Heaven. In this place to fancy a sphear of fire, is the shame of a Philosopher, which breaking the Laws of Nature, would have long ere this ruined the Fabrick of the Universe.

81. The Fire, as a fourth Element of Nature, was placed in the highest Region of the Air, as in its proper sphear, by the chief Philosophers, being led by an argument, from order and by conjecture, rather than truth. For let no man fancy any other fire of Nature than the celestial Light, therefore the blessed Philosopher in his *Genesis,* makes no mention of fire, because he had before told of the creation of the Light upon the first day, which is the genuine fire of Nature, and truly he would else not have omitted Fire, if it had been a principle of Nature, having specified Earth, Water, and the Fowls of the Heavens.

82. Let not any therefore fancy, unless sleeping, a Region of Fire burning next the Moon, for the whole Air would not be able to bear so great an abundance of intense fire, but it had long ago fed upon, and ruined the whole Fabrick of the World, for whatsoever it falls upon it feeds upon and devours, being the designed ruin of the World and Nature.

83. Such a Devourer of Nature is not lodged as an Element of Nature, neither above the Air, nor below the Earth. Onely he doth tyrannize in the kingdom of Nature, either in the height of the Air, or the depths of the Earth, or else being kindled, upon the superficies of the Earth. Therefore *Lullius,* a man of a raised wit, did justly account it amongst the Gyants and Tyrants of the World. It may also be termed to be an Enemy to Nature, because whatsoever is destructive to Nature, is an adversary of Nature.

84. Our common Fire is partly natural, partly artificial. It may be man borrowed it for the accommodation of life, and for his necessity, from the Celestial, by an unition of the beams of it, and a multiplication of its vigour, or else by attrition or the collision of two bodies, the Spirit of God suggesting the project

to man.

85. The Sovereign Creatour of all things, did place the fiery spirit of a kindly heat in the Globe of the Sun to inspire light, and an enlivening heat to the rest of the bodies in the Universe, wherefore many have thought him to be the heart of the whole Fabrick, for from him springs the principle of all generation and life. He that searcheth for any other Element of Fire in the world, doth shut his own eyes against the Sun.

86. The source therefore of the Fire of Nature, is seated in the Sun, whose heat is always of an equality, and temperate in it self, though it be felt by us either greater or less, according to his appropinquation or distance, or according to his direct or oblique beams, or according to the scituation or nature of places. The Sun hath been elevated by most Philosophers, as the Soul of the World, breathing in motion, and a faculty of generation to Nature.

87. The Sun is not the Eye of the World, as some Ancients termed it, but is the Eye of the Creatour of the World, by which he doth sensibly view his sensible creatures, by which he conveys to them the sweetly-affecting beams of his love, by which he renders himself viewable to them: For scarcely could a sensible Nature have comprehended an insensible Creatour, therefore he formed for himself, and us so noble a body roab'd in his own glory, whose rays, that nearest approach Divinity, are Spirit and Life.

88. From that universal Principle of life, all the in-bred heat of Elements or mixed Beings is derived, which hath gotten to be called by the name of *Fire,* for wheresoever a free heat, a natural motion or life lodges, there Nature hath hidden Fire, as the principle of them, and the first mover of the Elements, by which the sensible Elements, or the Portions of the World are elementated, and receive their animations, yet doth it cleave close to the womb of the Earth, being bound up by the Earths density and coldness, exciting an Antiperistasis.

89. That Fire of Nature which is seated in mixt bodies, hath chosen the radical moisture, as its proper seat, the principal residence of which is in the heart (although it be diffused through all the parts of the body) as in the prime organ of life, and

the centre of this little world, whence that Prince of nature, as commanding from its Castle, doth move concordantly all the faculties, and the rest of the organs, and doth in-breathe life to the humours of the mixed Being, to the spirits, and finally to the whole Elementary Mass. And being the Sun, and Vicegerent of the Sun doth act all in this little, that the Sun doth in that large World.

90.   As the Sun, being in the middest of the rest of the Planets, doth enlighten them with his light, replenish them with his influential virtues, beget an harmony of life by his enlivening spirit, so doth the solar spirit in the middle of the Elementary Nature, giveth it an influential light, and gathers the Elements together in the work of Generation and doth unite and enliven them.

91.   The first Agent in the World is the Fire of Nature, which being seated in the Globe of the Sun, doth diffuse that vivifical heat by means of his rays, through all the dominions of Nature, working in the seeds; a power of activity, and setling in them the principle of motion and action, at the removal of which all motion ceaseth, and also the faculty of life and action.

92.   The heat of Nature, and the light of Nature, are really one and the same, for they have a continual and uniform effluence from the same Fountain, *i.* the Sun, but are distinguished by their office, for the heat is to penetrate into the moist inward parts of Nature, but light is to manifest, and open the outward parts: the office of heat is to move the occult Natures of things, that of light, to set before the eyes sensible accidents: both of these is wrought by the rays of the Sun. The Sun therefore is the first Organ of Nature, by whose approach or distance, all the operations of Nature are variously governed, intended, or remitted, by means of light and heat.

93.   The second universal Agent is that same light; not so immediately issuing from the Fountain, but reflected from solid bodies, inlightened by it as the heavenly, yea, the Earth it self: for the light of the Sun beating upon those bodies, gives a motion to their dispositions and faculties, and alters them, and diffuseth their several and different virtues by the reflection of his rays, through the whole frame of Heaven and of our Air: for by those

rays, as by so many conveyances, are the various effects of several bodies dispersed every where for the benefit and harmony of Nature, which are called by us *Influences*. These are the true and first Elements of Nature, which because they are spiritual, do communicate themselves to us under some airy, or also some watry Nature, to whose good act, as to the roots of the Elements, we are beholding for the gift of every birth, and of all life.

94. Love, styled by *Plato* the Eldest of the gods, was breath'd into nature, begotten by the Divine Spirit, and hath the place of a *Genius* in her dispositions. In the first Division of the World, betwixt the first brothers, she gave the judgement for the partitions of their families, and after had alwayes the Præfecture in Generation.

95. The God of Nature did fix the first bond of Love in the things of Nature, between the first Matter and the universal Form, the Heaven and the Earth, Light and Darkness, Plenty and Poverty, Beauty and Deformity. The second degree of Love from the first couple, which is as it were the loving embraces of the Parents, issued into the Elements, which having a fraternal tye to bind them, have divided betwixt them the whole right of Nature. The third and last degree, is compleated in mixed bodies, which excites them by the in-born and in-bred sparkles of love, to a propagation and multiplication of their like. The Divine Love hath appointed this treble Love-knot, as a kind of Magical tye, that it might deliver it self by traduction into all and every part of his workmanship. Love is the Base of the Universe, the Cube of Nature, and the fastening bond of things above and below.

96. Let those avaunt therefore, who do attribute the concordant motions of Nature to Discord; for Nature is peaceable and pleasant in all her workings, yea, she is delightfully tickled in her actings. The very Elements of things in their coition are wholly lost in love, that they may knit themselves together by their mutual embraces, and of many be made one.

97. Let the Academies stand up, and tell us how the first Matter can be the first subject of contraries, and how Love can lye amongst the brawlings and jarres of Enmity! or that eager appetite, which the Prince of Philosophers acknowledgeth resid-

ing in the heart of this Matter, whereby it doth as earnestly lust for its form, as a man for a woman? Will not those enemies, constituting the seeds of Beings and the mixt bodies, by their eternal food, at length force Love and Concord to yield to their ruine.

98. They that placed a lust between the Matter and the Form, and yet an hatred and repugnancy in the Matter it self, and in the Elements, in making these contraries, have made themselves so: for according to the dictates of their School, the Soul in all things generated (onely man excepted) is brought forth out of the power and privy virtue of the Matter: But how can this be without love? If the Matter radically doth lye under the dissentions of contraries, must not the Form, which springs from her very root, feel the same portion? Nay, would it not be stifled by them in its first birth and cradle? What man therefore that stood right in his wits, would acknowledge the rule of these bandetties, to be chief in the nuptials of Love and Nature, in the very juncture of the mixture of the Elements, and of the information of the Matter? Yea, who would expect an uniform, and not a monstrous issue from the heterogeneous seed of opposite parents?

99. Let therefore the Philosopher surcease to place the cause of the alteration of the Elements, of the corruption and failing of mixt beings in the repugnancy of the Elements, but rather lay the fault upon the penurious weakness of the first matter. For in the first Chaos

> '*Twixt moist and drie there was no battel fought,*
> *Nor any enmitie 'twixt cold and hot.*

It is indeed the Vulgar conceit that there was, whereas onely two, no way contrary, of those four qualities, to wit, Cold and Moisture, agreed to the female, & the matter, and were in it: The other two, which are Heat and Drought, which are masculine and formal qualities, came forth out of the part of the informing light. And the Earth was not called *Drie Land* before the drawing off the Waters, and the coming on of the light Being, which was first moist and covered with Waters.

100. Therefore certainly reason it self doth evidence, that

those four qualities, which by the Vulgar are accounted repugnant, are not extant in the first matter, unless after information. And lest she might endure some contrariety in its solitude, she had other diseases, to wit, Darkness, Confusion, Deformity, Coldness, & an indigested Moisture, with an impotency, which are all evidences of a diseas'd and languishing body: Therefore being infected from its creation with that corruption, it derived it down to its posterity, lodged in this lowest and weakest Region of the elements. Therefore it is not set down in *Genesis* of that Abyss of Darkness, that it was very good, but reserv'd that gracefull Elogie for the Light, and for the rest that were created.

101. But who is there that hath the least dram of knowledge, will conceive that this contentious repugnancy did flow from the form into the matter, after the union of the four qualities in the matter being informed? Since it is essential to and the intent of the form, to adde a perfection to the matter, and compleately to perfect it into an harmony and consent, and a temperament according to its ability.

102. The first contraries through opposing qualities, were Light and Darkness; Light hath two qualities Heat and Drougth; Darkness as many, Cold and Moisture, wholly opposite each to other, because of their intention. But after those two aged principles of Nature came together, and the dark material and female principle was informed by the lightsom, formal and masculine principle, and impregnated by the light, the whole matter of the Universe, and all the Regions thereof received this priviledge of light, though distinct in the degrees and differences: for that fiery tincture of the Spirit of light left nothing unpierced, and the four qualities also at first being in their highest degree, were brought down to a remission in the informed matter, and so closing sweetly, contracted a fast friendship, and consented to a temperature: and so being made friendly, they were entered into the *homogeneous* family of the Elements, that so there might nothing of repugnancy or enmity lurk in the generation of mixt bodies, whereby the pleasing motion of Nature might be disturbed.

103. Neither in nature are those four qualities contrary one to another, but onely divers and unlike one to another, neither

do they ruin, but unite into a firm league one with another. So Heat and Cold in a remiss degree, do amicably agree and commix in one and the same subject, that a middle and temperate quality, to wit, a lukewarmness might be produced. But if in the intense degree they couple not without a fight and combat, this proceeds from the excess and tyranny of the intension, which cannot endure two qualities equally heightened and adverse, to be partners and sharers of one and the same Sovereignty, but there will fall out a tumult. But indeed Nature casteth out intense qualities, as bastards and strangers.

104. Let not therefore any fancy that Nature admits fire intense into the family of her Elements, for such a fire would be fit for destruction, not generation, would not be according to, but against Nature, which avoids violent things, and delights in a temperature, in which is no fighting, no contrariety. For the Rule of Nature cannot away with the rage of a scorching heat, or a wasting cold, or the distemper of moist and drie, but doth pleasingly lye down in a composed temperature. Let not any therefore search for the intense qualities in the Elements of things; he will find them in them either less or more remitted.

105. He is deceived therefore who says that hot and cold, moist and drie, are simple contraries. For the Earth, which by *Aristotle* is laid down as drie in the highest, should always quarrel with the Air, which is said by him to be moist in the highest: Also Water that is cold in the highest, according to his opinion, should be opposite to Fire, that is hot in the highest: and this repugnancy would inclose by force every one of the common Elements, or every Region of the World within the verge of its sphear, and by reason of this antipathie, would destroy all hospitality betwixt them. But we are convinced of the contrary, both by reason and experience. For ditches and all hollow places under the Earth, yea, the very bowels and pores of the Earth are replenished with Air, and the intrinsical moisture of the Earth, by which, as with their mothers milk, all Vegetables are nourished, is nothing else but an hot and moist Air, cleaving close to the Earth, and handing it as a nursive and nourishing faculty: the pores of the Earth are the dugs, and the airy moisture the milk, by which, she, the Mother and Nurse of things, doth

nourish her off-springs, and give them growth.

106. They, who settle four Elements in as many humours, do grant, that Nature being moist, is receivable, yea, is the subject of four Elementary qualities: how then can they hold a contrariety in them, which they place in one and the same subject? For though those four humours are distinguished by their respective differences, yet have they but one base, one common root to all, to wit, Humour: for yellow choller which resembles fire, is no less an humour than flegm, which resembles water: and the same may be said of adust Choller and Bloud, although they do not absolutely, but comparatively confound the four Elements in a moist Being.

107. If there were any repugnancey in the qualities and elements of Nature, the greatest would be betwixt hot and cold, and so betwixt Water and Fire, but the nature of these are not adversary, many generations which are under the Waters, do evidence: for wheresoever there is any generation or life, there must be fire, as the nearest intrinsical, efficient, moving and altering cause of the matter for generation:

> *Here Men, Beasts, and the Fowls their Being have,*
> *And ghastly Monsters rowling on a wave;*
> *A fiery vigour to their seeds is given,*
> *The homage for their birth is due to Heaven.*

108. Therefore certainly he will be in the right, who shall acknowledge those four first qualities, in-born and essential to the things themselves, and to their Elements, to be apt to a mixture by the direction of Nature, and not contrary, for they are as it were four organs or instruments which Nature makes use of in the perfecting of her alterations and generations.

109. Nature sets up a Potters trade, for she is wholly taken with making her matter circular, these four qualities are as the wheels, by which she doth by degrees and wisely inform her works through a circular and slow motion.

110. Of those four Wheels, two, *viz.* those of Moist and Drie, are most agreeable to the matter, because Nature doth turn and work the matter between these two: those two qualities are nearest the matter, because more subject to be passive, and

to a change. But the other two, to wit, of Hot and Cold, are more of action, because by their turns they alter and change the former; these are passive, those active, & are as it were the active instruments of Nature, working upon her passive matter.

111. Let us therefore cast off that tenent of Contraries, as contrary to natures concord, and dash out it with a pen of iron, with the good leave of learning, from the depraved table of Philosophy, and let us in the room of it, inscribe the Symbole of Concord, which Nature doth acknowledge of the same standing with her self, by whose help the delightfull copulation of actives with passives is procured in every Generation.

112. Those, who according to the flying opinion do stand for four Elements contrary each to other, do necessarily introduce a fifth, as the knot or bond-tye of concord, as the Peace-maker, otherwise they could not receive any perfect mixture, or any temperature in the work of generation, but without a rudder or a ruler would float a drift through the vast Ocean of Nature, never able to reach a port, or bring forth a birth: and so would they cheat the common Genius of Nature of her proper end.

113. For these four being acknowledged by reason of their repugnant qualities to keep up an eternal war betwixt themselves, cannot be united or appeased in the generation of mixt Beings, but rather with their mutual conflict rushing in, will procure an Abort, than a birth in Nature, unless their contrary actings be composed to a peaceable love by the part of some fifth heavenly and tempering Nature, which may introduce a temperature void of Hot and Cold, Drie and Moist.

114. That fifth Element, as they call it, or heavenly and incorruptible Spirit, springing from the light, motion, and virtue of the heavenly bodies upon these lower Beings, and preparing the Elements for motion and life, and stopping from ruin particular individuals, as far as their setledness will permit, hath merited the name of the salt Nature, the tie of the Elements, the Spirit of the world, to be given it by the searchers of occult Philosophie.

115. If there were any contrariety between the principles of things, certainly it was between Light and Darkness, by reason of their opposite qualities, but those qualities were tempered by

42

the coition of both principles, and from the extreams became a middle temper, and such were they when they dislodged from the first, and went into the second principles or Elements.

116. The extreams are contrary each to other, onely by reason of the intension of their opposite qualities, but those things that spring from the mixture of these extreams are not diverse, because they are of a middle nature, and the efflux of the union of the two extreams, to wit, of Light and Darkness.

117. That out of the mixture of the Contraries, to wit, of Light and Darkness, do not come contraries forth but in a temperature, is plain by that of the Kingly Prophet, breaking forth into these words of the Eternal Light, *He bowed the Heavens and came down, and Darkness was under his feet, &c. He made Darkness his Covert, his Pavilion in the middest of it, &c.* The very fountain of Eternal Light, that he might exhibit the brightnes of his infinite glory to mortal eyes, did wrap it up in a cloud and dark mask, and brought the Darkness to the Light, that he might make of the two Extreams a moderate light, and so allay the splendour of so great a light, as was not to be gazed on without the ruin of the Spectatour; yea, Philosophers do affirm, the Rain-bow that was given by God as a sign and token of a Covenant made with man, to be produced out of a mixture of Light and Darkness, that so that Symbole of the temperature of Gods wrath, existing out of contraries, might be tempered of various coherent and friendly colours.

118. Those that have delivered that the Earth, Water, Air and Fire, in their sphears are distinct Elements of the World, and are turned each into other, by mutual reciprocation, did but slightly look into the depths of Nature; for it is more safe to call them the compleating parts of Nature, or the Shops of the Elements: for the Elements of the world do not lye under our view or senses, as separated in their proper Regions, but do lye hid and keep close in their wombs, till they come together in the generation of mixt bodies, and make up a body. But those parts of the World, as so far mutually different, can never have a conversion in them, neither can that one common quality, whereby those natures are linked together, beget such a change, that out of things of a diverse, should be formed a like nature,

43

yea, that they should be turned into the same.

119. If those four Elements asserted by them, do change and barter their rooms, natures and offices, all the compact frame of the World, devoted to a chance and motion, would be in a perpetual fluctuation, which we know is established by God in a certain and constant order and scite, and distinction of parts: For Earth will quickly be made Water, Water Air, Air Fire, and so backward, and by this the Centre shall run out to Circumference, and the Circumference run into the Centre, the farthest and the middle parts of the World, shall of their own accord remove out of their places, that so after a long time the order of Nature shall be inverted, whilest the top and the bottom, and the bottom and the top change places, and clash together. He who doth fancy this so fair composure of a World, doth not deserve to have so fine a piece termed a World, but a Chaos, an Abyss, which Nature, a friend to Order, doth absolutely detest.

120. They which do say that those extream bodies of the lower World, Earth and Fire, (supposing, not granting a sphear of Fire) are turned into each other, do wrong themselves and truth too. For their distant and repugnant natures do disagree from such a charge, for the heightened cold, thickness, and gravity of the Earth are so opposite to the same degree or heat, subtility, and levity in Fire, that they can never be brought to change. Besides, the Earth, a fixed body, will not yield to fire, but slighteth its virtue, if we may believe the opinions of Chymists and common experience, neither doth any thing flie out from it, but a fat and watry humour, both of them not natural to the Earth: but if any thing is to be turned into elementary Fire, it must necessarily be light and volatile, that it may be translated into its Orb and Nature. The Earth therefore being most weighty, and so the Centre of all, being most fixt, and so least volatil, how can it be turned into Fire, and be carried up into the Sphear of Fire, or how can Fire, the highest and lightest of all, be beaten down to be essentially united with the Earth, contrary to the laws of Nature? It were a more easie conversion of Water and Fire, because they are nearer by one degree than Earth and Fire.

121. They that believed, the exhalations from the region of

the earth drawn up into the Air, and because kindled there, to be earthie, and converted into the Element of Fire, are far out of the way of truth, for they are not earthie, but rather airie natures: for our Air being moist, through the contagion of water lying in the drie bosom of the Earth, gather a fatness, and by the consortship of the Earth, doth temper the moist with the drie, but when it exhales through the pores and crevices of the Earth being drawn by heat, or else the abundance of the matter forcing out, it breaks not forth out of its prison without a noise & crack, whence proceed earth-quakes and openings not without much ruin; that exhalation, got loose, doth flie up into the region proper to light bodies, and there is set on fire, being digested by its errant motion and heat, more fully into a sulphureous matter. Therefore that matter is not truly earthie, since it is neither ponderous nor cold, but because it is made fat and combustible by the concourse of hot, drie, and moist; it may more properly be called the accidental food of fire, than the Fire of Nature, or the Elementarie Fire. That is a bastard, a spurious generation, which for that very reason ought not to have been placed amongst the natures, or been called by the names of Elements; therefore these Firings are rightly called by *Aristotle,* imperfectly-mixed things. The same we must conceive of the smoke of combustibles: For Smoke being unctious, doth quickly take fire, which is nothing else but smoke kindled.

122. Fire feeds upon fat and unctious matter, but the fat moisture of the Air is contempered with drought, whence we often may see a sulfureous matter, extrinsecally drie and terminated with drought, as our ordinarie sulfur, gun-powder, and the like; which though they seem to be outwardly drie, do close within them a fat moisture, and upon the firing are resolved into it.

123. And truly they slip to purpose, that have taken an opinion, seeing stones and heavie bodies sometimes generated in the Air, and shot down thence by lightnings, thunders, and breaking of the clouds, that the Fire turns to a stone, or is converted into earth, or have a conceit, that the Earth is carried up thither. This is done far otherwise; for that hardened matter was never fire or earth, nor proceeded from the Orb of Fire (if

45

there be any) or from the bodie of the earth, but an unctious and viscous humour, in a manner clayish, shut up in a cloud as in a fornace, is so hardened and decocted, as an earthen vessel by the heat of the burning exhalations, that it turns a stone: Hence proceed those darted Thunder-bolts. Such meteors as these are the wens, weaknesses, and diseases of Nature, not Elements. In the same, though after a slower manner, is the stone generated in the bodie out of flegm in the reins or bladder. For the Microcosm hath also his meteors.

124. The fire of nature is far different from our artificial or accidental fire. The fire of nature is double, either Universal and Particular, or Individual. The Universal is diffused through all the parts of the Universe, doth sweetly excite and move the propensive virtues of the celestial bodies, doth impregnate and supply with engendering seed this Globe of ours, designed for the generation of things; doth infuse virtues into the seeds; doth untwist the intangled power of nature; mingles the Elements; informs the Matter; and finally doth unlock the secret of Nature: but the fountain of it is in the Sun, who as the Heart of the World doth stream forth his enlivening heat as his love through all regions. But the particular Fire of Nature, is in-born and in-bred in every mixed bodie, and individual, which flows as a rivulet from that General, and doth work all things in this Microcosm or little World MAN, according to an Analogie with the Sun in the Macrocosm or greater World. But who is there that would not stile our common fire, being an opposite of all generation, living onely upon prey, subsisting upon the ruins of other Beings, the destruction of life, deputing all things to ashes, rather a foe than a friend to nature, its enemie, not its inmate; and rather the ruin than the raising of Life? But those fires that are bred in the Airie region, are rather engendred by chance, than by any intention of Nature.

125. Neither are those two bodies of the Earth and Water, situated next one to the other, convertible each into the other, but onely by reason of their neighbourhood are mingled together; so that the Water washeth the Earth, and the Earth thickens the Water; and hence is made Clay, being a bodie of neither, but a middle betwixt both; which if resolved by the force of fire, will

separate it self into both these natures. The water flying out, the earth settles: neither will there be any conversion of each into the other, for that cannot be effected by that single common qualitie of cold, since the drieness and moisture are not less powerful to resist, than the mutual consent of cold can bring them to a conversion. Besides the driness and fixation of the Earth, are quite opposite to the moist and volatile nature of the Water, so there is but one qualitie agreeing to an alteration, and many disagreeings, which will prevail in the combate. Besides, here is the help of nature always readie to conserve it self, and doth never incline, unless upon force and conquest to its ruin or change.

126. We may guess the whole Globe of the Earth, not to be of a less settled nature than the Heaven, the Moon, or the Stars, for it, if it be the centre of the World, as it is generally received, then certainly the constancie is not less necessary to it than to the rest of the bodies of the World. Besides the earth is the same without any essential immutation of what it was from the beginning, and what it will be to the end of ages. But if it did suffer any notable detriment by the universal deluge in the general, or any accidental in particular, as by some chasme, or by the breakings in of rivers, or the Sea; this falls out by the supream order of him that doth change at list, the laws of the whole and every region: or by the discordant harmonie of the World, or by some disease of some distempered nature, rather than by any propensiveness or viciousness of the Earth. For all the bodies of the Universe do lie under their burdens and diseases, although they be diversified according to the disagreement of Nature, and difference of perfection, yet the accidents do not change the nature and constancie of them in respect of the whole. Absolute constancie and impassibilitie do onely suit to God alone: but the Heaven, Water, Earth, and the rest of the bodies of the Universe shall stand firm, in regard of their essence to the designed period of their age.

127. If any one of those four natures have a propensitie to conversion, it will be strongest in the mean qualities; for Water and Air are joyned in greater affinitie between themselves than with the rest, or the others amongst themselves. For they seem

47

not to differ so much in their qualities, as in the intension and re-mission of them, not so much naturally as accidentally. For since Water doth by a right of nature challenge to it self moisture and coldness, it doth also communicate them to the lower region of the Air by way of commerce, (for Air obtains no proper qualitie almost besides the highest tenuitie, yet capable of receiving the rest, therefore is it of an heavenly nature, being of it self most temperate, and not addict to any proper qualitie, doth readily receive and dispence the dispositions, influences, and virtues of the heavenly bodies.) Densitie and raritie, which in a remiss degree are of kin, seem to make the principal difference between Water and our Air; for which reason God is said in *Genesis*, to have separated the Waters from the Waters; as if by reason of the unity of their nature, it seemed more truely to be a division of their situation, than a mutation in respect of their essence.

128. Yet these bordering natures, do not entertain any true and essential reciprocation, but onely according to some respect, not altogether changed, but after some manner; and this change is acted in the lower region of the Air, which is bound in by the cover of the clouds, and reacheth not the middle, much less the highest region. Water being rarified into a vapour flies up, and is rather raised then turned into Air; and that vapour condensed doth resolve, and fall down again. The ancients, being led by the legerdemain of sence, more than the light of reason, conceived this circulation, and returning into it self of one and the same nature, to be the turning of nature into another: but it is found to be otherwise by those that have and use a sharp insight into the depths of Nature. He is also deceived that shall call the Air simply a thin Vapour, because a Vapour is a middle and imperfect bodie betwixt the two Waters, those above, and these below, betwixt our Water and Air, yet it is neither of them, because although it rarifie, yet will it never be heightened to the great degree of the nobilitie of the Air. It may be made a spurious but never a pure Air: neither will the refined nature of the Air be so depressed and fall from its puritie, as to thicken into a vapour, cloud, or Water. For the right of Nature never got that first separation of the Waters, which was really and actually done by that Architect spirit, and that the established

bounds of the parts of the World, which God hath sealed with an indelible signature, should either be blurred or removed by any new confusion.

129. But those that dive deeper into things, will acknowledge the Earth to be the womb of the World, the vessell of Generation, the mother of a multiplied, and almost numberless issue, which being rescued in the beginning of the Creation from the power of the covering Waters, and priviledged to it self, was made and remained drie land; and her bodie being condensed, sunk to the foundation and the centre of the whole, and spread out her lap as a Parent to all vegetables, and all other creatures; yet did she want moisture, whereby she might be made apt for a fruitful generation. Gods providence set out a remedie for this exigence: Therefore from the beginning was the water made volatile, that so it might be carried up in vapours, which being frozen by cold in this cloud, might by heat be thawed again into Waters. By this master-piece of Divine providence, was this exigence of the Earth supplied, and that driness, which threatened barrenness, was tempered with a large moisture, and the womb of our mother conceived. Therefore onely Water hath the circulation, to the intent that it might moisten the bosom of the Earth, or more truly it is distilled up in the lower region of the Air as in its Alembick; that so by often pouring in, and reiterated distillations, it being abounded, and having gotten virtues both from above and below, and endued with that celestial Nectar, it might more effectually soften the bosom of the Earth, and endue it with a prolifical virtue. The chief worker of all, who maketh use of the art of Nature, hath added nothing superfluous to his work, nor left any thing defective in it.

130. But the Water being the menstruum of the World, doth cherish and contain in it the seeds of things and their elements; but she having this circulation, the true and genuine Elements of things which are in the Earth, as in the matrix and vessel of Generation; and in the Water, as in the menstruum, are also whirled about. In the vapour therefore, are the Elements of the Earth, the Water, and the Air; & have their sublimation, and exuberation with it. They are not the bodies of Earth, Water, and Air, which have their proper sphears, and constitute the

several Regions of the World, but they are the very spiritual Elements of Nature, which lye hid and inhabit in them, out of which many bodies, as stones may be generated and excocted in the Air. For where all the Elements well mixt, do meet, as they do in a vapour, there bodies may be generated; but when they find not a convenient matrix, as in the Air, there are ingendered imperfect mixtures, not by reason of any fault in the mixture, but in the Matrix.

131. The Water being seated as middle, betwixt the Earth and the Air, doth trouble both by its flowing, and always moving inconstancy, infesting the Air with a black soote, and noisom vapours, and often drowning the Earth by flouds; causing tempests in the Air, ruines to the Earth, and corruption to both; and it doth assault the Region of the one with its levity, and of the other with its gravity; and doth cross the order of Nature, and the nature of Times by its defect or excess, yet, doth shake all her borderers with her terrible claps and tumultuous ragings. Her nature being altogether female, the supream Creatour seems to have bestowed her on the World in the nature of a Woman, or a necessary Evil, even so doth she arrogate all things as subject to her, and turns those things that were given her for a general good, to a publick ruin. Finally, it is the scourge of divine Justice, revenging *Nemeses,* which being designed to the vengeance of sin, doth break out to punish, and sets the hopes and wealth of many the very roots of pride, under several shapes of judgements, the scoff and blast of the world.

132. The universal Natures, the more thick they are, the more impure, the more endued with tenuity; the more purity. The Earth, because more thick than Water, therefore is less noble, and so Water than Air; and Air than Heaven: and so the highest Region of the Heavens is the most noble, because it is most subtile. For it is an undoubted truth, that spiritual Natures are more excellent than corporeal, and the more bordering upon the spiritual Natures, the more they draw nigh to perfection.

133. The foundation of Generation and Corruption is in Moisture, for in both the travails of Nature, Moisture, of all the Elements, is the first patient, receiving the first seal of the form. The natural Spirits are easily united with it, because flow-

ing from it, do lightly return to it, because the root of them, in that, and by that, are the rest of the Elements mixed. The moist Element hath its circulation no less in mixed and individual bodies, than in the World, both in the work of Generation and of Nutrition, for it was Natures pleasure, that both these works should be performed by the same instruments of condensation and rarefaction, and by the same means, to wit, Spirits.

134. The Earth is the Vessel of Generation, Water the menstruum of Nature, containing in it the formal and seminal virtues, which it borrows from the Sun, the male and the formal universal Principle; from him is derived into all things the influence of the fire of Nature, and of formal Spirits, in which are all things necessary for generation, the in-bred heat being wrapt up in the moist: Therefore *Hippocrates* did rightly affirm, That these two Elements, Fire and Water, could do all, contained all things in them: For from them do issue two masculine qualities of Hot and Drie, from the other two more of Cold and Moist, being the female qualities, which so concurring and mixing, perfect the generation of mixed bodies. Over those two principal Elements, the two greater Lights were set, the Sun the authour of Fire, and the Moon the Lady of Moisture.

135. Nature perfects the circulation of the volatile Element, by a three-fold action or instrument, by Sublimation, Demission or Refusion, and by Decoction, which stand in need of a divers temperament. So doth the rightly ordered intention of Nature, wandering through various motions, directeth her interrupted actions to their designed end, and attaineth the same mark, though it trades through divers wayes.

136. Sublimation is the conversion of a moist and a ponderous nature, into a light, or the exhalation of it into a vapour. The end and benefit of it is three-fold: First, that a gross and impure body might be mundefied by attenuation, and might by degrees be drawn off the dregs; then that by sublimation it might gain the higher virtues, which continually flow down. Lastly, that by such an evacuation the Earth might be disburthened of its superfluous and loading humours, which seizing upon its passages, do hinder the action of the heat, and the free pass of the natural spirits, yea, do violently choak them. This drawing away of the

51

superfluous moisture, takes away the cause of obstructions, and gives ease to the squeazy stomach of the Earth, and makes it more fit for digestion.

137. But the Moisture is sublimated by the impulsive operation of heat. For Nature useth her fire as its proper instrument for rarefaction of moist bodies. Therefore the Vapours that generates Clouds & Rain, are most frequently drawn up in the Fall and Spring, because then the womb of the Earth doth more abound with hot and moist; now Moisture is the material, and Heat the efficient cause of exhalations. Nature doth shew a kind of intense heat in sublimation, whilest it is bound in within the terms and latitude of temperature.

138. Demission is the second wheel of Nature; in the work of Circulation is the returning of the spirituous Vapour into a gross and watry body: or the Refusion of a rarefied and sublimated humour, being again condensed, and its descent into Earth, that it may dilute it of its exuberant liquour, and suck it up by a sweet and celestial draught.

139. Nature doth intend three things by irrigation. First, that it might not pour out, but by degrees distil its abundant humour, lest there fall out a gulf, and by the abundance of water, the passage for the vivifical spirit in the bowels of the earth be dammed up, and the intrinsecal heat of the Earth be extinguished, for that wise and righteous Governess doth dispense all her benefits in number, weight, and measure. Secondly, that it might distribute the humour by divers drops, and by a various manner, to wit, a Rain sometimes larger, sometimes less, sometimes a dew, sometimes a hoar frost, sometimes pouring out a greater, sometimes a less plenty, that so it might water the Earth according to its appetite or necessity, thirsting for more or less. Thirdly, that these irrigations or waterings may be not continual, but by turns and betwixt other works; for the Sun doth in its course succeed the Showers, and the Showers in theirs the Sun, the day the night, and the night the day.

140. The lightest Cold or the departing Heat, doth unloose and make fit to fall those vapours that are brought up into the middle Region, and there frozen. For an immoderate heat doth dissipate and hinders their condensation, and an intense cold

doth so knit and freeze them, that they cannot produce a humour that may be fit to fall down.

141. The last wheel or action of the Circulation of Nature, is Decoction, which is nothing else but the digestion, ripening, and conversion into aliment of a crude humour instilled on the bosom of the Earth. This seemeth to be the end and the scope of the others, because it is the release of their labour, and a receiving of the food, attained by the former labours. For that crude humour, by force of that internal heat, is chewed, concocted, and digested by it, being as it were without motion and in a trance, silently and without noise, moving that secret fire as the proper instrument of Nature, that it may turn that crude liquour tempered with driness into a food. This is the compleat circle of Nature, which she rowls round by various degrees of labour and heat.

142. These three operations of Nature are so knit together, and have such a relation each to the other, that the beginning of the one is the end of the other, and according to Natures intention, they do in a necessary order succeed one another by turns. And the orders of these vicissitudes, are so interwoven and linkt together, as that combining to the good of the whole, they do in their operations prove serviceable each to other.

143. Yet Nature is forcedly sometimes drawn out of her bounds and verges, and ranges in an uncertain path, especially in the guidance of the moist Element, whose orders being interrupted do deceive, and they do easily as well as suffer wrong, by reason of the inconstancy of its volatile and flitting nature, as also by reason of the various disposition of the superiour bodies, which do bend these things below, especially Moisture, and draw them from their setled track, according to the beck of the Sovereign Moderatour, who doth use them as Organs and Instruments to the motion of the frame of the Universe. Hence is raised the deceitfull and inconstant temperature of this our Mansion, and the changed seasons of the year. So doth the womb of the Earth, being diversly affected, bring forth either more plentifully or more sparingly, generous or castling births. So doth the bordering Air being either pure or impure, produce either health or sickness, the moist Nature rowling and tossing

all things amongst us.

144. The Rule of our Heavens is uncertain and deceitful to us, because things below receive their orders from things above, whose natures and affections are for the most part unknown to us, yet let the Philosopher set always before his eyes the intention rather than the action of Nature, the order rather than the disturbance of the order.

145. We may observe the volubility or flittingness of the moist Nature, not onely in the general harmony of the World, but also in the particular of mixed Beings. For they are generated by the revolution of Moisture, they are nourished and grow by drying, moistening, and digesting; wherefore those three operations of nature are resembled to food, drink, and sleep, because meat answers to driness, drink to moisture, and sleep to concoction.

146. Lest man should dream fancies to himself, glory in divers priviledges, assume to himself as proper onely to him the name of *Microcosm,* or the Worlds lesser draught, because there are discernable in his material workmanship, an Analogie of all the natural motions of the *Macrocosm,* or the larger Volume of the World, let him consider that every creature, even a worm, that every plant, even the weed of the Sea, is a lesser world, having in it an epitome of the greater. Therefore let man seek for a world out of himself, and he shall find it every where, for there is one and the same first Copy of all creatures, out of which were made infinite worlds of the same matter, yet in form differenced. Let therefore man share humility and lowliness of spirit, and attribute to God glory and honour.

147. The inferiour natures are leavened by the superiour: But the Water not enduring delay, doth hast to meet the operations of the Heavens, for the Air, giving way to the vapour that flies up to it, receives it to lodge in the Region of the Clouds, as in a large Hall, but ere it comes thither, its body being in a manner spiritualized, the moist Being is divested of its ponderous nature, that so it might by this addition of agility, the sooner compass its desire, and enjoy the priviledge of an ambiguous nature.

148. In the mean time the Sun, the Prince of the celestial Quire, and the rest of the superiour Natures, taking care of the

inferiour, do instil by continual breathings enlivening spirits, as so many trilling rivulets from their most clear and pure Fountains: But the Vapours being thin, and so swimming in the Air, or else bound up into a Cloud, do most eagerly suck in that spiritual *Nectar,* and attract it to them by a Magnetick virtue, and having received it, they grow big, and being impregnated and quickened with that ingendering seed, as being delivered of their burden, do freely fall down back into the lap of the Earth in some Dew, hoar Frost, Rain, or some other nature; and this Mother of the Elements doth receive into her womb the returning moisture, and being quickened by this Heavenly seed, sends forth in her due time innumerable issues, according to divers degrees, more or less generous, according to the goodness of the seed, or the disposition of the womb: and the inferiour Waters also are made partakers of the benevolence of the Superiour and Celestial, because she goes with the Earth to the making up of one and the same Globe, and so they receive joynt and common benefits. But by the nature of Water is the fermentation of the rest of the Elements.

149. But this ferment or leaven is a vivifical spirit, flowing down from the superiour Natures upon these inferiour, without which the Earth would be again void and empty. For it is the seed of Life, without which neither man, nor any creature, nor any growing thing could enjoy the benefit of a generation or life; *for man lives not by bread alone,* but especially by that Heavenly food by Air, *to wit,* by such a spirit so breathed in, and fermented.

150. The three material Elements being remote in the composition of things, do onely obey God and Nature, and come not under the laws of Art, or of humane Invention: but there are three others that issue from the copulation of these, which being extracted by resolution, do sufficiently shew that they are the nearest in the composition of mixt Beings, *to wit,* Salt, Sulphur, and Mercury. And so it is manifested, That there is a Trinity of Elements, and a Signature of the universal NATURE.

151. These three last Elements are the issue of a threefold copulation of the three former, Mercury of the mixture of Earth and Water, Sulphur of the copulation of Earth and Air,

Salt produced out of the condensation of Air and Water, and there can be no more combinations of them named. The Fire of Nature is in all of them as their formal principle, the virtue of the celestial bodies contributing their influence and co-operation.

152. Neither are these latter produced out of any copulation of the former bodies, for Mercury comes forth of an unctious Earth and clear Water well diluted and mixt. Sulphur is generated of the most subtile and driest Earth coupled with the moist Air; Finally Salt is congealed of salt and thick Water, and crude Air.

153. It may be lawfull to affirm that *Democritus* his opinion, That all bodies were composed out of Atoms, is not far distant from truth: for both reason and experience do vindicate him from biting tongues, for the knowing Philosopher would not wholly conceal, but would unfold in an obscure and dark term, the mixture of the Elements, which that it might be agreeable to the intention of Nature, must necessarily be done by the smallest, and by actually indivisible Beings: otherwise the Elements could not combine into a continuous & natural body. Experience teacheth us in the artificial resolution & composition of mixt Beings, which are tryed by distillations, that the perfect mixtion of two or more bodies, is not done but in a subtile vapour. But Nature doth make her mixtions far more subtile, and as it were spiritual, which we may safely believe was the opinion of *Democritus*: for the grosseness of bodies is an impediment to Mixtion, therefore the more any thing is attenuated, the more apt and fitted it is for mixtion.

154. The three-fold degree of Existence in mixt Beings, doth offer to us three supream kinds of mixt Beings, *to wit,* of Minerals, Vegetables, and of Animal Beings. Natures law hath appointed a Being for Minerals in the Earth, for Vegetables in the Earth and the Water, for Animals in the Earth, Water, and Air; yet to all the Air is the principal food and foster of life.

155. Minerals, are thought simply not to have an existence or a life, although Metals from Minerals may be said to be endowed with a principal life, both because in their generation there is a kind of a copulation, and a commixiton of a double seed, male and female, *viz.* Sulphure and Mercurie, which two, by a long

and multiplied circulation, are turned and purged, and being seasoned with the salt of Nature, and fermented by it, and being perfectly mixed in a most subtile vapour, are formed into a clay or soft mass, the spirit of Sulphure by degrees closing in the Mercurie, at length that Mass doth grow hard, and is confirmed to a metallick body.

156. As also, because perfect Metals, especially do contain in them a principle of life, *to wit*, in-set fire infused from heaven, which being dulled by being bound in with the hard outside of the Mettal, lies hid as void of motion, and as an enchanted treasure, till getting libertie by philosophical solution, and the subtile artifice of the work-man, it doth powerfully display its refined spirit and celestial soul, by a motion of vegetation, & in the issue, heightened to the sudden perfection of art & nature.

157. Vegetables also are invested with a vegetative soul or spirit, they grow by a vegetative motion, and multiply, yet want an animal sence and motion. Their seeds are of an Hermaphroditical nature, for every particular grain doth contain in it a fruitfull seed, without copulation or mixture of a double seed, although in every kind, almost, of Vegetables, experience sheweth, there are both sexes to be found.

158. God also hath wrapt up in the seeds of Vegetables, a secret spirit, the authour of generation ennobled with a special character, which is wholly celestial, and a ray of the heavenly light, void of corruption, in which is preserved the specifical form under the bodie of every individual subsistance, which being through corruption resolved & lost, that immortal spirit being called out by the vivifical and homogeneal heat of the Sun, doth rise up in a new stalk, and doth bring into it the form of the former.

159. Animals, besides their existence and faculty of vegetation, do exceed in a sensitive soul, which is in them the principle of life and motion. Therefore an Animal, seated in the highest degree of things below, doth compleat the work of Nature in her Elementary kingdom, doth live properly, generate properly, and in it hath Nature truly distinguished each Sex, that from two, a third, *to wit*, their issue might be produced. So in the more perfect Beings the most perfect Symbole of the Trinity is most

apparent.

160. Man, the Prince of all creatures, and of the lower World, is accounted the Summary of Universal Nature: For his Soul is an immortal ray of the Divine Light, his Body is a beautied Composure of the Elements. The inward and unperceiveable faculties of the Sense, by which man doth comprehend all things obvious, are alogether celestial, and as it were Stars, giving the influence of knowledge of things; the motions and perturbations of the mind, are as it were the Winds & Tempests, Lightenings and Thunders; the Meteors, which break forth in the Aerial Region of the Spirit, do trouble the heart and the bloud. Therefore was man deservedly called a *Microcosm,* and the accomplisht Draught of the Universe.

161. But not onely man, but even every living creature, yea, every Plant is a *Microcosm.* So is every Grain or Seed a Chaos, in which are the seeds of the whole World compendiously bound up, out of which in its season a little World will spring.

162. Whatsoever Beings of Nature have a perfect mixture and life, they have a body, spirit, and soul. The body is made of clay, in which are all things necessary for the matter of generation, for it is most agreeable to reason, that Bodies should be made of two corporeal Elements especially, *viz.* Earth and Water.

163. The Spirit is a small portion of the purest Air, or the Heaven, a middle nature betwixt the Body and the Soul, the knot and bond of both, the case of the Soul, and the conduit of the more subtile and spiritual parts of the body.

164. The soul or form of a mixt body, is a spark of the Fire of Nature, and undiscernable Ray of Celestial Light, brought into act from the power of the seed, by the motion of generation, bound to an Elementary body by the mediation of the Spirit, giving its individual Being to the mixt body, the nearest principle and the efficient cause of life. It acts according to the disposed matter, and the qualities of the Organs.

165. The nature or form of the Soul, because it is altogether full of light in living creatures especially, hath so great a distance from the dark and earthy matter of bodies, that this is wholly irrational in respect of that, and this unproportionably more no-

ble, and therefore is fastened by that strictest tye which Nature makes use of in her works to the body, by reason of the disconveniency and distance, unless the conjunction and knot had been made by the virtue and efficacy of a peculiar and powerfull mean, therefore did the provident Creatour assign a subtile mean, which is the Ætherial spirit, which receives and retains the begotten form, and is the tye of it to the body, communicating in its nature with both. These things are to be conceived to be spoken of the celestial Soul of Natural things, not of the Super-celestial and divine Soul of man, which notwithstanding is according to the good pleasure of the Creatour, brought into a consortship with the body of man by natural *mediums.*

166. The specifical forms from the first day of the Creation, were imprinted in the first individual and particular persons, by the character of the Idæal copie, and that divine and indelible impress was according to the direction of the Creatour, by the way of generation traduced to posterity, that so by the perpetual succession of particular individual natures, the priviledge of immortality might be continued in the kind.

167. It cannot, nor must be conceived, that Forms do generate in the matter their like, for to generate is the alone property of bodies, but by an harmonious motion of their Organs, they do by them dispose the seminal matter for generation, and shut up in it a ray of Light, or a secret spark of life, as a treasure: This is the office and priviledge of the Form, as also to imprint its own specifical character on that vivifical spirit, wrapt up close in the seed, which in its set season, doth in the work of generation by the engendering heat, display it self into a soul, whether Vegetative or Animal, so that what was a formal and hidden spirit in the seed, is now a Form in the mixt body. So that occult thing that was closed in the bosom of Nature, is now made manifest, and brought forth from a power to an act.

168. The Form issues not forth onely out of the power and virtue of the seed, because there is an influence of celestial virtues in the generations of Beings, which do heighten the efficacies of the matter, do multiply them, and as it were midwife it to groaning Nature, yea, they do get into, and mixe themselves with, and bring in auxiliary strength to the formal and seminal

spirit that is the matter, which is also by its original, celestial.

169. There do not onely meet in the generation of every mixt Being, the corporeal Elements, but also all the Virtues, all the Powers of Natue in general, and these do contribute something of their own; so are the parts of the Universe bound up together, that they have an unanimous combination for life, and couple by a mutual affection.

170. The natural Forms of things though they are potentially in the seeds, yet are they neither of, nor generated by the substance of the lower Elements, for they have their rise from a more noble spring, their original is from Heaven, for their father is the Sun, the heavenly Nature the bond whereby these matters are knit together.

171. The specifical Forms of mixt Beings have within themselves closed a dark kind of knowledge of their original, and are carried up by their own strength, and by a secret motion, like unto Waters, to the height of their Fountain head. So the Soul of man being derived from the divine Spring of the uncreated Light, is reflected to the same by the sharp sight of his mind, and by the soaring contemplations of his soul, but the forms of other living creatures being taken out of the privy Treasury of the Heavens and the Sun, do by the instinct of Nature, and by a weak kind of reminiscency, glance back thither. Hence we may observe the frequent Prognosticks of several creatures concerning the courses of the Sun, and the changes of the Heavens. But the forms of Vegetables, being for the most part airy and inspired from the lowest Region of our Air, therefore they are not able to extend or reach forth their power, or faculties beyond it, they do, according to their abiliity, lift up their heads into the Air, as willing to visit their Countrey, but they are stopped so, as that they are not able to pass the narrow confines of their bodies, wanting the sense and life of a Soul, because there is so little of the Suns virtue in them, as will not carry them above the motion of a Vegetation. For in the order of creation, the Vegetables were first before the Sun, wherefore creatures are not equally indebted to him for their originals, and the aged principles of their life, but must acknowledge them received from the lightsom Air, as a nearer Agent. For the disposition of their matter was adjudged

by Nature as too weak to receive so sublime a form.

172. But for Stones, since they are not so much generated out of a true mixture of the Elements, as from a concourse of Earth and Water, by an external force of Heat and Cold, they are decocted as an earthen Work or Vessel, therefore they are altogether senseless, having borrowed a feeble form from the dark and cold nature of the Earth and Water.

173. Concerning precious Stones and Gems, we must conceive otherwise, for they derive their forms from the Chrystal Fountains of the Heavens and the Sun, and their bodies are the purest drops of a refined dew, engendered by celestial influences, and as it were the congealed tears of Heaven, whence they possess and contain many sublime virtues.

174. But the matter of Metals, because it is watry and earthy, and most compacted, by reason of the principal & subtile commixtion of weighty Elements, is therefore heavy and exceedingly ponderous, and of it self capable of no motion: but because it is sublimated and mundefied by the wonderfull artifice of Nature, in an earthy and stony Matrix, as in a Limbick, and its mixture is compleated in a most thin vapour, by reiterated distillations, that by reason of its exceeding subtility and exuberancy, the influential helps of the Sun and the Heavens, get in and mix with it, especially in the generation of perfect mettals; for this cause, though they fetch their bodies from Water and Earth, yet Nature performing the office of workman, doth so ingeniously make up the bodies, especially of a perfect mettal, that it delivers them to the heavenly Deities, as those that deserve to be informed with the most eminent form. It is a work of long travail, but an absolute one, & heightened to the utmost of Natures actings, in which Heaven and Earth seem rather to copulate, than to consent. But the formal spirits of metals being bound up in a hard cover, do stick immoveable, till released of their bands by Philosophical Fire, they do produce by their heavenly Seed in their matter, that noble son of the Sun, and at length that Quint-essence of admirable Virtue, in which the Heavens seem to lodge with, and come down to us.

175. It was provided by the Decree of the supream Creatour, that a Nature more noble should not degenerate into one less no-

ble, or that one more eminent, into a nature that is more base, or that it should, abjuring its native priviledge or birth-right, come under a servile vassalage. Superiour Beings are coupled with these below, and those of greater power do communicate themselves with those of a less, that they may inform and compleat them by their emissary spirits, which notwithstanding in this do no way derogate from their stock or kind. Nay, when they work themselves into the seeds of things, or also into mixed Beings, they subject not themselves to a bondage, but do attain a new honour and priviledged power. For every mixt Being of whatsoever kind it is, is a kind of an Empire, yea the whole world, who hath a spiritual form of her own to rule her, whose office it is to have dominion over the organs and faculties of Nature, yea over the whole frame, so that that, which being void and without distinction, did drift it rowling hither and thither in the vast Ocean of Nature, is now called to an Empire.

176. The formal act of the first matter, as also of the Elements, doth inform nothing besides the verie principles of Nature, therefore the specifical form doth constitute a perfect mixt Being, neither is it to be thought to contain any more forms, since the very Elements in their mixtion, have the charge of the fashioning, not of the informing of the bodie.

177. It is most improbable, that the virtue of multiplication, which lyes in the seeds of Beings, doth not flow from the Elementary matter as its efficient cause, but from a celestial form: for to multiply, is the most natural and proper action of light, for from one ray are almost an infinite number darted forth; from whence it proceeds, that the Sun, who is the Fountain of immortal Light, is also in nature the first efficient cause of generation and multiplication: that therefore every form receives a natural power of multiplication from the celestial light, is prov'd by this weighty Argument, because it is lightfull and furnished with its native endowments, *Ergo* multiplying; It is lightfull, because it doth enlighten with its rays the sensitive and imaginative faculties in creatures, that so out of that double faculty, springs a double apprehension & knowledge of things; an external by the senses, an internal by imagination; but all knowledge is a light, as all ignorance is a darkness: but there peeps up some enlightening

and lightsomness, when there is an apprehension of the images of things, and when that, which lay unknown in the dark, is now manifested by a light of knowledge, for it is onely by the good office of light, that obscure things receive a revelation. God did adde to man a third light, *to wit,* his Understanding, by the help of which he attains by their causes, a far more perfect way of knowledge. All these things are produced by the operation of light, and of a perspicuity flowing out of an enlightened Soul. This last action of light is onely proper to man, the two former are shared with beasts as well as by him, for their souls are also partakers of celestial light. Therefore reason doth convince, that the virtue of multiplication in the individual Beings of Animals and Vegetables, doth proceed from the Souls multiplication of light, and that some rays of it are included in the seed with the Ætherial spirit, until at length they are set upon the rising of the Sun of Life.

178. Light and Darkness are the principles of Life and Death, for the rays of Light are the forms of mixt Beings, their bodies a dark Abyss. By Light all things live, yea Light is life; but those that loose their life, loose their light, and are hurried into their former darkness, in which they lay close and hidden, before they were drawn to light by the fatal wheel of Predestination.

179. The specifical forms of Animals, as also of Vegetables, are rational, though not after the manner of men, but after a property of their own, according to the virtues and impress of their nature. For they have their vital endowments, their cognizances, knowledge, and their predestinations. The vital endowments of Vegetables, are an endeavour of generating the like, the multiplying virtues, nutritive, augmenting, motive and sensitive, and the like. But their knowledge is experienced by their wise fore-knowledge of times, their strict observation of change, as of the orders of Nature, in a variety agreeable to the motion of the Sun and Heaven, in the fastening the Roots, the erecting the Stalk, spreading the Branches, in the opening the Leaves and the Flowers, in the forming the Fruit, in their beautifying, in their ripening, in the transmutations of Elements into aliments, in the inspiring of a vivifical virtue into the Seeds; lastly, in constituting a various difference of Nature and parts, according to

the benign or malign concurrence of the Sun or Soil.

180. That the souls of Bruits are endowed with knowledge, is sufficiently evinced, by their copulations and generations upon set times, their just distributions in the forming and nourishing of the parts of the individual Beings, the distinct offices of those parts free from any confusion, the various motions of their souls, the nimble faculties of their senses, the secret spirits, harmoniously moving the members as organs, their proneness to discipline, their obsequious reverence to their Masters, the presaging instinct of things to come; in most a devout worship, an art in getting their provision, in choice of their raunges, providing their sence, their prudence in the avoiding dangers, and the rest actions so agreeable to knowledge and reason, bestowed upon them by Nature. But Nature in every individual, is nothing else but the form it self, which is the principle of motion, and rest of action, and life to it, in which it is, to which is committed the charge, direction and conservation of its body, as a Ship to a Pilot.

181. But who will deny the certain predestination of Times for the birth of things, unless he fancy a confusion and disorder in the Nature of the Universe, for she draws forth all those things out of her bosom, according to setled and fore-appointed order, for she had a prescript from her Maker for the Law of Order, and the times of production; their quickening, birth, life and death have their set times, and do fulfil their designed seasons; those things that either this or that year receive their Being, or return to darkness, are pre-ordained to it, which pre-ordination, Nature, Gods Vicegerent in the rule of the Universe, doth fore-know by the suggestion of the Divine Spirit, that she might be ministerial to the compassing of it; neither do those things casually fall out, but they have a necessary, though unknown cause, yet the Grand Ruler of all is not comprized within the Law of Necessity, but appoints all things, and changeth them according to his own will. He it is that decrees concerning all, even the least things, whose Decrees want neither certainty nor order. Therefore that Order, that runs through the series and succession of things & times, hath the law of its necessity from the divine Decrees.

182. As all things which afterwards were actually produced

and separated, in respect of their matter were potentially in the Chaos, so all individuals before they came to light, are in the World in their matter and potentiality, and will in their time and order come forth and break into act, but when they fail and die, they return as Rivers into the Sea, into that general Mass from whence they came, every nature recovering its proper Region, and being to be brought again and again into Natures shop, are wrought into new Beings upon her Anvile. It may be this was that opinion of the *Pythagoreans,* therefore exploded, because not comprehended concerning their Tenet of Transanimation.

183. When the mixt body is dissolved, and the corruption of the frail Elements come to a loss, the Ætherial nature returns to its native home, and there is nothing left in the carkass but a perturbation and confusion of the Elements, having lost their Governour, then there reigns nothing but corruption, death, and darkness in the widowed matter, untill she through corruption be made fit for generation, and the virtue of Heaven do again flow down into the matter thus disposed, and gathering and mingling the wandering Elements, do rekindle the weak light of a new form, which at length breaks forth, the forces of the Elements being corroborated, and so compleats the new mixture.

184. In that corruption which tends to generation, which is a corruption in the mean, and is done with the conservation of the specifical form potentially inherent in the seed or matter, that sublime spirit departs not, but being weak and impotent, is excited by external heat, and begins to move, and withal give motion to the matter, till at length it works more vigorously, and gives information to the perfectly mixed body.

185. The Elements as well as the Aliments of Nature, do begin their generation and nutrition, which are in most respects the same from Corruption. For both must necessarily be putrified, and by putrefaction be resolved into a moist, and as it were a first matter, then is there made a Chaos, in which are all things necessary for generation and nutrition. So doth the birth and repair of every *Microcosm* bear with an Analogical resemblance with the creation and conservation of the *Macrocosm.*

186. The insensible seeds of things, and those mixed bodies which are begot from them, do consist of a three-fold Nature, of

65

a Celestial, Elementary, and Mixt Nature. The Celestial is a ray of Light of the Sun, endued with all heavenly vigour, the principle of action, motion, generation and life, by whose help the seeds, by their renewed vigour, do resemble the constant permanency of the Stars, and being in a manner as so many immortal grafts of celestial plants, ingrafted upon corruptible nature, as upon a strange stock, do by a kind of an eternal succession, vindicate it from death: The Elementary, corporeal and sensible portion, which in creatures is called the *Sperm,* is the Case and keeper of the seed, which putrifies and is corrupted, and generates an invisible seed. The Radical Moisture, or the Ferment of Nature, in which lyes the spirit, is a middle substance, coupling the Celestial and Elementary, in the material part answering the Elements; in the spiritual, the Form. Like the Day-break, whose cheek being covered with a duskie light, doth knit together the two extreams of Light and Darkness, and being neither, doth hold forth a mixture of both.

187. Life is an harmonical act, proceeding from the copulation of the Matter and the Form, constituting the perfect Being of an individual nature. Death is the term or end of this act, the separation of the matter and form, and a resolution of the mixt body.

188. These mixt bodies have the roots of their generation and life in Heaven, from whence springs their Causes and Principles, whence also as inverted Trees, they do suck their juice and aliment. Neither is it suitable for the Understanding, to be envassaled to the Rule of the Senses, which comprehend nothing but what is sensible. But the mind rangeth far abroad beyond the Cloysters of the Senses, and searcheth to a greater height, for the hunting out of the bounds of Nature. The bodies are as it were the barks, the grosser parts of the Elements the accidents of things, under which lye hid the pure and sprightly Essences, which acknolwedge not the subjection and censure of the Senses, and which it was a necessity to cloth under a dark Cloud, that they might pass from their heavenly, to their earthly province of the corporeal Beings. The supream Creatour of Nature enacted this copulation of spirituals with corporeals, whereby his uncreated spirit communicating it self, first to the more spiritual

and simple Natures, might be conveyed through them, as by so many conduits, to corporeal Beings, and in this manner diffusing it self gradually and orderly, through all the Regions of the World, through all and every Being, doth sustain all things by the Divine presence, as also that by a sensible creature, the insensible CREATOUR might be apprehended through corporeal and sensible resemblances.

189. Whatsoever lives either an Animal or Vegetable life, stands in need of food, that the natural spirits might be recruited, which do continually slide forth through the pores, and that so the loss of Nature might have a successive repair. For the nourishing juice is made by the more succulent substance of the meat, whereby the parts and humours of the body are re-inforced. The radical Moisture is renewed out of the purer portion of the humours, especially of the bloud, the celestial influence intermingling it self by respiration with it.

190. Living things have a two-fold nourishment, *to wit*, a Corporeal and a Spiritual, the former being of small avail to life without the latter. For Vegetables do evidently referre the benefit of their increase and nourishment no less to the Air and Heaven, than to the Earth: yea the Earth it self, unless suckled with the milk of Heaven, would quickly find her own breast to flag drie, this that holy Diver into Natures secrets, when he blessed *Joseph,* doth thus express: *Blest be the Lord for his Earth, for the apples of Heaven, for the Dew, and for the Deep that coucheth beneath, for the pleasant apples of the Sun and of the Moon, for the top of the everlasting Mountains, for the fruits of the eternal Hills,* &c. By which mystical speech, the Prophet fore-ensureth the Earths plenty, by the abundant influence of the Sun, Moon, and of the rest of the celestial bodies.

191. The spiritual Diet, as far as it conduceth to the life of creatures, is acknowledged by every vulgar capacity, that sees the renewed respiration, and the frequent sucking in of the external Air. For not onely according to the opinion of ordinary Physicians, hath Nature so workmanlike framed those bellows, bordering upon the heart to cool it, but also that by their continued fanning, they might breath in an æthereal Air, and hand to it celestial spirits, that so by their recruits the vital spirits

may be kept in repair, and by alwayes multiplied.

192. Philosophers do not onely call those spiritual Natures, which being created without matter, are onely comprehended by the Understanding, as the intelligencies, Angels, and Devils are accounted to be: but also those that, which although they have their original from matter, yet in respect of their great tenuity & nobility, do not subject themselves to the search of the Senses, and nearer approching to spiritual Beings, are rather under stood by reason, than found by sense. Such is the pure part of the Air, such are the influencies of heavenly bodies, such the in-set fire and seminal virtues, such the vegetable spirits, such the animal, and the vital, and the like, in which consists the very nature of Beings, than in grosser bodies. Such like natures spring from Heaven, and in relation to sensibles, do assume to themselves the name and right of spirits.

193. It is suitable that we should give the Fire of Nature a place amongst the spiritual Beings, for in it self it is not perceivable by any sense, but discovers it self onely in bodies, by heat and other effects and accidents. This is apparent in living creatures, into which by this unperceiveable fire, is infused a sensible heat, and that Fire with the life stealing away, the Elementary body or the carkass, yet the mixed being dissolved, remains sound and unhurt. In Vegetables, because this Fire is weaker, it doth elude the sense, and is not to be perceived by any heat.

194. Reason also convinceth, that our common Fire is to be sorted amongst the spiritual, rather than corporeal Beings. For if it were corporeal, it should have from it self a peculiar and inseparable body, no less than Earth, Water, or Air, and the rest of the sensible Natures, which do consist and are bounded within their proper bodies, which do exist in them and by them, which do act according to their virtues, and produce them to the Senses. But Fire hath not a peculiar and sensible body, lodgeth onely in anothers, for a Coal is not Fire, but Wood fired, neither is the flame Fire, but smoke inflamed; finally, that Robber onely feeds upon what is not his own, lives upon the prey, and is extinguished when this fails, having nothing in it self to feed it. Besides, a body super-added to another body, doth augment the

quantity of it, but this not found in fire put into wood or smoke, for the smoke or wood is no way increased by the accession of fire in their quantities, from which it is evident, that a fiery spirit rather than a body, doth invade the wood or smoke. A sword melted, the scabbard being untouch't, the bones shattered by the fiery bolt of Thunder, and yet the flesh unhurt, do sufficiently argue the spiritual nature, even of that thundering fire. Yet we must know that Fire is not wholly immaterial, for it hath a matter, though a very subtile and light one, whereby it cleaves to the encompassing air, whereby it may be kept in by a more gross body. Yet doth it rather deserve the name of a spirit, than of a body, because it hath not a sensible quantity, neither can it be comprehended, but when it is arrayed in another body.

195. For Light the original of it doth evince, that it ought to be seated amongst those things that are truly spiritual. There was no light but in God before the informing of the first matter, & the birth of the world. But when Nature received her Being, then began there a spiritual light to issue forth from the fiery spirit of God upon the matter, and there to settle as in its lamp, and this was the creation and original of Light: that was the first act of the Deity upon the matter; the first copulation of the Creatour with the creature, of a spirit with a body. Therefore the first informing Light, was a meer Spirit, which did kindle with its fiery virtue, as with heat, the nearest matter, being exceedingly rarefied by its spiritual Light, and so were the darkness converted to light. The Heaven, being distinguished by the first light, although it be not material and fiery, yet is nevertheless invisible, because in respect of the matter, it is brought to the highest degree of tenuity, and in respect of its form, is endowed with spirituality. But the Light that was scattered in the middle Heaven, being bounded into a narrower compass, was cast into the Globe of the Sun, which was necessarily to be formed into a kind of a thick body, as it were into a smoke fit to be kindled, yet not combustible, that so it might be setled, being kindled by that immortal Light, and be in the room of the general Lamp of Nature, or as a fiery Mass. The light of the Sun therefore is nothing else but a lightsome spirit, deriving its rise from the Spirit of eternal Light, gathered in, and inseparably cleaving to

the body of the Sun, and made sensible by reason of the thickness of the body, communicating to all the natures of the Universe, light, and a manifold virtue: constituting the spirit of the World by its non-intermitted influence: and bound up in a body for the good and welfare of the corporeal Nature.

196. Yet the Sun-beams that are perceivable by our eyes, are not pure spirits, for issuing continually from the Sun, have their progress, being clothed with the encompassing Air. They are therefore nothing else but a continued flowing forth of the spirit of Light, which springing forth as so many rivulets from their Eternal Fountain, and working themselves into the ætherial Nature, as a flame into a most thin smoke, do over-spread the whole face of the Universal World with their light.

197. It is natural to Light to flow continually from its Fountain. We call those Rays issuing forth, and mixing themselves with the airy nature, and they are the first actings of light in the Sun, and the conveyance of it from the Sun. For it is the property of a lightfull body, to act by its rays, and to send forth heat and light, and that might spread its light abroad by a darting forth, and multiplying of its beams. We do by light signifie both the first act of the lightsom body, as also a secondary lightsomness which floweth out from the former.

198. The Lamp being out, either for want of matter, or blown out by the wind, the fiery and lightsom spirit that kindled the Lamp doth not perish, neither is it extinguished, as it commonly seems, but onely loosing what it feeds on, and being stript from it, is scattered in and vanisheth to Air, which is the Abyss and universal Receptacle of all lights and spiritual natures of the material World: from whence we may learn, that the nature of this Lightsomneness is spiritual, and is derived from the spiritual Fountain, not otherwise than natural forms from their Matrix, which is the spirit of the Universe, perpetually flowing from the Sun, as from an eternal and immortal Spring. For as the bodies of mixt Beings in their making, do rise from the first matter, and the Elements, and do gradually at their departure, slide into the same again, so the natural forms of individuals in their approch, do flow from the universal form (which in the manner of a Form of forms, doth inspire a formal virtue into

the seeds) and in their recess do again return into it. But that form is the Spirit of the light of the Universe, to which, as to their principle, and as to a nature of the same kind, do all single forms and sparks of light got loose from their tyes, return. So are all mixt Beings resolved into their first principles, but these principles do return to that Eternal Spring of Nature, as to their proper centre and peculiar countrey.

199. But that Spirit of the Universe is from the Sun, yet not the very light of the Sun, conspicuous to us by reason of the presence of its body; but that invisible spirit, which is continually dispersed by the beams of the Sun, through the universal Region of the Air, and doth extend it self perpetually by communication through our Heaven, yea, even to the centre of the Earth, and that in the absence of the Sun, and in the darkest night, pouring out all gifts for generation and life, through all the bodies of the Universe.

200. The divine Love was not able to contain it self within it self, but did wholly go out of it self in the creation, by multiplication of it self, and pouring out himself wholly also in the conservation of creatures in themselves. Light also, which is the exactest Copie of the Deity, doth also imitate the divine Love: for it is not able to be comprized within its own lightsom body, but is diffused far and near for the good of other Beings, by a strong multiplication of its beams, being not so much born for it self as for others, being as it were the token of Divine Love, communicating it self to its power, and reaching forth into the most remote places, unless it meet with a stop from a thick bodie.

201. Light also doth hold forth to us the infinite Nature of God; for the small light of a lamp or candle cannot, as long as it is fed, by all its continued effluence of rays, and by its infinite communication of its flames, be exhausted or diminished. As many beams so many streams flow from it. Yet though it gives, though it diffuseth it self, although much be taken from it, yet is it not brought to nothing, neither receives loss, which is the alone property of a spiritual nature, and is altogether unappliable to a corporeal. So the intellectual endowments, as the understanding and knowledge of things, which are justly esteemed spiritual lights, are of the same kind, that though alwayes be-

stowed abroad, yet are preserved entire at home. Therefore must we confess that there is something divine in Light.

202. The beams of a lightsom body, although they be of a spiritual nature, yet are they stopt by a thick body, because their conveyance is by means of the Air, without which they are not perceivable by us, by which copulation also they are in a manner made corporeal, and therefore cannot pierce or enter into the bodies that are not porous. So spiritual things do act with us by some sensible mean, that so we may perceive them to act. But the lightsom body being absent, the beams also depart, neither do they part from his presence, because they immediately flow from him.

203. But the Air is without enlightened, not onely by the presence of a body of light, and of the beams from it, but also the body being gone, and the beams withdrawn, by a lightsom spirit flowing from them: as is clear in the darkest Eclipse, or the Heavens over-cast with the blackest clouds, or wrapt up in the mask of night, yea, the Sun being sunk under the Horizon: for that act of present light cannot proceed from the body of light, and its beams being absent, but from the access and presence of a spiritual light.

204. A transparent body as glass, being pointed with the Sun beams, doth gather them, and receives in it the image of the Sun, and is made lightsom, & as it were a brief draught of the Sun, which sends forth its beams on the farthest side opposite to the Sun, from which the beams of the Sun being refracted, by the concourse of the glass, seem to pass through the glass, which yet indeed they do not, for the rays by reason of the Air that cleaves to them, are setled about the glass, the spirit of light onely passing forward, but by the beams which are darted out on the other side, are the beams of the Sun, or of the glass being kindled by the Sun-beams into a lightsom bodie.

205. Every transparent body, especially glass, is a *medium* of light, because it receives light into it, and having received it, doth communicate it to the Air that is beyond it, not by the sending forth of lightsom Air about it, which is repugnant to Nature, but by another double way. First, because a transparent body yields to, and lets pass the spirit of light, and doth send it

forth abroad being received by it, which sent forth, gets into the adjoyning Air, hence springs that plentifull light; and besides, because that transparent *Medium* is made by the benefit of the light, it receives not onely light in it self, but lightsom to others, and by the spirit of Light, which is in love with transparent bodies, becomes as it were a lighted lamp. But now every lightsom body hath the priviledge and power to scatter its light, which is not granted to thick and dark bodies, unless by reflection.

206. Those which are the pure natures of mixt Beings, are mearly spiritual, the bodies are as it were the Barks and Vessels, in which they are contained and kept. And not otherwise could those sublime Natures, unless tied to the corporeal Elements, and so bound in by their weight, pass this lower Sea, and lodge in the Centre of this Abyss. They come subject to sense by their bodies, the bodies are moved and acted by them, so do they do interchangeable offices. This that secret of *Homers Juno,* whom *Jupiter* let down with a weight at her heels.

207. Since the whole frame of the Universe is but one onely body, one onely universal Nature, consisting of many natures and bodies, bound together by their proper *Mediums* and bonds, it should not be wondered at, that such parts & members are knit together by a strong, but secret tye, and do give a mutual assistance each to other, for they have not onely a mutual relation to, but also a communication with one the other, and these various natures do exercise a kind of a commerce, the extreams by the middle, the middle by the nearest. But this communication is performed by spirits sent forth: for all the parts of the world, all the individual natures of the world do abound in spirits; many of which flowing forth, leave room and give way for those that flow in, and so is there by the continual ebbing out and flowing in of spirits, a continual reparation of the world, and of the natures thereof. This is the scale of general Nature presented in a vision to the Patriarch *Jacob,* these are *Mercuries* wings, by whose help being mistically termed by the Ancients, the Messenger of the Gods, he was thought frequently to visit the coasts of the Earth, and the courts of Heaven.

208. The active principles of every kind of Vegetables or Animals are spiritual, their bodies are the passive organs of the

spirits, by which they exercise the faculties of the senses, and do by various actings put forth their powers, as the authours of actions, so that in the general life may be termed a concent of actions, or a continued act diversified by the multiplicitie of actions, flowing from a spiritual fountain, and brought forth by corporeal organs.

209. It is the propertie of the spiritual nature to act, of the corporeal to be passive, where therefore there is a concourse of both, as in mixed bodies, that as the more noble doth act and rule this as passive doth obey. For the power of act is the priviledge of ruling, but the burden of being passive is the mark of being servile; so the in-set fire in the seed, is the principle of generation and life, the highest operating spirit, the Archæus of Nature, the orderer in the preparing and forming the matter in the mixtion and distribution of the Elements. So doth the Form in the mixt Being exercise its rule at his will, as the fountain of all actions. So do the virtues of the heavenly Beings dispose and seal all inferiour Elements and corporeal matter.

210. Natural bodies which have an active vigour, and an occult cause of acting, do not, as is commonly thought, act alone by their qualities, but by secret spirits. For the fire doth not heat and burn by the single qualitie of heat, but by the continual flux of spirits and rayes. Neither do the Earth and Water refrigerate or moisten by the alone qualities of cold and moist, but by their vapours and in-nate spirits sent forth, do affect the sense from without. Neither do poysons onely by cold or hot qualities, but by malignant spirits bring death or infection sooner or later. Concerning Plants or Herbs, we must judge alike, because their active virtues do not lie hid in their qualities, but in their essence, which Nature hath made abundant in spirits, whose basis and principle powers are concerning spirituals, for the bodies are as the shadows or the investments of things, under which the invisible Nature is hidden, but since qualities are the accidents of things, are not therefore able to constitute their essence, nor shew forth in their actings those wonderful virtues, but are onely as the in-set instruments of actions & passions, which the working spirits, that are the workers of all actions make use of in their actings, but yet Nature indures them not as principles

and efficient causes of actions.

211. The natural tinctures, odours and tasts of things are special and spiritual gifts of Nature, with which it hath suitably inriched her Beings, & which do not onely contribute to their ornament, or onely are inherent in them, as extrinsecal accidents, but also have an in-set and radical cause, and are not so much to be termed accidents, as demonstrative tokens of inward virtues, by which the occult and formal signatures of things discover themselves.

212. Rarefaction and condensation are the two instruments of Nature, by which spirits are converted into bodies, and bodies into spirits, or also by which corporeal Elements are changed into spiritual Beings, and spiritual into corporeal; for Elements do suffer these changes in mixt bodies. So the Earth doth minister spiritual food to the roots of vegetables, which being fed upon, doth go into the stalk, the bark, the boughs, the branches, the flowrs, and into the corporeal substance. The same is done by Nature in Animals. For the meat and drink, which they diet on, or at least the better part, is terminated into humours, and at length into spirits, which getting through the pores, and knit to the flesh, nerves, bones, and the rest of the parts of the bodie, do nourish and augment them, and do by the never-tired work of supply, repair decaying nature. So the spiritual and the portion of the purer substance, is curdled to the frothie bodie of seed. Art the Ape of Nature, doth experience the like in her resolutions and compositions.

213. The life of individuals is in a rational and strict union of the matter and form: but the knot of both natures, their tie and base lieth hid in the fortified embraces of the in-nate heat and fire, and the radical moisture. For that formal fire is an heavenly ray, which is united with the radical moisture, which is the purest and best digested portion of the matter, and as it were an oyl defæcated, exuberated, and turned as it were into a spiritual nature, by the organs of Nature, as by so many Alembicks.

214. There is much of the radical moisture in the seed of things, in which, as in its food, is kept a celestial Spark, which doth act all things necessarie to generation in a convenient ma-

trix. But wheresoever there is a constant principle of heat, there is conceived to be a fire, because the natural principle of heat is his in which it is.

215. A man may observe something immortal in the radical moisture, which doth neither vanish by death, nor consume by the force of the most violent fire, but remains unvanquished in the carkases and ashes of bodies burnt.

216. There is a double moisture lies in every mixed Being, to wit, an Elementarie and a Radical. The Elementarie, being partly of an aeriall, partly of a watrie nature, yields not to fire, but flies away into a vapour or smoke, which being drawn forth, the bodie is resolved into ashes; for by it, as by a glue, the Elements in their mixture are knit together. But the radical moisture scorns the tyrannical assaults of common fire, but it neither dies in the martyrdom, nor flies away in the combat, but surviving the mixt bodie, doth stubbornly stick to its ashes, which is an evidence of its exact puritie.

217. The experience of this radical moisture, hidden in the ashes, did teach a secret to the glas-makers, being ignorant of the nature of things, for by bringing Glass out of Ashes by the sharp point of their casting flames, they have made a hidden thing evident, beyond which, neither the strength of fire or art are able to stretch it. But the ashes must necessarily run, that there might be a continued quantitie, and a solid bodie made as glass is, which could not be otherwise, for there can be no flowing of any thing without moisture. Therefore that moisture being inseparable from its matter, is at length brought to terminate into that noble and as it were ætherial transparent bodie.

218. The extraction of Salts out of Ashes, in which is the chief virtue of mixt Beings, the fertilitie of ground increased by the burning of stubble, and by ashes, doth evidence, that that moisture preserved free from fire, is the radical principal of generation, & the root of nature. Although this virtue lies hid, solitarie and idle, till being received by the Earth, the common matrix of Natures principles, yet shew forth a hidden facultie convenient for generation and multiplication, as it is also accustomable in the seed of things.

219. The Radical Balsame, is Natures ferment or leaven,

infecting the whole mass of the bodie. It is an indelible and multiplying tincture, for it pierceth and tingeth even the more loathsom excrements, which is evident by the frequent, although imperfect generation, that is made from out of them, as also by the frequent dunging of the ground, which is known by the most unskilfull husbandmen, that so the languishing land may be set forward to pay its due, and that with an advantage to the expecting labourer.

220. We may guess, that that root of Nature, which survives the ruin of the mixt bodie, is a foot-step, and the purest and immortal portion of the first matter informed, and signed with the divine character of Light. For that ancient matrimonie betwixt the first Matter and its Form, is not to be untied, from which copulation the other bodies drew their original. Moreover, it was necessarie that this incorruptible base of corruptible things, and as it were the cube-root of them should lie hid, always remaining and immortal in the depth of bodies, that it might be constantly and perpetually a material Principle, having a potentiality and aptitude to life, about which, as about an immoveable Axle-tree, there might be a continual turning of the Elements and things. And if we may have the liberty in dark things, to guess at what is most likely truth, that immortal Substance is the foundation of the material World, and the Ferment of its immortality, which the Eternal Measurer of all things hath fore-established to survive the day of the conflagration of all things, when the Elements shall be purified by that refining fire, that so he might renew and repair out of this pure and ever-remaining Matter, his work vindicated from original sin, and the taint of corruption.

221. That this radical Basis is not of the kind of special forms, is evident, because every individual hath its individual and singular form, which doth depart the body upon the dissolution of the mixt Being, yet that radical principle remaining unextinguished, although it abide much weakened, and of little efficacy, by reason of the absence of the form, yet do those vital sparkles remain apt for the production of more debased and imperfect births, which production belongs not so much to Nature, as to the matter in its birth; this attempteth, but is not able to generate without a companion, by reason of the absence

of the formal and specifical virtue. So the carkass of a man or an horse, by reason of the defect of seed is not capable for the generation of a man or an horse, but of loathed worms and other insects, from whence we may guess, that that feeble principle of life proceeds from the scarcity of the first matter, and rather to be of the family of the lower Elements, than of the higher and celestial, yet that there is in it some of that tincture of light.

222. For certainly that slight spark of that former light, which did in the beginning inform the dark matter of the lower Abyss, may be sufficient for the generation of insects: for it doth work the matter by a confused and disordered motion, that it might bring forth the power into a feeble act, but the matter warmed by this spark, and as it were languishing, being corrupted rather by the fancy than the copulation of a male, doth rush into the lustfull act, and being unable to bring forth a just issue of Nature, doth form loathsom phantasms, as Worms, Hornets, Beetles, and the like, in the filthy excrements. Therefore that radical Moisture is the nearest and never-ceasing subject of generation and life, in which is first kindled the fire of Nature, and the formal act in a well disposed and prepared matter. But in a confused and ill ordered matter, where that humour doth act the part of the male, it begets spurious and bastard births of Nature, for that generation which is made without specifical seed, seems to be made rather by chance and default, than by the intention of Nature, although in it seems to be a dark and confused kind of copulation of actives with passives, which is required also to the production of every, though imperfect, Being.

223. That radical Ferment constantly abiding in the depth of mixt Bodies, seem to be the Band, Seat and Tye of that matrimony contracted between Light and Darkness, between the first Matter and the universal Form, finally of all the Contraries: otherwise the Matter and Form, by reason of their repugnant natures, would not be knit together. But that dark unbridledness of the first matter and its averseness from light was tamed, and its hatred turned into love, by the good office of that lightsom tincture, which doth reconcile things repugnant.

224. The inbred Heat and the radical Moisture are of a

divers kind, for that is wholly spiritual and of the Sun, this of a middle nature, betwixt a spiritual and a corporeal, both participating of an æthereal and elementary Nature; that is of the degree of things above, this of things below, in which was celebrated the first marriage of Heaven & Earth, by which also Heaven hath its abode in the very Centre of the Earth. They are therefore deceived, that do confound the inbred heat and the radical Moisture, for they differ no less than smoke and flame, the light of the Sun and the Air, Sulphur and Mercury: In mixt Beings, the radical Moisture is the seat and food of the inbred and celestial Fire, its bond with the Elementary body: but that power of Fire is the Form and Soul of mixt Beings. In seeds, that moisture is the immediate Keeper and Case of that Spirit of Fire inclosed in the seed, till it be set on to generation in a disposed Matrix, by an adventitious heat. Finally, that radical Substance is *Vulcan's* Shop in every mixt Being, the Chimney in which is kept that immortal Fire, which is the first mover of all the faculties in an individual nature.

225. That radical Moisture is the Catholical Balsam, the most precious Elixar of Nature, the Mercury of Life, having a perfect sublimation by Nature, a dose of which is administered to every individual of her family, weighed to a just quantity by plenteous Nature. They that have attained the happiness to fetch out this hidden Treasure of Nature, wrapt up close in the heart, and in the closets of Natures birth, and can get it out of those close coverts of the Elements, let him boast that he hath attained the chiefest staff and help of life, and a most precious Treasure.

226. The order of Reason and of Creation doth require, that the first Copies of things, being first of all concealed in the celestial Natures, were transmitted into inferiour Beings: but in the first they are of a far greater perfection, both because of their greater tenuity and dignity, as also because of their neighbouring seats to the Eternal Being: but with us they are much meaner, because carved in a grosser and less valuable matter, and more distant from their eternal Principle. There is nothing therefore printed in this lower Margin of the World, which was not at first copied in the heavenly Being: neither is there any particular kind

of Being of the inferiour natures, which doth not acknowledge the dominion of one Superiour agreeable to it, and which it hath not the secret seal and signature of it. So do things below depend on things above.

227. The World is a creature of an ambiguous nature, for it is of both Sexes, the higher part, *to wit,* the celestial, is active and masculine; the lower Elementary nature, is the passive and feminine nature. The Globe of the Earth is the womb, in which the engendering seed of Heaven is received and kept. From the masculine part proceed life and strength; from the female part corruption and death do issue.

228. Since superiour and inferiour bodies have their original from the same Principles, as from their parts, yet are they not such as have their equal lot: it is equal, that those things that have the honour of being nobler substances, and advanced to higher offices, should distribute to their brethren of a lower degree, being poor and in want, some of their wealth, and so provide for their life and conservation. For it was provided by the fore-sight of the Deity, that since there was a necessity that the World should be made up of unequal natures, the more powerfull Natures should aid the weaker, & hand help to the fainting Natures. So Love is the indissoluble knot of the parts of the Universe.

229. In this sublunary Region, diseased Nature sickens out of a defect of the proportion and temperament of the Elements, either by reason of the quantity, or of the qualities, either out of a too great intension or remission, and so is there a dissonancy in Natures musick, and a distemper in her bodies. Therefore the consonancy of the Elements, which riseth from a proportion, and constitutes their temperament, being gone, the matter and form of the whole mixt Being hath a bad coherence; Nature is troubled and staggers with a perplexed confusion, and hence do first diseases, and then death assault disordering and falling Nature.

230. That discord of those Principles, have either an intrinsecal and radical cause, as from a vicious seed, an evil generation, or age; or an extrinsecal and accidental, as from a too great repletion or emptiness, from whence either an excess or defect in

humours and spirits; or from putrefaction, mortal poison, infection, grief, hurt, or some other impediment brought upon the Organs of life with the like, which do hurt Nature.

231. The four radical Qualities of the Elements, are as so many harmonious Tones of Nature, not contrary but divers, and distant each from other by certain pauses, from whose rational difference, intension and remission, is made a perfect consent of Nature, perceivable by the understanding, bearing an Analogy to that vocal Musick which is heard by the Senses. Sharp and Flat in Musick, though they are extreams, yet are not Contraries in Musick, they are the terms of those means, which lye betwixt them, and are composed and tempered after a divers manner by these two extreams. So Heat and Cold, Driness and Moisture, are the extream Qualities in Nature, yet not therefore contrary, but onely the bounds of the middle and interjacent Qualities, from whose mixture and temperament, do the middle proceed.

232. The motion of Nature is continual and not tyred, no less in every part than in the whole. For she always acts, never idle, so that if she were but out of action for a moment, it would ruine the whole frame of the Universe, which is addicted to a decree of a perpetual motion. For neither doth the setled Earth, the calm Sea, the quiet Air, therefore altogether rest, because they are not seen to be moved, they rest no more than a sleeping man: that rest is a remission of action, not an omission or cessation. Nature acts within, neither doth it ever desist its action or motion of the Organs. Even a very carkass hath a motion, *to wit,* of corruption: but living Beings, though they are not acted by a local, yet are they by an organical motion.

233. Nature doth move the frame of the Universe in a uniform and orderly motion, yet so that it wheels things unequal and unlike, by an unequal unlike motion. This unequality of the motion is required by a Geometrical equity, and so all the motions of all the heavenly bodies, may be Geometrically termed equal, considering the difference of the magnitude, distance, and nature of them.

234. Nature being no less powerfull than wise, in the informing and governing of her Works, doth attain her certain end by many wanderings and windings, which is most evident in the

births of the Earth, for she handling the Elements in an unequal temper, doth, especially in the Winter, replenish the womb of the Earth with a fruitfull seed, in the Spring brings forth an easie birth, in the Summer ripens the fruit, and in the Autumn all fall.

235. This diversity doth especially proceed from the approach and recess of the Sun, appointed to this end by the Creatour: for he hath destined the Sun to the Rule of the Elements, that by his various distance, inflection and reflection, they may have a divers and various temperament, and so there might be some help for Nature, working divers things by divers means, and that she might perfect her changes, by the various changes of Times. This variety of Nature is worth the exactest thoughts of the most acute Philosophers.

236. The heavenly bodies, though not subject to that stain of alteration, do notwithstanding introduce manifold changes in the Elementary Region, and do inspire various affections by their divers propension, and the various motions of the planetick bodies, which do alter their fire and distance between themselves, and also the figure of the Heavens, which actions do diversly form and incline the pliable natures of the Elements, and they never cease to ferment them by their continual influence.

237. The whole substance of the Heaven, hath parts continuous, though not contiguous; let not any therefore fancie the World to be the works of Art, which is the work of Nature, which cannot endure any section into Sphears and Circles; for they that first divided the ætherial region into many orbs and circles, did propose to themselves rather the easie teaching by it, than to shew the truth of the thing. For the divine nature being an unitie, is desirous of and endeavours unitie, and so avoideth multiplicitie: wherefore we must conceive she created not many Heavens, separated by their matter and superficies, when one bodie, in respect of the continuitie of the matter, though distinct in the dignitie and virtue of the parts, might suffice. Neither is this taken off by the motions of the Stars in their courses and customs, which because we know not, we therefore make a fancied Astrologie, and do too boldly bring the power of God under the weakness of man, though the continuitie of the Heaven hin-

der not the motion of the Stars, and there might be some help for mans reason to find out their orders.

238. That there should be a first moveable above the Heavens, by whose hurying motion the lower Heavens are turned about, is not an invention of the wisdom of God, but onely a fancied help for mans ignorance: for if we assign the principle of motion to that first mover, why do we denie it to the globe of heaven? why should we fancie an external cause of motion, which may be all this time intrinsecal?

239. As this lowest province of the World is subject to the rule of the middle, so is the middle, *viz.* the ætherial to the highest and supercelestial for its priviledges and deputieship. For the Empyrean heaven, and the quire of the intelligible Beings, do inspire into the celestial orb those virtues, which they receive from the Archetype, in order of succession, and do move those natures that lie nearest them, not without a concent, as the first organs of the material world: by which motion the inferiour bodies, being also moved, do exercise their turns, as so many dances to a set pace, and do borrow whatsoever is excellent from the superiour bodies.

240. But Intelligences are illuminated at hand, according to their orders from the mind of God, as from the spring of eternal light, by which illumination they are fed, as with an immortal food, and in it, as in a glass, do they read, receive the commands and will of the Divine Majestie, and by it are enkindled to an honourable obedience. This is the manner and union of the threefold nature of the Universe, the knot and Herculean bond of this union is the love of God. So in a ternarie is compleated the whole state of the World, whose Creatour is by no means part of it, no otherwise than Unitie is neither a Number, nor the part of a Number, although it constitutes all number, but is the principle and measure of Number, neither is the Musician or Lutonist a part, but the authour of the Concent.

241. They which believe that an almost innumerable multitude of heavenly bodies, were created for the commoditie of the globe of the Earth, and for her inhabitants, as to their proper end, are deceived, for reason will denie, that natures, so far more noble and transcendent, were enslaved to the service of more

vile and low-born Beings. Is it not rather more likely, that every Globe doth rather of it self make a peculiar world, and that so many worlds as feodaries to the eternal Empire of a God, are diffused through the vast range of the heaven, and there do hang as bound each to the other by the common bond of the heaven, and that the whole large Universe doth consist of those manifold natures? These, though so far severed in nature and place, yet do joyn in a mutual love, so as to make up a perfect harmonie in the Universe. The heaven is the common place of all, yet is it more pure about those more perfect Beings, therefore it is of great tenuitie and almost spiritual, and so fils up the places between, that so it may the better receive the various affections of so many natures, and the secret virtues continually issuing from them, and having received them, it might swiftly communicate them to others, though far distant. For the heaven is Natures conveyance, by the mediation of which, all the Cities of Nature do traffique one with another, and are made partakers of each the others wealth and store. So are they linked together by a most powerfull bond of friendship and nearness, as it were by some magnetick virtue.

242. What hinders, but that we may reckon the Globe of the Earth, as well as the Moon amongst the Stars? For both are naturally dark bodies, both do borrow light from the Sun, both are solid bodies, and reflect the beams of the Sun, both send forth spirits and virtues, both hang in their heaven or their air. But the doubt is, whether it moves or no. But to what end is her motion needfull? why may not she also stand fixt amongst so many fixt bodies? And it may be the Moon hath her inhabitants, for it is not credible, that Orbs of so immense and vast a compass, should be idle and useless, not inhabited by any creatures; that their motions, actions, and travels should onely tend the good of this lowest and most despicable Globe: since God himself, not liking Solitude, did go out of himself in the Creation, and poured out himself upon the creatures, and gave them a Law for Multiplication. Is it not more for Gods glorie, to assert the intire Fabrick of the whole Universe to be like a great Empire, graced with the various natures of many worlds, as with so many Provinces or Cities? and that the Worlds themselves are

as so many habitations & tenements for innumerable Citizens of divers kinds, and all created to set forth the superlative glorie of the great Creatour.

243. And who will not admire the Sun as an immortal Lamp, hanging up in the middle of the hall of the Great Lord, and enlightening all the corners & recesses of it, or else as the Vicegerent of the Divine Majestie, infusing light, spirit and life into all the creatures of the World? For it was fit that God, being altogether immaterial, should rule and order his material works by an organ, which should be of a middle and most excellent material Being, which also ought to be full of vivifical spirits, and so to set over sensible things, a sensible Monarch.

244. This Doctrine of many Worlds is not repugnant to Scripture, which doth onely relate to us the Creation of our World, describing all things concerning the others in a mystical, rather than an open & clear way, onely touching at them, that so mens feeble souls, that had alreadie fallen, as too curious of knowledge, might rather sit and admire, than rise and understand. The clouding of this truth, this darkness of mans soul, was part of the punishment of sin, by which he fell from the pleasures of Paradise, the delights of knowledge, the knowledge of Nature and heavenly things, that so he that would stretch himself to a sinfull desire of a forbidden knowledge, might be nipt by a just deprivement of what was given: and so he having brought in a multiplication and confusion of knowledge, might be punished with the loss of that true Knowledge, which was one of all things. That is the Cherub, the guardian of the Garden, he that hath his flaming faulcheon, striking blind the guiltie souls of men with the brightness of his light, and forcing us off from the secrets of Nature, and the truth of the Universe.

245. The Divine nature, although it be a most perfect unitie, yet seems to consist of, and to be perfected by two things, *viz.* Understanding and Will. By his Understanding, he knows all things from eternitie; by his Will, he acts all; and both he doth most absolutely. His Knowledge and Wisdom belong to his Understanding: but his Goodness, Mercy, Justice and the rest of those virtues, which are accounted Moral with us, belong to his Will; yea so doth also Gods Omnipotencie, which is nothing

else but his Omnipotent Will. The Intelligible natures, *viz.* the Angelical nature, and the Soul of Man, which are small draughts of the Divine nature, have also these two faculties, according to their weight and measure. For in them the understanding is the organ of Knowledge, the will of Working, and beyond these can they not act.

FINIS.

Fasciculus Chemicus : *Whit: Bulwork*
p. 3. 6

OR

Chymical Collections.

EXPRESSING

The Ingreſs, Progreſs, and Egreſs,
of the Secret Hermetick Science,
out of the choiſeſt and moſt
Famous A u t h o r s.

Collected and digeſted in ſuch an
order, that it may prove to the advantage,
not onely of the Beginners, but Proficients
of this high Art, by none hither-
to diſpoſed in this Method.

Whereunto is added, The *Arcanum* or
Grand Secret of Hermetick Philoſophy.

Both made Engliſh

By *James Haſolle*, Eſquire,

Qui eſt Mercuriophilus Anglicus.

*Our Magiſtry is begun and perfected, by onely one
thing; namely, Mercury.* Ventur. p.26.

London, Printed by *J.Fleſher* for *Richard Mynne*,
at the ſign of St. *Paul* in Little *Britain.* 1650.

Figure 4. Title-page from the English translation of
Arcanum (1650).

These Hieroglyphicks vaile the Vigorous Beames
Of an vnbounded Soule: The Scrowle & Scheme's
The full Interpreter: But how's conceal'd .
"Who through Ænigmaes lookes, is so Reveal'd .

T. Cross sculp: T: W: M: D.

Figure 5. Frontispiece from *Arcanum* (1650).

ARCANUM:

OR,
The grand Secret
OF
HERMETICK
PHILOSOPHY.

WHEREIN,

The Secrets of NATURE and ART, concerning the Matter and Manner of making the Philosophers Composition, are orderly and methodically manifested.

The Work of a concealed Author.

Penes nos unda Tagi.

The third Edition amended and *enlarged.*

To the Students in, and well

affected unto HERMETICK

Philosophy, health and prosperity.

AMongst the heights of hidden Philosophy, the production of the
Hermetick Stone hath of a long time been strongly believed to
be the chiefest, and nearest a Miracle, both for the Labyrinths
and multitudes of operations, out of which the minde of man,
unlesse it be illuminated by a beam of Divine light, is not able
to unwinde her self; as also because of its most noble end which
promiseth a constant plenty of health and fortunes, the two main
pillars of an happie life. Besides, the chief Promoters of this Science have made it most remote from the knowledge of the vulgar
sort by their Tropes and dark expressions, and have placed it on
high, as a Tower impregnable for Rocks and Situation, whereunto
there can be no accesse, unlesse God direct the way. The study
of hiding this Art hath drawn a reproach upon the Art it self
and its Professors: for when those unfortunate Plunderers of the
Golden Fleece by reason of their unskilfulnesse felt themselves,
beat down from their vain attempt, and far unequall unto such
eminent persons; they in a furious rapture of desperation, like
mad-men, waxed hot against their fame and the reknown of the
Science, utterly denying any thing to be above their cognizance
and the spheare of their wit, but what was foolish and frothy:
And because they set upon a businesse of damage to themselves,
they have not ceased to accuse the chief Masters of hidden Philosophy of falshood, Nature of impotency, and Art of cheats, not
for any other reason, then that they rashly condemne what they
know not: nor is this condemnation a sufficient revenge, with-

out the addition of madness to snarl and bite the innocent with infamous slaunders. I grieve (in truth) for their hard fortune, who whilest they reprove others, give occasion of their own conviction, although they justly suffer an hellish fury within them. They moil and sweat to batter the obscure principles of the most hidden Philosophy with troops of arguments, and to pull up the secret foundations thereof with their devised engines: which yet are onely manifest to the skilfull, and those that are much versed in so sublime Philosophy, but hid from strangers: Nor doe these quick-sighted Censors observe, that whilst they malign anothers credit, they willingly betray their own. Let them consider with themselves, whether they understand those things which they carp at; What Author of eminency hath divulged the secret elements of this Science, the Labyrinths and windings of operations, and lastly, the whole proceedings therein? What *Oedipus* hath sincerely and truly explained unto him the figures and intangled dark speeches of Authors? With what Oracle, what Sibyll, have they been led into the Sanctuary of this holy Science? In fine, how were all things in it made so manifest, that no part remains yet unveiled? I suppose they will no otherwise answer my question, then thus, that they have pierced all things by the subtilty of their wits; or confesse that they were taught (or rather seduced) by some wandring Quack or Mountebank, who hath crept into a good esteem with them, by his feigned countenance of a Philosopher. O wickednesse! who can silently suffer these Palmer-worms to gnaw upon the fame, labour, and glory of the wise? who can with patience hear blinde men, as out of a Tripode judging of the Sun? But it is greater glory to contemne the hurtlesse darts of bablers, then to repell them. Let them onely disdain the treasure of Nature and Art, who cannot obtain it. Nor is it my purpose to plead the doubtfull cause of an unfortunate Science, and being condemned, to take it into tuition: Our guiltlesse Philosophy is no whit criminous: and standing firm by the aid of eminentest Authors, and fortified with the manifold experience of divers ages, it remains safe enough from the fopperies of pratlers, and the snarlings of envy. However Charity hath incited me, and the multitude of wanderers induced me, taking pity on them, to present my light, that so they may escape the hazard of the night: by help whereof they may not onely live out, but also procure an enlargement both to their Life and fading Fortunes. This small Treatise penn'd for your use (ye Students of Hermetick Philosophy) I present unto you, that it may be dedicated to those, for whose sake it was writ. If any perhaps shall complain of me, and summon me to appear as guilty of breach of silence for divulging secrets in an itching style, ye have one guilty of too much respectfulnesse towards you, confessing his fault, sentence him if you please; so that my crime may supply the place of a reward to you: The offence will not bee displeasing unto you, and the punishment (I doubt not) pleasant unto mee, if I shall finde my self to have erred in this onely, whereby you may put an end to erring for the future.

Hermetick Secrets.
CANON 1.

GODS fear is the entrance into this Science. Its end is good will towards our Neighbour, the all-satisfying Crop is the rearing and endowing religious entertainment, with certainty; that whatsoever the Almighty freely bestoweth on us, we may submissively offer again to him. As also Countreys grievously oppressed, may be relieved; prisoners miserably captivated, released; and souls almost starved, comforted.

2. The light of this knowledge is the gift of God, which by his freenesse he bestoweth upon whom he pleaseth: Let none therefore set himself to the study hereof, untill having cleared and purified his heart, he devote himself wholly unto God, and be emptied of all affection unto things impure.

3. The Science of producing Natures grand Secret, is a perfect knowledge of Nature universally and of Art, concerning the Realm of Metals, the practise whereof is conversant in finding the principles of Metals by Analysis, and after they are made much more perfect, to conjoyn them otherwise then before they have been, that from thence may result a catholick Medicine, most powerfull to perfect imperfect Metals, and for restoring sick and decaied Bodies, of what sort soever.

4. Those that are in publick Honours and Offices, or be always busied with private and necessary occupations, let them not strive to attain unto the top of this Philosophy, for it requireth the whole man, and being found, possesseth him, and being possessed, challengeth him from all long and serious imploiments, esteeming all other things as strange unto him, and of no value.

5. Let him that is desirous of this Knowledge, clear his minde from all evil motions, especially pride, which is abomination to Heaven, and the gate of Hell: let him be frequent in prayers,

94

and charitable; have little to do with the world; abstain from company keeping; enjoy constant tranquility; that the Minde may be able to reason more freely in private, and be higher lifted up; for unlesse it be kindled with a beam of Divine Light, it will not be able to penetrate the hidden mysteries of Truth.

6. The *Alchymists,* who have given their minds to their welnigh innumerable Sublimations, Distillations, Solutions, Congealations; to manifold Extraction of Spirits and Tinctures, and other Operations more subtill then profitable, and so have distracted them by variety of errors, as so many tormentors; will never be bent again by their own Genius to the plain way of Nature and light of Truth, from whence their industrious subtilty hath declined them, and by twinings and turnings, as by the Lybian Quicksands, hath drowned their intangled Wits: the onely hope of safety for them remaineth in finding out a faithfull Guide and Teacher, that may make the clear Sun conspicuous unto them, and vindicate their eies from darknesse.

7. A studious *Tyro* of a quick wit, constant minde, inflamed with the study of Philosophy, very skilfull in naturall Philosophy, of a pure heart, compleat in manners, mightily devoted to God, though ignorant of practicall Chymistry, may with confidence enter into the highway of Nature, peruse the Books of best Philosophers; let him seek out an ingenious and sedulous Companion for himself, and not despair of obtaining his desire.

8. Let a Student of this secret, carefully beware of reading or keeping company with false Philosophers; for nothing is more dangerous to a learner of any Science, then the company of an unskilfull or deceitfull wit, by which false principles are stamped for true, whereby an honest and too credulous a minde is seasoned with bad Doctrine.

9. Let a Lover of truth make use of a few Authors, but of best note and experienced truth; let him suspect things that are quickly understood, especially in mystical Names and secret Operations; for truth lies hid in obscurity; nor doe Philosophers ever write more deceitfully, then when plainly, nor ever more truly then when obscurely.

10. As for the Authors of chiefest note, which have discoursed both acutely and truly of the secrets of Nature, and hid-

$\mathcal{ARCANVM}$:

OR,

The grand Secret

OF

HERMETICK

PHILOSOPHY.

WHEREIN,

The Secrets of N A T U R E and
A R T, concerning the Matter
and Manner of making the
Philoſophers Compoſition, are orderly and methodically manifeſted.

The Work of a concealed Author.

Penes nos unda Tagi.

The third Edition amended and
enlarged.

Figure 6.   Separate title-page for *Arcanum* (1650).

den Philosophy, *Hermes,* and *Morienus Romanus,* amongst the Ancients, in my judgement are of the highest esteem: amongst the Modern, *Count Trevisanus, & Raimundus Lullius,* is in greatest reverence with me: for what that most acute Doctour hath omitted, none almost hath spoken: let him therefore peruse him, yea let a Student often reade over his former Testament, and Codicil, and accept them as a Legacy of very great worth. To these two Volumes let him adde both his Practicks, out of which Works all things desirable maybe collected, especially the truth of Matter, the degrees of Fire, and the ordering of the Whole, wherein the whole Work is finished, and those things which our Ancestors too carefully laboured to keep secret. The occult causes of things, and the secret motions of nature, are demonstrated more clearly and faithfully. Concerning the first and mysticall Water of Philosophers he hath set down few things, yet very pithy.

11. As for that clear Water sought for by many, found out by few, yet obvious and profitable unto all, which is the Base of the Philosophers Work, a noble *Polonian* not more famous for his learning then subtilty of wit (not named, whose name notwithstanding a double Anagram hath betraied). In his *Novum lumen Chymicum, Parabola* and *Ænigma,* as also in his Tract of *Sulphur,* he hath spoken largely and freely enough; yea he hath expressed all things concerning it so plainly, that nothing can be satisfactory to him that desireth more.

12. Philosophers do usually expresse themselves more pithily in types and ænigmaticall figures (as by a mute kind of speech) then by words; for example, *Senior's* Table, the allegorical Pictures of *Rosarius,* the Schemes of *Abraham Judæus* in *Flamellus:* of the later sort, the rare Emblemes of the most learned *Michael Maiërus,* wherein the mysteries of the Ancients are so fully opened, that as new Perspectives they can present antiquated truth, and remote from our age as near unto our eies, and perfectly to be seen by us.

13. Whosoever affirmeth that the Philosophers grand Secret is above the stength of Nature and Art, he is blinde, because he knows not the Sun and Moon.

14. As for the Matter of their hidden Stone, Philosophers

have writ diversly; so that very many disagreeing in Words, do neverthelesse very well consent in the Thing; nor doth their different speech, argue the science ambiguous or false, since the same thing may be expressed with many tongues, divers expressions, and a different character, and also one and many things may be spoken after a divers manner.

15. Let the studious Reader have a care of the manifold significations of words, for by deceitfull windings, and doubtfull, yea contrary speeches, (as it should seem) Philosophers vent their mysteries, with a desire of keeping in and hiding, not of sophisticating or destroying the truth: And though their writings abound with ambiguous and equivocall words; yet about none doe they more contend, then in hiding their golden branch:

> —— *Quem tegit omnis*
> *Lucus; & obscuris claudunt convallibus umbræ.*
> Which all the Groves with shaddows overcast,
> And gloomy Valleys hide.

Nor yeeldeth it to any Force, but readily and willingly will follow him, who

> *Maternas agnoscit aves*
> —— *& geminæ cui fortè Columbæ*
> *Ipsa sub ora viri cœlo venêre volantes,*
> Knows Dame *Venus* Birds ——
> And him to whom of Doves a lucky paire
> Sent from above shall hover 'bout his Eare.

16. Whosoever seeketh the Art of perfecting and multiplying imperfect Metals, beyond the nature of Metals, goes in errour, for from Metals the Metals is to be derived, even as from Man, Mankinde; and from an Oxe, that species is to be fetcht.

17. Metals (we must confesse) cannot be multiplied by the instinct and labour of Nature onely; yet we may affirm that the multiplying virtue is hid in their profundity, and manifesteth it self by the help of Art: In this Work, Nature standeth in need of the aid of Art; and both doth perfect the whole.

18. Perfect Bodies are endued with a more perfect seed: and therefore under the hard bark of perfect Metals the perfect seed

lies hid, which he that knows to take out by the Philosophers solution, hath entred into the high way, for

—— *In auro*
Semina sunt auri, quam avis abstrusa recedant
Longius.
In Gold the seeds of Gold do lie,
Though buried in Obscurity.

19. Most Philosophers have affirmed that their Kingly Work is wholly composed of the Sun and Moon; others have thought good to adde Mercury to the Sun: some have chosen Sulphur and Mercury; others have attributed no small part in so great a Work to salt mingled with the other two. The very same men have professed that this clear Stone is made of one thing onely, sometimes of two, otherwhiles of three, at other times of four, and of five; and thus though writing so variously upon the same subject, doe neverthelesse agree in sense and meaning.

20. Now that (abandoning all Cheats) we may deal candidly and truly, we hold that this entire Work is perfected by two Bodies onely, to wit, the Sun and Moon rightly prepared, for this is meer generation which is by nature, with the help of Art, wherein the copulation of male and female doth intercede, from whence an off spring far more noble then the Parents, is brought forth.

21. Now those Bodies must be taken, which are of an unspotted and incorrupt virginity; such as have life and spirits in them; not extinct as those that are handled of the vulgar, for who can expect life from dead things; and those are called corrupt which have suffered copulation; those dead and extinct which (by the enforcements of the chief Tyrant of the world) have poured out their soul with their bloud by Martyrdome, fly a fratricide from whom the greatest imminent danger in the whole Work is threatned.

22. The Sun is Masculine, forasmuch as it sendeth forth active and inforcing seed, the Moon is Feminine, called the matrix and vessel of Nature, because she receiveth the seed of the male in her womb, and fostereth it by her monthly provision yet doth it not altogether want its active virtue; for, first of all

99

(being ravished with love) she climbs up unto the male, untill she hath wrested from him the utmost delights of *Venus,* and fruitfull seed: nor doth she desist from her embraces, till that being great with childe, she slip gently away.

23. By the name of the Moon Philosophers understand not the vulgar Moon, which also is masculine in its operation, and in copulation acts the part of a male. Let none therefore presume to try the wicked and unnaturall conjunction of two males, neither let him conceive any hope of issue from such copulation, but he shall join *Gabertius* to *Beia,* and offer the sister to her own brother in firm Matrimony, that from thence he may receive Sol's noble Son.

24. They that hold Sulphur and Mercury to be the Matter of the Stone, by the name of Sulphur, they understand the Sun and common Moon; by Mercury the Philosophers Moon: so (without dissimulation) holy *Lullius* adviseth his friend, that he attempt not to work without Mercury and Luna for Silver, and Mercury and Sol for Gold.

25. Let none therefore be deceived by adding a third to two: for Love admitteth not a third; and wedlock is terminated in the number of two; love further extended is adultery, not matrimony.

26. Neverthelesse, Spirituall love polluteth not a virgin, *Beia* might therefore without crime (before her promise made to *Gabritius*) have contracted spirituall love, to the end that she might thereby be made more cheerfull, more pure, and fitter for the businesse of matrimony.

27. Procreation of children is the end of lawfull Wedlock. Now that the Infant may bee borne more vigorous and gallant, let both the combatants be clensed from every scab and spot, before they both go up to their marriage bed, and let nothing unnecessary cleave unto them; because from pure seed comes a purifyed generation, and so the chast wedlock of *Sol* and *Luna* shall be finished when they shall enter into Loves bed-chamber, and be conjoyned, and she shall receive a soul from her husband by imbracing him; from this copulation a most potent King shall arise, whose father will bee *Sol,* and his mother *Luna.*

28. He that seeks for a physicall tincture without *Sol* and *Luna,* loseth both his cost and pains: for the Sun affordeth a

most plentifull tincture of rednesse, and the *Moon* of whitenesse, for these two are onely called perfect; because they are filled with the substance of purest Sulphur, perfectly clarified by the skill of nature: Let thy *Mercury* therefore have its tincture from both of these Lights; for things must of necessity receive a tincture before they can give one.

29. Perfect metals containe in them two things, which they are able to communicate to the imperfect, Tincture and Fixation; for those, because they are dyed and fixed with pure Sulphur, to wit, both white and red, they doe therefore perfectly tinct and fix, if they be fitly prepared with their proper Sulphur and Arsenick, otherwise they have not strength of multiplying their tincture.

30. *Mercury* is for imperfect metals, fit only to receive the tincture of the *Sun* and *Moon* in the work of the Philosophers Stone, that being full of tincture, it may give forth other things in aboundance: yet ought it (before that) to be full of invisible Sulphur, that it may be the more coloured with the visible tincture of perfect bodies, and so repay it with sufficient Usury.

31. Now the whole tribe of Philosophers sweat much, and are mightily troubled to extract tincture out of gold: for they beleeve that tincture can be separated from the Sun, and being separated encrease in virtue; but

> *Spes tandem Agricolas vanis eludit aristis.*
> Vaine hope, at last the hungry Plough-man cheats
> With empty Husks,*in stead of lusty meats*

For it is impossible that the Suns tincture can at all be severed from his naturall body, since there can be no elementary body made up by nature more perfect then gold, the perfection whereof proceedeth from the strong and inseparable union of pure colouring Sulphur with *Mercury,* both of them being admirrably pre-disposed thereunto by Nature; whose true separation nature denieth unto Art: But if any liquor remaining be extracted (by the violence of fire or waters) by the Sun, it is to be reputed a part of the body made liquid or dissolved by force. For the tincture followeth its body, and is never separated from it. That is the deluding of Art, unknowne to Artificers themselves.

101

32. Neverthelesse it may be granted, that tincture is separable from its body, yet (we must confesse) it cannot be separated without the corruption of the tincture: when as Artists offer violence to the gold, or *Aqua fortis* rather corroding then dissolving. The body therefore spoiled of its tincture and golden fleece, must needs grow base, and as an unprofitable heap turne to the damage of its Artificer, and the tincture thus corrupted to have a weaker operation.

33. Let them in the next place cast their tincture into *Mercury,* or into any other imperfect body, and as strongly conjoyne both of them as their Art will permit; yet shall they fail of their hopes two wayes; First, because the tincture will neither penetrate nor colour beyond Natures strength; and therefore no gaine will accrue from thence to recompence the expence and countervaile the losse of the body spoiled and of no value, so

> *Cum labor in damno est, crescit mortalis egestas.*
> Want is poor mortals wages, when his toyle
> Produces only losse of paines and Oyle.

Lastly that banished Tincture applied to another body will not give a perfect fixation and permanency to endure a strong tryall, and resist searching *Saturne.*

34. Let them therefore that are desirous of *Chymistry,* and have hitherto followed Impostors and Mountebanks, sound a retrait, spare time and cost, and give their minde to a work truly Philosophicall, lest the *Phrygians* be wise too late, and at length be compelled to cry out with the Prophet, *Strangers have eaten up my strength.*

35. In the Philosophers work more toyle and time then cost is expended; for he that hath convenient matter, need be at little expence: besides, those that hunt after great store of mony, and place their chief end in wealth, they trust more to their riches, then their own art. Let therefore the too credulous Fresh-man beware of these pilfering pick-pockets, for whilst they promise golden mountains, they lay in wait for gold; they demand bright ushering Sol, *(viz. mony before hand)* because they walk in darknesse.

36. As those that sayle between *Scilla* and *Charybdis* are in

danger on both sides: unto no lesse hazard are they subject who pursuing the prey of the Golden fleece, are carried between the uncertaine Rocks of the Philosophers *Sulphur* and *Mercury*. The more acute by their constant reading of grave and credible Authors, and by the irradiant Sun have attained unto the knowledge of *Sulphur,* but are at a stand in the entrance of the Philosophers *Mercury*; for Writers have twisted it with so many windings and Meanders, involved it with so many æquivocall names, that it may be sooner met with by the force of the Seekers intellect, then be found by reason or toyle.

37. That Philosophers might the deeper drown their *Mercury* in darknesse, they have made it manifold, and placed their *Mercury* (yet diversly) in every part and forefront of their worke, nor will he attaine unto a perfect knowledge thereof, who shall be ignorant of any part of the work.

38. Philosophers have acknowledged a threefold *Mercury* especially, to wit, after absolute preparation of the first degree, and Philosophicall sublimation; for then they call it their *Mercury*, and *Mercury* sublimated.

39. Againe, in the second preparation, that which by Authors is stiled the First (because they omit the First) Sol being now made crude again, and resolved into his first matter is Mercury, properly called of such like bodies, or the Philosophers Mercury; then the matter is called *Rebis, Chaos,* the whole world, wherein are all things necessary to the work, because that onely is sufficient to perfect the Stone.

40. Lastly the Philosophers do sometimes call perfect *Elixir* and colouring medicine, their *Mercury*, though improperly; for the name of *Mercury* doth onely properly agree with that which is volatile; besides that which is sublimated in every region of the work, they call Mercury: but Elixir because it is most fixed, cannot have the simple name of Mercury, and therefore they have stiled it their own Mercury, to difference it from that volatile. A straight way is only laid downe for them to find out and discerne so many Mercuries of the Philosophers, for then onely

———— *Quos æquus amavit*
Iupiter, aut ardens evexit ad æthera virtus.
———— Whom just and mighty Jove
Advanceth by the strength of love;
Or such whom brave heroick fire,
Makes from dull Earth to Heav'n aspire.

41. Elixir is called the Philosophers Mercury for the likenesse and great conformity it hath with Heavenly Mercury; for this, being void of elementary qualities is beleeved most propense to receive influence from them, and that changeable *Proteus* puts on and encreaseth the genius and nature of other Planets, by reason of opposition, conjunction and aspect. The like this uncertaine Elixir worketh, for that being tyed to no proper quality, it imbraceth the quality and disposition of the thing wherewith it is mixed, and wonderfully multiplyeth the virtues and qualities hereof.

42. In the Philosophicall sublimation or first preparation of Mercury, Herculean labour must be undergone by the workman; for *Jason* had in vaine attempted his expedition to *Colchos* without *Alcides*.

Alter in auratam noto de vertice pellem
Principium velut ostendit, quod sumere possis;
Alter onus quantum subeas ————
One from on high a Golden Fleece displayes
Which shewes the Entrance, another says
How hard a taske you'l find.

For the entrance is warded by horne-pushing beasts; which drive away those that approach rashly thereunto to their great hurt; onely the ensignes of *Diana* and the doves of *Venus* are able to asswage their fiercenesse, if the fates favour.

43. The naturall quality of Philosophicall Earth and the tillage thereof, seems to be touched by the Poet in this Verse,

Pingue solum primis extemplo à mensibus anni
Fortes invertant Tauri ————
———— *Tunc Zephyro putris se gleba resolvit.*
Let sturdy Oxen when the yeare begins
Plough up the fertile soyle ————

For *Zeph'rus* then dissolves the rotten clods.

44. He that calleth the Philosophers Luna or their Mercury, the common Mercury; doth wittingly deceive, or is deceived; so the writings of *Geber* teach us, that the Philosophers Mercury is Argent vive, yet not of the common sort, but extracted out of it by the Philosophers skill.

45. That the Philosophers Mercury is not Argent vive in its proper nature, nor in its whole substance, but in the midle and pure substance thereof, which thence hath taken its originall and made by it, the grand Philosophers opinions being founded in experience.

46. The Philosophers Mercury hath divers names, sometimes it is call'd Earth, sometimes Water in a divers respect, because it naturally ariseth from them both. The earth is subtle, white, sulphurous, in which the elements are fixed & the philosophicall gold is sowne: the water is water of life, burning, permanent, most clear, call'd the water of gold and silver; but this Mercury, because it hath in it Sulphur of its own, which is multiplyed by art, it deserves to be cald the Sulphur of Argent vive. Last of all the most precious substance is *Venus* the ancients Hemaphrodite, glorious in each sex.

47. This Argent vive, is partly naturall, partly unnaturall, it being intrinsecall and occult hath its root in nature, which cannot be drawne forth unlesse it be by some precedent clensing, & industrious sublimation, it being extrinsecall is præternaturall and accidentall: separate therefore the clean from the unclean, the substance from the accidents, and make that which is hid, manifest, by the course of nature, otherwise make no further progresse, for this is the foundation of the whole worke, and nature.

48. That dry and most precious liquor doth constitute the radicall moisture of metals, wherefore of some of the ancients it is called Glasse; for glasse is extracted out of the radicall moisture, closely lurking in ashes which will not give place, unlesse it be to the hottest flame; notwithstanding our inmost or centrall Mercury discovers it selfe by the most gentle and kindly (though a little more tedious) fire of nature.

49. Some have sought for the latent Philosophicall earth by Calcination, others by sublimation; many among the glasing vessels, and some few between vitrial and salt, even as among their naturall vessels: other enjoyne to sublime it out of lime and glasse. But we have learned of the Prophet, that *in the beginning God created the Heaven and the Earth, and the Earth was without form and void, and darknesse was upon the face of the Deep; and the spirit of God moved upon the Waters, and God said, Let there be Light, and there was Light; and God saw the Light that it was good, and he divided the light from the darknes, &c.* Josephs blessing spoken of by the same Prophet will be sufficient to a wise man (Deut. 33.) *Blessed of the Lord be his Land, for the * Apples of Heaven, for the dew, and for the Deep that lyeth beneath; for the Apples of fruit both of sun and moon, for the top of the ancient mountains, for the Apples of the everlasting hills, &c.* pray the Lord from the ground of thy heart (my son) that he would bestow upon thee a portion of this blessed land.

50. Argent vive is so defiled by originall sin, that it floweth with a double infection; the first it hath contracted from the polluted Earth, which hath mixed it selfe therewith in its generation, and by congelation hath cleaved thereunto: the second borders upon the dropsie, and is the corruption of intercutal Water, proceeding from thick and impure water, mixed with the clear, which nature is not able to squeeze out and separate by constriction; and because it is extrinsecall, it goes away with a gentle heat. The Mercuries leprosie infesting the body, is not of its root and substance, but accidental, and therefore separable from it; the earthly part is wiped off by a moist Bath and the laver of nature: the watery part is taken away by a dry bath with the pleasant fire of generation. And thus by a threefold washing and clensing the Dragon putting off his old scales & ugly skin is renewed.

51. The Philosophicall sublimation of Mercury is compleated in two things; namely by removing things superfluous from it, and by introducing things wanting: the superfluities are the externall accidents, which in the dark spheare of *Saturne* doe make cloudy ruddy *Jupiter*. Separate therefore the blewnesse of *Sat-*

urne coming up, untill *Iupiters* purple star smile upon thee. Add hereunto the sulphur of nature, whose grain and leaven it hath in it selfe, so much as sufficeth it; but see that it be sufficient for other things also. Multiply therefore that invisible Sulphur of the philosophers until the Virgins milk come forth: and so the first gate is opened unto thee.

52. The entrance of the Philosophers garden is kept by the Hesperian Dragon, which being laid open, a fountaine of the clearest water proceeding from a seaven-fold spring floweth forth on every side the threshold, wherein make the Dragon drink thrice the magicall number of Seven, untill being drunk he put off his hideous garment: may the divine powers of light-bringing *Venus* and horned *Diana,* be propitious unto thee.

53. Three kinds of most beautifull flowers are to be sought, and may be found in the garden of the wise: Damask coloured Violets, the milk-white Lilly, and the purple and immortal flower of love, *Amaranthus.* Not far from that fountaine at the entrance, fresh Violets do first salute thee, which being watered by streams from the great golden river, put on the most delicate colour of the dark Saphir: the Sun will give thee signs. Thou shall not sever such precious flowers from their root, untill thou makest the Stone: for the fresh ones cropt off, have more juyce and tincture: and then pick them carefully with a gentle and discreet hand; if fates frown not, they will easily follow, and one flower being pluck't, the other golden one will not be wanting: let the Lilly and the *Amaranthus,* succeed with greater care and labour.

54. Philosophers have their Sea also, wherein small fishes, fat and shining with silver scales, are generated; which he that shall catch in and take out of a smal and fine net, shall be accounted a most expert fisher.

55. The Philosophers Stone is found in the oldest mountaines, and flowes from everlasting brooks; those mountaines are of silver, and the brooks of gold: from thence gold and silver, and all the treasure of Kings are produced.

56. Whosoever is minded to obtaine the Philosophers Stone, let him resolve to take a long peregrination, for it is necessary that he go to see both the Indies, that from thence he may bring the most precious gems and purest gold.

57. The Philosophers extract this their Stone out of seven stones, the two chiefe whereof are of a divers nature and efficacy, the one infuseth invisible Sulphur, the other spirituall Mercury; that bringeth heat and drinesse, and this cold and moisture: thus by their help, the strength of the elements is multiplyed in the Stone; the former is found in the Easterne coast, the latter in the Westerne: both of them have the power of colouring and multiplying, and unlesse the Stone shal take its first tincture from them, it will neither colour nor multiply.

58. Rx The winged Virgin very well washed and clensed, impregnated by the spirituall seed of the first male, and gravidated with the permanent glory of her untoucht virginity, will be discovered by her cheeks dyed with a whitish red colour: joyne her to the second male, without Jealousie of adultery, by whose corporeall seed she shall conceive againe, and shall in time bring forth a reverend off-spring of either sex, from whence an immortall Race of most potent Kings shall gloriously arise.

59. Keep up and couple the Eagle and Lion well clensed in their transparent cloister, the entry door being shut and watched, lest their breath go out, or the aire without do privily get in. The Eagle shall snap up and devoure the Lion in the copulation; afterwards being affected with a long sleep, and a dropsie occasioned by a foule stomach, she shall be changed by a wonderfull metamorphosis into a cole-black Crow, which shall begin to fly with wings stretched out, and by its flight shall whisk downe water from the clouds, untill being often moistned, he put off his wings of his owne accord, and falling downe againe it be changed into a most white Swan. Those that are ignorant of the causes of things, may wonder without astonishment, when they consider that the World is nothing but a continuall Metamorphosis, they may marvel that the seeds of things perfectly digested should end in greatest whitenesse. Let the Philosopher imitate Nature in his work.

60. Nature proceedeth thus in making and perfecting her works, that from an inchoate generation it may bring a thing by diverse meanes as it were by degrees, to the ultimate terme of perfection: she therefore attaineth her end by little and little, not by leaps; confining and including her work between two

extreams, distinct and severed as by spaces. The practice of Philosophy, which is the Ape of Nature, ought not to decline from the way and example of Nature in its working and direction to finde out its happy stone, for whatsoever is without the bounds of Nature, is either an errour or nearest one.

61. The extreams of the Stone are naturall Argent vive, and perfect Elixir: the middle parts which lye between, by helpe whereof the work goes on, are of three sorts; for they either belong unto matter, or operations and demonstrative signes: the whole work is perfected by these extreams and means.

62. The materiall means of the Stone are of divers kinds; for some are extracted out of others successively: The first are Mercury Philosophically sublimated, and perfect metals, which although they be extream in the work of nature, yet in the Philosophical worke they supply the place of meanes: of the former the seconds are produced; namely, the four elements, which againe are circulated and fixed: of the seconds the thirds are produced, to wit, either Sulphur the multiplication whereof doth terminate the first worke: the fourth and last meanes are leaven or ointments weighed with the mixtion of the things aforesaid, successively produced in the worke of the Elixir: By the right ordering of the things aforesaid, the perfect Elixir is finished, which is the last term of the whole work, wherein the Philosophers Stone resteth as in its centre, the multiplication whereof is nothing else then a short repetition of the premised operations.

63. The operative meanes (which are also called the Keys of the work) are foure: The first is Solution or Liquefaction; the second is Ablution; the third, Reduction; the fourth, Fixation. By Liquefaction bodies returne into their ancient matter, things concocted are made raw agine, and the copulation between the male and female is effected, from whence the Crow is generated: Lastly the Stone is divided into 4 confused elements, which happeneth by the retrogradation of the Luminaries. The Ablution teacheth to make the Crow white, & to create *Jupiter* of *Saturn*, which is made by the conversion of the body into Spirit. The office of Reduction is to restore the soule to the Stone examinated, and to nourish it with dew and spirituall Milk, untill it shall attaine unto perfect strength: In both these latter opera-

tions the Dragon rageth against himselfe, and by devouring his tayle, doth wholly exhaust himselfe, and at length is turned into the Stone. Lastly, the operation of the Fixation fixeth both Sulphurs upon their fixed body, by the mediation of the spirits tincture; it decocteth the leavens by degrees, ripeneth things raw, and sweetneth the bitter; In fine, by penetrating and tincturing the flowing Elixir, generateth, perfecteth; and lastly, riseth up to the height of sublimity.

64. The Meanes or demonstrative signes are Colours, successively and orderly affecting the matter and its affections and demonstrative passions, whereof there are three speciall ones (as criticall) to be noted, to these some adde a Fourth. The first is black, which is called the Crowes-head, because of its extreame blacknesse, whose crepusculum sheweth the beginning of the fires action of nature and solution, and the blackest night the perfection of liquefaction, and confusion of the elements. Then the graine putrefies & is corrupted, that it may be the more apt for generation. The white colour succeedeth the black, wherein is given the perfection of the first degree, and of white Sulphur. This is called the blessed stone: this Earth is white and foliated, wherein Philosophers doe sow their gold. The third is Orange colour, which is produced in the passage of the white to the red, as the middle and mixt of both, and is as the morning with her safron-haire a fore-runner of the Sun. The fourth colour is ruddy and sanguine, which is extracted from the white fire onely: Now because whitenesse is easily altered by any other colour, before day it quickly faileth of its candor. But the dark rednesse of the Sun perfecteth the worke of Sulphur, which is called the Sperme of the male, the fire of the Stone, the Kings Crown, and the son of Sol, wherein the first labour of the workman resteth.

65. Besides these decretory signes which firmely inhere in the matter, and shew its essentiall mutations, almost infinite colours appear, and shew themselves in vapours, as the Rainbow in the clouds, which quickly passe away and are expelled by those that succeed, more affecting the aire then the earth: the operatour must have a gentle care of them, because they are not permanent, and proceed not from the intrinsecall disposition of the matter, but from the fire painting and fashioning every thing

after its pleasure, or casually by heat in small moisture.

66. Of the strange colours, some called out of time, give an ill omen to the work, as the Blacknesse renewed: for the Crowes young ones having once left their nest are never to be suffered to returne. Too hasty Rednesse; for this once and in the end onely gives a certaine hope of the harvest; if before it make the matter red, it is an argument of the greatest aridity, not without great danger, which can onely be averted by Heaven alone, forthwith bestowing a shower upon it.

67. The Stone is exalted by successive digestions, as by degrees, and at length attaineth to perfection. Now foure Digestions agreeable to the foure abovesaid Operations or Government do compleat the whole worke, the author whereof is the fire, which makes their difference.

68. The first digestion operateth the solution of the Body, whereby comes the first conjunction of male and female, the commixtion of both seeds, putrefaction, the resolution of the elements into homogeneall water, the eclipse of the Sun and Moon in the head of the Dragon, and lastly it bringeth back the whole World into its ancient Chaos, and dark abysse. This first digestion is made as in the stomack, of a melon colour and weak, more fit for corruption then generation.

69. In the second digestion the spirit of the Lord walketh upon the waters; the light begins to appear, and a separation of waters from the waters; the Sun and Moon are renewed; the elements are extracted out of the chaos, that being perfectly mixt in Spirit they may constitute a new world; a new Heaven and new Earth are made; and lastly, all bodies are become spirituall. The Crowes young ones changing their fethers begin to passe into Doves, the Eagle and Lion embrace one another with an eternall League. And this generation of the World is made by the fiery Spirit descending in the forme of Water, and wiping away Originall sin; for the Philosophers Water is Fire, which is moved by the exciting heat of a Bath. But see that the separation of Waters be done in Weight and Measure, lest those things that remaine under Heaven be drowned under the Earth, or those things that are snatched up above Heaven be too much destitute of aridity.

Hic, sterilem exiguus ne deserat humor arenam.
Here, lest small moisture, leave a barren Soyle.

70. The third digestion of the newly generated Earth drinketh up the dewy Milk, and all the spirituall virtues of the quintessence, and fasteneth the quickning Soul to the Body by the Spirits mediation. Then the Earth layeth up a great Treasure in it selfe, and is made, like the coruscant Moon, afterwards to ruddy Sun; the former is called the Earth of the Moon, the latter the Earth of the Sun; for both of them is begot of the copulation of them both; neither of them any longer feareth the pains of the Fire, because both want all spots; for they have been often clensed from sin by fire, and have suffered great Martyrdome, untill all the Elements are turned downwards.

71. The Fourth digestion consummateth all the Mysteries of the World, and the Earth being turned into most excellent leaven, it leaveneth all imperfect bodies because it hath before passed into the heavenly nature of quintessence. The vertue thereof flowing from the Spirit of the Universe is a present *Panacea* and universall medicine for all the diseases of all creatures, the digestions of the first worke being repeated will open to thee the Philosophers secret Furnace. Be right in thy works, that thou mayest finde God favourable, otherwise the plowing of the Earth will be in vaine; Nor

Illa seges demum votis respondet avari
Agricolæ ——
With the expected Harvest e're requite
The greedy High-shooe ——

72. The whole Progresse of the Philosophers work is nothing but Solution and Congelation; the Solution of the body, and Congelation of the Spirit; neverthelesse, there is but one operation of both: the fixed and volatile are perfectly mixed and united in the Spirit, which cannot be done, unlesse the fixed body be first made soluble and volatile: By reduction is the volatile body fixed into a permanent body, and volatile nature doth at last change into a fixed one, as the fixed Nature had before passed into volatile. Now so long as the Natures were

confused in the Spirit, that mixed Spirit keeps a middle Nature between Body and Spirit, Fixed and Volatile.

73. The generation of the Stone is made after the patterne of the Creation of the World; for it is necessary, that it have its Chaos and First matter, wherein the confused Elements do fluctuate, untill they be separated by the fiery Spirit; they being separated, the light Elements are carried upwards, and the heavie ones downwards: the light arising, darknesse retraits: the waters are gathered into one, and the dry land appeares. At length the two great Luminaries arise, and minerall virtues vegetable and animal, are produced in the Philosophers Earth.

74. God created *Adam* of the mud of the Earth, wherein were inherent the virtues of all the Elements, of the Earth & Water especially, which doe more constitute the sensible and corporeall heap: Into this Masse God inspired the breath of Life, and enlivened it with the Sunne of the Holy Spirit. He gave *Eve* for a Wife to *Adam,* and blessing them he gave unto them a Precept and Faculty of multiplying. The Generation of the Philosophers Stone, is not unlike the Creation of *Adam,* for the Mud was made of a terestriall and ponderous Body dissolved by Water, which deserved the excellent name of *Terra Adamica,* wherein all the virtues and qualities of the Elements are placed. At length the heavenly Soule is infused thereinto by the Spirit of the quintessence and Solar influx, and by the Benediction and Dew of Heaven; the virtue of multiplying *in infinitum* by the intervening copulation of both sexes is given it.

75. The chief secret of this worke consisteth in the manner of working, which is wholly imployed about the Elements: for the matter of the Stone passeth from one Nature into another, the Elements are successively extracted, and by turnes obtaine dominion; every thing is agitated by the circles of *humidum* and *siccum,* untill all things be turned downwards, and there rest.

76. In the work of the Stone the other Elements are circulated in the figure of Water, for the Earth is resolved into Water, wherein are the rest of the Elements; the Water is Sublimated into Vapour, Vapour retreats into Water, and so by an unwearied circle, is the Water moved, untill it abide fixed downwards; now that being fixed all the Elements are fixed: Thus into it

they are resolved, by it they are extracted, with it they live and dye: the Earth is the Tombe, and last end of them all.

77. The order of Nature requireth that every generation begin from *humidum* and in *humidum.* In the Philosophers work, Nature is to be reduced into order, that so the matter of the Stone which is terrestriall, compact and dry, in the first place may be dissolved and flow into the Element of Water next unto it, and then *Saturne* will be generated of *Sol.*

78. The Aire succeeds the Water drawne about by seven circles or revolutions, which is wheel'd about with so many circles and reductions, untill it be fixed downwards, and *Saturne* being expell'd, *Jupiter* may receive the Scepter and Government of the Kingdome, by whose coming the Philosophers Infant is formed, nourished in the wombe, and at length is borne; resembling the splendor of *Luna* in its beautifull serene countenance.

79. The Fire executing the courses of the Nature of the Elements, extream Fire promoving it, of hidden is made manifest: the Saffron dyeth the Lilly: rednesse possesseth the cheeks of the whitening Child now made stronger: A Crowne is prepared for him against the time of his Reigne. This is the consummation of the first work, and the perfect rotation of the Elements, the signe whereof is, when they are all terminated in *Siccum,* and the body void of Spirit lyeth downe wanting pulse and motion: And thus all the Elements do finally acquiesce in *Terra.*

80. Fire placed in the Stone is Natures Prince, Sol's Son and Vicar, moving and digesting matter, and perfecting all things therein, if it shall attain its liberty; for it lieth weak under an hard bark, procure therefore its freedome that it may secure thee freely; but beware that thou urge it not above measure, for it being impatient of Tyranny it becomes a fugitive, no hope of returne being left unto thee; call it back therefore by courteous flattery, and keep it prudently.

81. The first mover of Nature is Externall Fire, the Moderator of Internall Fire, and of the whole work; Let the Philosopher therefore very well understand the government thereof, and observe its degrees and points; for from thence the welfare or ruine of the worke dependeth. Thus Art helpeth Nature, and the Philosopher is the Minister of both.

82. By these two Instruments of Art and Nature, the Stone lifteth it selfe up from Earth to Heaven with great ingenuity, and slideth from Heaven to Earth, because the Earth is its Nurse,and being carried in the wombe of the wind, it receiveth the force of the Superiours and Inferiours.

83. The Circulation of the Elements is exercised with a double Wheel, by the greater or extended, and the lesse or contracted: The Wheel extended fixeth all the Elements of the Earth, and its circle is not finished unlesse the work of Sulphur be perfected. The revolution of the minor Wheel is terminated by the extraction and preparation of every Element; Now in this Wheel there are three Circles placed, which always and variously move the Matter, by an Erratick and Intricate Motion, and do often (seven times at least) drive about every Element, in order succeeding one another, and so agreeable, that if one shall be wanting the labour of the rest is made void. These are Natures Instruments, wherby the Elements are prepared. Let the Philosopher therefore consider the progresse of Nature in the Physicall Tract more fully described for this very end.

84. Every Circle hath its proper Motion, for all the motions of the Circles are conversant about the Subject of *Humidum* and *Siccum,* and are so concatenated, that they produce the onely operation, and one only concent of Nature: two of them are opposite, both in respect of the causes & the effects; for one moveth upwards, drying by heat; another downwards, moistning by cold; a third carrying the form of rest and sleep by digesting, induceth the cessation of both in greatest moderation.

85. Of the three Circles, the First is Evacuation, the labour of which is in subtracting the superfluous *Humidum,* and also in separating the pure, cleane, and subtile, from the grosse and terrestriall dreggs. Now the greatest danger is found in the motion of this Circle, because it hath to doe with things Spirituall, and makes Nature plentifull.

86. Two things are chiefly to be taken heed of in moving this Circle; First, that it be not moved too intensly; the other, that it be not moved longer then is meet. Motion accelerated raiseth confusion in the matter, so that the grosse, impure and indigested part may fly out together with the pure and subtile,

and the Body undissolved mixed with the Spirit, together with that which is dissolved. With this precipitated motion the Heavenly and Terrestriall Nature are confounded, and the Spirit of the Quintessence corrupted by the admixtion of the Earth, is made dull and invalid. By too long a motion the Earth is too much evacuated of its Spirit, & is made so languishing, dry, and destitute of Spirit, that it cannot easily be restored and recalled to its Temperament. Either errour burneth up the Tinctures, or turns it into flight.

87. The Second Circle is Restauration; whose office is, to restore strength to the gasping and debilitated body by Potion. The former Circle was the Organ of Sweat and labour, but this of Refreshment and Consolation. The action of this is imployed in the grinding & mollifying the Earth, (Potter like) that it may be the better mixed.

88. The motion of this Circle must be lighter then that of the former, especially in the beginning of its Revolution, lest the Crow's young ones be drowned in their nest by a large floud, and the growing world be overflowne by a deluge. This is the Weigher and Assayer of Measures, for it distributeth Water by Geometricall Precepts. There is usually no greater Secret found in the whole practice of the Worke, then the firme and justly weighed Motion of this Circle; for it informeth the Philosophers Infant and inspireth Soul and Life into him.

89. The Lawes of this Circles Motions are, that it run about gently; and by little and little, and sparingly let forth it selfe, lest that by making hast it fall from its measure, and the Fire inherent overwhelmed with the Waters, the Architect of the Work grow dull, or also be extinguished: that meat and drink be administred by turnes, to the end there may be a better Digestion made, and the best temperament of *Humidum* and *Siccum*; for the indissoluble colligation of them both is the End and Scope of the Worke. Furthermore see, that you add so much by Watering, as shall be wanting in assation, that Restauration may restore so much of the lost strength by corroborating, as Evacuation hath taken away by debilitating.

90. Digestion the last Circle acteth with silent and insensible motion; and therefore it is said by Philosophers, that it is made

in a secret furnace; it decocteth the Nutriment received, and converteth it into the Homogeneal parts of the body. Moreover, it is called Putrefaction; because as meat is corrupted in the Stomack before it passe into Bloud and Similar parts: so this operation breaketh the Aliment with a concocting and Stomack heat, and in a manner makes it to putrefie, that it may be the better Fixed, and changed from a Mercuriall into a Sulphurous Nature. Again, it is called Inhumation, because by it the Spirit is inhumated, and as a dead man buried in the ground. But because it goes most slowly, it therefore needeth a longer time. The two former Circles do labour especially in dissolving, this in congealing, although all of them work both.

91. The Lawes of this Circle are, that it be moved by the Feaverish and most gentle heat of Dung, lest that the things volatile fly out, and the Spirit be troubled at the time of its strictest Conjunction with the Body, for then the businesse is perfected in the greatest tranquillity and ease; therefore we must especially beware lest the Earth be moved by any Winds or Shewers: Lastly, as this third Circle may alwayes succeed the second straight-wayes and in its order, as the second the first: so by interrupted works & by course those three erratick Circles doe compleat one intire circulation, which often reiterated, at length turnes all things into Earth, and makes peace between enemies.

92. Nature useth Fire, so also doth Art after its example, as an Instrument and Mallet in cutting out its works. In both operations therefore Fire is Master and Perfect. Wherefore the knowledge of Fires is most necessary for a Philosopher, without which as another Ixion (condemn'd to labour in vaine) he shall turne about Wheel of Nature to no purpose.

93. The name Fire is Equivocall amongst Philosophers; for sometimes it is used Metonymically for heat; and so, as many fires as heats. In the Generation of Metals and Vegetables, Nature acknowledgeth a three-fold Fire; to wit, Celestiall, Terrestriall, and Innate. The First flowes from Sol as its Fountaine, into the Bosome of the Earth; it stirreth up Fumes or Mercuriall and Sulphurous vapours, of which Metals are created, and mixeth it selfe amongst them; it stirreth up fire, placed and snorting in the

117

seeds of the Vegetables, and addeth sparkles unto it (as Spurres) for vegetation. The Second lurketh in the bowels of the Earth, by the Impulse and action whereof the Subterraneous vapours are driven upwards through Pores and Pipes, and thrust outwards from the Centre towards the Superficies of the Earth, both for the composition of Metals, where the Earth swelleth up, as also for the production of Vegetables, by putrefying their seeds, by softning and preparing them for generation. The third of the former, *viz.* Solar, is generated of a vappid smoak of Metals, and also infused with the monthly provision grows together with the humid matter, & is retained as in a Prison within the strength of it; or more truely, as forme is conjoyned with the mixt body: It firmely inhereth in the seeds of Vegetables, untill being solicited by the point of its Fathers rayes it be called out, then Motion intrinsecally moveth and informeth the matter, and becomes the Plastes and Dispensator of the whole Mixture. In the generation of Animals, Celestiall Fire doth insensibly cooperate with the Animall; for it is the first Agent in Nature: but the heat of the *Femella* answereth Terrestrial heat, untill it putrefie the Seed, and prepare it: The Fire implanted in the Seed, Sols son, disposeth the matter, and being disposed informeth it.

94. Philosophers have observed a three-fold Fire in the matter of their work, Naturall, not Naturall, against Nature. The Naturall they call the Fiery Celestiall Spirit Innate, kept in the profundity of matter, and most strictly bound unto it, which by the sluggish strength of metall growes dull, untill being stirred up and freed by the Philosophers discretion and externall heat, it shall have obtained a faculty of moving its body dissolved, and so it informeth its humid matter, by explication, Penetration, Dilatation and congelation. In every mixt body Naturall Fire is the Principle of Heat and Motion. Unnaturall Fire they name that which being called and coming extrinsecally, is introduced into the matter wonderfull artificially; that it may increase and multiply the strength of naturall heat. The Fire contrary to Nature they call that, which putrefies the Compositum, & corrupteth the temperament of Nature; It is imperfect, because being too weak for generation, it is not carried beyond the bounds of corruption: such is the Fire or heat of the menstruum: yet it hath

the name improperly of Fire against Nature, because in a manner it is according to Nature, for salving the specifical form, it so corrupteth the matter, that it disposeth it for generation.

95. It is more credible neverthelesse, that the corrupting Fire, called Fire against Nature, is not different from the Innate, but the first degree of it, for the order of nature requireth, that corruption precede generation: the fire therefore that is innate agreeable to the Law of Nature performeth both, by exciting both successively in the matter: the first of corruption more gentle stirred up by feeble heat, for to mollifie and prepare the body: the other of generation more forcible, moved by a more vehement heat, for to animate and fully informe the Elementary body disposed by the former. A double Motion doth therefore proceed from a double degree of heat of the same fire; neither is it to be accounted a double Fire. But far better may the Name of Fire contrary to Nature be given to violent and destructive Fire.

96. Unnaturall fire is converted into Naturall or Innate Fire by successive degrees of Digestion, and increaseth and multiplyeth it: Now the whole secret consisteth in the multiplication of Naturall Fire, which of it selfe is not able to Work above its proper strength, nor communicate a perfect Tincture to imperfect Bodies; for it is sufficient to it selfe; nor hath it any further power; but being multiplyed by the unnaturall, which most aboundeth with the virtue of multiplying, doth act far more powerfully, and reacheth it selfe beyond the bounds of Nature colouring strange and imperfect bodies, and perfecting them, because of its plentifull Tincture, and the abstruse Treasure of multiplyed Fire.

97. Philosophers call their Water Fire because it is most hot, and indued with a Fiery Spirit; againe, Water is called Fire by them, because it burneth the bodies of perfect Metals more than common fire doth; for it perfectly dissolveth them, whereas they resist our Fire, and will not suffer themselves to be dissolved by it; for this cause it is also called Burning Water: Now that Fire of Tincture is hid in the belly of the Water, and manifests it selfe by a double effect, *viz.* of the bodies Solution and Multiplication.

98. Nature useth a double Fire in the Work of generation,

Intrinsecall, & extrinsecall: the former being placed in the seeds
& mixtures of things, is hid in their Centre; & as a principle
of Motion and Life, doth move and quicken the body: But the
latter, Extrinsecall, whether it be poured down from Heaven or
Earth, raiseth the former, as drowned with sleep, and compels
it to action; for the vitall sparks implanted in the seeds stand in
need of an externall mover, that they may be moved and actuate.

99. It is even so in the Philosophers worke; for the matter of the Stone possesseth his Interiour Fire, which partly Innate, partly also is added by the Philosophers Art, for those two
are united and come inward together, because they are homogeneous: the internall standeth in need of the externall, which
the Philosopher administreth according to the Precepts of Art
and Nature; this compelleth the former to move. These Fires
are as two Wheels, whereof the hidden one being smitten of the
sensible one, it is moved sooner or later: And thus Art helpeth
Nature.

100. The Internall Fire is the middle between the mover and
the matter, whence it is, that as it is moved by that, it moveth
thus; if so it shall be driven intensly or remisly, it will work after
the same manner in the matter. The Information of the whole
worke dependeth of the measure of externall Fire.

101. He that is ignorant of the degrees and points of externall Fire, let him not set upon the Philosophicall Worke; for
he will never pull light out of darknesse, unlesse the heats passe
through their mediums, like the Elements, whose extreams are
not converted but onely by mediums.

102. Because the whole work consisteth in Separation and
perfect Preparation of the foure Elements, therefore so many
degrees of Fire are necessary thereunto; for every Element is
extracted by the degree of Fire proper to it.

103. The foure degrees of Fire are called the Fire of the
Bath, of Ashes, of Coales, and of Flame, which is also called
Optetick: every degree hath its points, two at least, sometimes
three; for the Fire is to be moved slowly and by points, whether
it be increased or decreased, that Matter (after Natures example) may goe on by degrees and willingly unto Information and
completion; for nothing is so strange to Nature as that which is

violent; Let the Philosopher propound to his consideration the gentle accesse & recesse of the Sun, whose Light & Lamp indulgeth its heat to the things of the world, according to the times and Lawes of the Universe, and so bestoweth a temperament upon them.

104. The first point of the Bath of heat is called the heat of a Feaver or of Dung; the second of both simply. The first point of the second degree is the simple heat of Ashes, the second is the heat of Sand: Now the points of Fire, of Coales and Flame, want a proper Name, but they are distinguished by the operation of the Intellect, according to intention and remission.

105. The degrees onely of Fire are sometimes found amongst Philosophers, *viz.* of the Bath of Ashes and the hot Bath, which comprehendeth the Fire of Coals and Flame: the Fire of Dung is sometimes distinguished from the Fire of the Bath, in degree. Thus for the most part Authors doe involve the light in darknesse, by the various expressions of the Philosophers Fire; for the knowledge thereof is accounted amongst their chief secrets.

106. In the White Work, because three Elements onely are extracted, three degrees of Fire also do suffice; the last, to wit the Optetick, is reserved for the fourth Element, which finisheth the Red Work. By the first degree the eclipse of *Sol* and *Luna* is made, by the second the light of *Luna* begins to be restored: by the third *Luna* attaineth unto the fulnesse of her splendour: and by the fourth *Sol* is exalted into the highest apex of his glory: Now in every part the Fire is administred according to the rules of Geometry, so as the Agent may answer to the disposition of the Patient, and their strength be equally poised betwixt themselves.

107. Philosophers have very much set upon their Fire with a desire of Secrecy, so as they scarce have been bold to touch it, but shew it rather by a description of its qualities and proprieties, then by its name: as that it is airie Fire, vaporous, humid and dry, clear, star-like, because it may easily by degrees be intended or remitted as the Artificer pleaseth. Hee that desireth more of the knowledge of Fire; may be satisfied by the Works of *Lullius*, who hath opened the Secrets of Practice to candid minds candidly.

108. Of the conflict of the Eagle and the Lion they write

diversly, because the Lion is the strongest animall of all others; and therefore it is necessary that more Eagles concur, (three at least, or else more, even to ten) to conquer him: the fewer they are the greater the contention, and the slower the Victory; but the more Eagles, the shorter the Battaile, and the direption of the Lyon will more readily follow. The happyer number of seven Eagles may be taken out of *Lullius,* or of nine out of *Senior.*

109. The Vessell wherein Philosophers decoct their worke, is twofold; the one of Nature, the other of Art; the Vessell of Nature which is also called the Vessel of Philosophy, is the Earth of the Stone, or the *Femella* or *Matrix,* whereinto the Seed of the Male is received, it putrefies and is prepared for generation, the Vessell of Nature is of three sorts: for the secret is decocted in a threefold Vessell.

110. The First Vessell is made of a transparent Stone, or of stony Glasse, the forme thereof some Philosophers have hid by a certain Enigmaticall description; sometimes affirming that it is compounded of two peeces, to wit, an Alembick, and a Bolts head, sometimes of three, othertimes of the two former with the addition of a Cover.

111. Many have feigned the multiplying of such like Vessels to be necessary to the Philosophicall Work, calling them by divers names, with a desire of hiding the secret by a diversity of operations; for they called it Solutory for solution; Putrefactory for putrefaction; Distillatory for distillation; Sublimatory for sublimation; Calcinatory for calcination, &c.

112. But that all deceit being removed we may speak sincerely, one onely Vessell of Art sufficeth to terminate the Worke of either Sulphur, and another for the Work of the Elixir; for the diversity of digestions requireth not the change of Vessels; yea we must have a care lest the Vessell be changed or opened before the First work be ended.

113. You shall make choise of a forme of the glassy Vessell round in the bottom or cucurbit, or at least ovall, the neck an hand breadth long or more, large enough, with a straight mouth, made like a Pitcher or Jugg, continued & uncutt and thick in every part, that it may resist a long, and sometimes an acute Fire: The cucurbit or Bolts head is called blind, because its eye

SENIO-

Figure 7. "Senior's Table" from *Theatrum Chemicum*, vol. 5 (1660).

SENIORIS ANTIQUISSI-
MI PHILOSOPHI LIBELLVS, VT
Brevis, ita artem discentibus & exercentibus
utilissimus, & verè aureus,

Dixit Senier Zadith filius Hamuel.

Nᴛʀᴀᴠɪ ego & Oboel, charissima barba, in dominum quidam subterraneam, & postea intuim summd ego & Elhalam universos canceros Joseph ignaros, & vidi in recto im ginis novem aquilarum pictas, habernes alas expansas, asi voluntem, pede verio extentos & apertos, & in pede unuscujusque, aquila similitudo arcui amply, quem violenter serie sagittam, & in pariete domus à dextra & à sinistra intranti, imagines hominum illantium, prout possent esse, perfectiores & pulchriores, in feri diversis vestimentis & coloribus; habentes in anus extensas ad meruorem thalamum, annunciebant ad quandam statuam sedentem in throno, in Lucre juxta parietem thalami interiorus, à sinistris int: anns thalamum contra faciem suam. Et sedebat sub cathedram simii cathedra M: dicorum extraêm à statua illa, & habebat in gremio suo uper brachiis suis, & in manibus extensis super genua suis, tabulam marmoream certrafam ab ea, cujus longitudo brachii unius, & latitudo unius palmæ, & digen manuum ejusdem sub tabula resiexu delsuper acsi tenerer eam, & erat tabula sicur liber apertus cuilibet intranti, veluti si innueret respicere in eam, & in parte thalami in qua sedebat erant imagines diversiarum rerum insualite, & literæ de barbaria. Erat tabula quam habebat in gremio in una ejus medietate divisa. Erat enim quædam linea per medium, imago duarum avium in inferiore parte ejus præiuce inclinato, quarum avium una habebat alas abscissas, & altera habens alas duas, & utraque tenebat rostro caudam alterius, acsi volant vellet volare cum altera, & illa vellet retinere volantem secum. Erant autem illæ duæ aves colligatæ, homogenæ, depictæ in una sphæra, quasi imago duarum in una, & erat pinctam per volantem ex duobus sphæra, & supra has duas aves præicebatur tabulæ, proximè digeris statuæ im:go Lunæ lucentis: Et ex altera parte tabulæ alia sphæra, respiciens ad avem inferius. Erant autem universa tempora quinque, uni ruis videlicet aves duæ, scilicet imago Lunæ, & alia sphæra.

In alia autem medietate in capite tabulæ declinater ad digitos statuæ, erat im:go Solis emittens radios, vebis imago docen-

Vol. 5. N

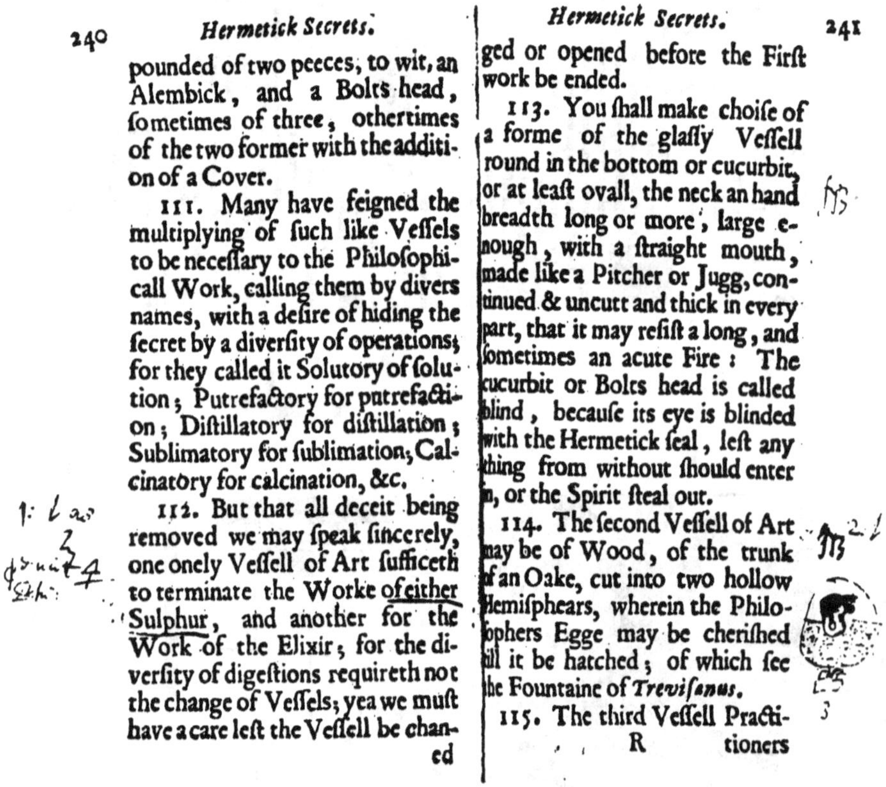

pounded of two peeces, to wit, an Alembick, and a Bolts head, fometimes of three, othertimes of the two former with the addition of a Cover.

111. Many have feigned the multiplying of fuch like Veffels to be neceffary to the Philofophicall Work, calling them by divers names, with a defire of hiding the fecret by a diverfity of operations, for they called it Solutory of folution; Putrefactory for putrefaction; Diftillatory for diftillation; Sublimatory for fublimation; Calcinatory for calcination, &c.

112. But that all deceit being removed we may fpeak fincerely, one onely Veffell of Art fufficeth to terminate the Worke of either Sulphur, and another for the Work of the Elixir; for the diverfity of digeftions requireth not the change of Veffels; yea we muft have a care left the Veffell be changed

ged or opened before the Firft work be ended.

113. You fhall make choife of a forme of the glaffy Veffell round in the bottom or cucurbit, or at leaft ovall, the neck an hand breadth long or more, large enough, with a ftraight mouth, made like a Pitcher or Jugg, continued & uncutt and thick in every part, that it may refift a long, and fometimes an acute Fire : The cucurbit or Bolts head is called blind, becaufe its eye is blinded with the Hermetick feal, left any thing from without fhould enter in, or the Spirit fteal out.

114. The fecond Veffell of Art may be of Wood, of the trunk of an Oake, cut into two hollow Hemifphears, wherein the Philofophers Egge may be cherifhed till it be hatched; of which fee the Fountaine of *Trevifanus.*

115. The third Veffell Practitioners

R

Figure 8.   A reader's notes in *Arcanum* (1650).

is blinded with the Hermetick seal, lest any thing from without should enter in, or the Spirit steal out.

114. The second Vessell of Art may be of Wood, or the trunk of an Oake, cut into two hollow Hemisphears, wherein the Philosophers Egge may be cherished till it be hatched; of which see the Fountaine of *Trevisanus.*

115. The third Vessell Practitioners have called their Furnace, which keeps the other Vessels with the matter and the whole work: this also Philosophers have endeavoured to hide amongst their secrets.

116. The Furnace which is the Keeper of Secrets, is called *Athanor,* from the immortal Fire, which it alwayes preserveth; for although it afford unto the Work continuall Fire, yet sometimes unequally, which reason requireth to be administered more or lesse according to the quantity of matter, and the capacity of the Furnace.

117. The matter of the Furnace is made of Brick, or of fatt Earth, or of Potters clay well beaten, and prepared with horse dung, mixed with haire, that it may stick the faster, and may not be chincked by the long heat; let the walls be thick, of three or foure fingers, to the end that it may be the better able to keep in the heat and withstand it.

118. Let the form of the Furnace be round, the inward altitude of two feet or thereabouts, in the midst whereof an Iron or Brazen plate must be set, of a round Figure, about the thicknesse of a Penknife's back, in a manner possessing the interiour latitude of the Furnace, but a little narrower then it, lest it touch the walls, which must leane upon three or foure props of Iron fixed to the walls, and let it be full of holes, that the heat may be the more easily carried upwards by them, and between the sides of the Furnace and the Plate. Below the Plate let there be a little door left, and another above in the walls of the Furnace, that by the lower the Fire may be put in, and by the higher the temperament of the heat may be sensibly perceived; at the opposite part whereof let there be a little window of the Figure of a Romboides fortifyed with glasse, that the light over-against it may shew the colours to the eye. Upon the middle of the foresaid plate, let the Tripode of secrets be placed with a double

Vessel. Lastly let the Furnace be very well covered with a shell or covering agreeable unto it, and that alwayes the little doores closely shut, lest the heat go out.

119. Thus thou hast all things necessary to the first Work, the end whereof is the generation of two sorts of Sulphur; the composition and perfection of both may be thus finished.

Rx. Take a Red Dragon, couragious, warlike, to whom no Naturall strength is wanting; and afterwards seven or nine noble Eagles [Virgins,] whose eyes will not wax dull by the rayes of the Sun: cast the Birds with the Beast, into a clear Prison and strongly shut up, under which let a Bath be placed, that they may be incensed to fight by the warm vapour: in a short time they will enter into a long and harsh contention, untill at length about the 45 day or 50. the Eagles begin to prey upon and teare the beast to pieces; this dying it will infect the whole Prison with its black and direfull poyson, whereby the Eagles being wounded, they will also be constrained to give up the ghost. From the putrefaction of the dead Carcasses a Crow will be generated, which by little and little, putting forth its head, and the Bath being somewhat increased it will forthwith stretch forth its wings and begin to fly; but seeking chincks from the Winds and Clouds, it will long hover about; take heed that it find not any. At length being made white by a gentle and long Raine, and with the dew of Heaven it will be changed into a White Swan, but the new borne Crow is a sign of the departed Dragon. In making the Crow White extract the Elements, and distill them according to the order prescribed, untill they be fixed in their Earth, and end in Snow-like, and most subtile dust, which being finished thou shalt enjoy thy first desire to the White Worke.

120. If thou intendest to proceed further to the Red, adde the Element of Fire, which is wanting to the White Work: the Vessell therefore being fixed, and the Fire strengthned by little and little through its points, force the matter untill the occult begin to be made manifest, the signe whereof will be the Orange colour arising: order the Fire of the Fourth degree by its points, untill by the helpe of *Vulcan* purple Roses be generated of the Lilly, and lastly the *Amaranthus* dyed with the darkish Rednesse of bloud: but thou mayest not cease to bring out Fire by Fire,

untill thou shalt behold the matter terminated in Reddest ashes, and insensible to the touch. This Red Stone may reare up thy minde to greater things, by the blessing and assistance of the holy Trinity.

121. They that thinke they have brought their worke to an end by perfect Sulphur, not knowing Nature or Art; and to have fulfilled the Precepts of the secret; are much deceived, and will try their Project in vaine: for the Praxis of the Stone is perfected by a double Worke; the First is, in creating the Sulphur, the other in making the Elixir.

122. The Philosophers Sulphur is most subtile Earth, most hot and dry, in the belly whereof the Fire of Nature abundantly multiplyed is hidden; Moreover, Fire deserveth the name of the Stone; for it hath in it selfe the virtue of opening and penetrating the bodies of Metals, and of turning them into their own temperament and producing something like it selfe, wherefore it is called a Father and Masculine seed.

123. That we may leave nothing untouched, let the Students in Philosophy know that from that first Sulphur, a second is generated which may be multiplyed *in infinitum*: let the wise man, after he hath got the everlasting minerall of that Heavenly Fire, keep it diligently. Now of what matter Sulphur is generated, of the same it is multiplyed, a small portion of the first being added, yet as in the Ballance. The rest may a freshman see in *Lullius,* this may suffice onely to point at it.

124. The Elixir is compounded of a threefold matter, namely of Metallick Water or Mercury sublimated as before; of Leaven White or Red, according to the intention of the Operator, and of the Second Sulphur, all in Weight.

125. There are Five proper and necessary qualities in the perfect Elixir, that it be fusile, permanent, penetrating, colouring and multiplying; it borroweth its tincture and fixation from the Leaven, its penetration from the Sulphur, its fusion from Argent vive which is the medium of conjoyning Tinctures, to wit of the Ferment and Sulphur, and its multiplicative virtue from the Spirit infused into the Quintessence.

126. Two perfect Metalls give a perfect Tincture, because they are dyed with the pure Sulphur of Nature, and therefore no

Ferment of Metals may be sought besides these two bodies; dye thy Elixir White and Red with *Sol* and *Luna, Mercury* first of all receives their Tincture, and having received it, doth communicate it to others.

127. In compounding the Elixir take heed you change not or mix any thing with the Ferments, for either Elixir must have its proper Ferment, and desireth its proper Elements; for it is provided by Nature, that the two Luminaries have their different Sulphur and distinct tinctures.

128. The Second work is concocted as the First, in the same or like Vessell, the same Furnace, and by the same degrees of fire, but is perfected in a shorter time.

129. There are three humours in the Stone, which are to be extracted successively; namely, Watery, Airy, Radicall; and therefore all the labour and care of the Workman is employed about the humour, neither is any other Element in the Worke of the Stone, circulated, besides the humid one. For it is necessary in the first place, that the Earth be resolved and melted into humour. Now the Radicall humour of all things, accounted Fire, is most tenacious, because it is tyed to the Centre of Nature, from which it is not easily separated; extract therefore those three humours slowly, successively, dissolving and congealing them by their Wheels; for by the multiplyed alterne reiteration of Solution and congelation the Wheel is extended, and the whole work finished.

130. The Elixir's perfection consisteth in the strict Union and indissoluble Matrimony of *Siccum* and *Humidum,* so that they may not be separated, but the *Siccum* may flow with moderate heat into the *Humidum* abiding every pressure of Fire. The signe of perfection is, if a very little of it cast in above the Iron or Brazen Plate being very hot, it flow forth without smoake.

131. Rx. Let three weights of Red Earth, or Red Ferment, and a double weight of Water and Aire, well beaten, be mixt together: let an *Amalgama* be made like Butter, or Metalline Paste, so as the Earth being mollifyed may be insensible to the touch; Add one weight and an halfe of Fire: Let these be ordered in their Vesell, the Fire of the first degree being most closely sealed; afterwards let the Elements be extracted out of

their degrees of Fire in their order, which being turned downwards with a gentle motion they may be fixed in their Earth, so as nothing Volatile may be raised up from thence, the matter at length shall be terminated in a Rock, Illuminated, Red and Diaphanous; a part whereof take at pleasure, and having cast it into a Crucible with a little Fire by drops give it to drink with its Red Oyle, and incere it, untill it be quite poured out, and goe away without smoake. Nor mayst thou feare its flight, for the Earth being mollifyed with the sweetnesse of the Potion will stay it, having received it, within its bowels: then take the Elixir thus perfected into thine owne power, and keep it carefully. In God rejoyce, and be silent.

132. The order and method of composing & perfecting the white Elixir is the same, so that thou usest the white Elements onely in the composition thereof; but the body of it brought to the terme of decoction, will end in the plate; white, spendid, and crystall-like which incerated with its White Oyle will obtaine the help of Fusion. Cast one weight of either Elixir, upon ten weights of Argent vive well washed, and thou wilt admire its effect with astonishment.

133. Because in the Elixir the strength of Naturall Fire is most aboundantly multiplyed by the Spirit infused into the Quintessence, and the naughty accidents of bodies, which beset their purity and the true light of Nature with darknesse, are taken away by long and mainfold sublimations and digestions; therefore Fiery Nature freed from its Fetters, and fortifyed with the aid of Heavenly strength, workes most powerfully being included in this our fift Element: Let it not therefore be a wonder, if it obtaine strength not onely to perfect imperfect things, but also to multiply its force and power: Now the Fountaine of Multiplication is in the Prince of the Luminaries, who by the infinite multiplication of his beams, begetteth all things in this our Orbe, and multiplyeth things generated, by infusing a multiplicative virtue into the seeds of things.

134. The way of multiplying the Elixir is threefold: By the first; Rx Mingle one weight of Red Elixir, with nine weights of its Red Water, and dissolve it into Water in a solutory Vessell, curdle the matter well dissolved, and unite by decocting it with a

gentle Fire, untill it be made strong into a Rubie or Red Lamell, which afterwards incere with its Red Oyle, after the manner prescribed untill it flow; so shalt thou have a medicine ten times more powerfull then the first. The businesse is easily finished in a short time.

135. By the Second manner Rx what Portion thou pleasest of thy Elixir mixed with its Water, the weights being observed; seale it very well in the Vessell of Reduction, dissolve it in a Bath, by inhumation, being dissolved, distill it, Separating the Elements by their proper fires, and fixing them downwards, as was done in the first and second work, untill it be a Stone; lastly, incere it and project it. This is the longer, but yet the richer way, for the virtue of the Elixir is increased unto an hundred fold; for by how much the more subtile it is made by reiterated operations, by so much more both of superiour and inferiour strength it retaineth, & more powerfully operates.

136. Lastly, take one Ounce of the said Elixir multiplyed in virtue, and project it upon an hundred of purifyed *Mercury,* and in a little time *Mercury* made hot amongst burning Coals, will be converted into pure Elixir; whereof if thou castest every ounce upon an other hundred of the like *Mercury, Sol* will shine most purely to thine eyes. The multiplication of White Elixir may be made the same way. Take the virtues of this Medicine to cure all kinds of diseases, and to preserve good health, as also the use thereof, out of the Writings of *Arnoldus de villa nova, Lullius* and of other Philosophers, may be fetched.

137. The Philosophers Signifer will instruct him that seeketh the times of the Stone; for the first Work *ad Album* must be terminated in the House of *Luna*; the Second, in the second House of *Mercury*; the first Work *ad Rubeum,* will end in the Second House of *Venus,* and the last in the other Regall Throne of *Jove,* from whence our most Potent King shall receive a Crowne deckt with most Precious Rubies:

> *Sic in se sua per vestigia volvitur Annus.*
> Thus does the winding of the circling Yeare
> Trace its owne Foot-steps, and the same appeare.

138. A three-headed Dragon keeps this Golden Fleece; the

first head proceedeth from the Waters, the second from the Earth, the third from the Aire; it is necessary that these three heads do end in one most Potent, which will devour all the other Dragons; then a way is laid open for thee to the golden Fleece. Farewell diligent *Reader,* in Reading these things invocate the Spirit of Eternal Light; Speak little, Meditate much, and Judge aright.

Textual Notes

Enchyridion Physicæ Restitutæ

"Epistle"

¶3   *Test*] ; *Text* 1651. (Latin *exercitio*.)
¶10   *envenomed*] ; *environed* 1651. (Latin *ferocia*.)

Canons

4   Not numbered in 1651. interpolation.)
13   unperceiveable; covetous]; unperceiveable covetous 1651.
      include "sealing" and "seeding.")
75   follows] ; flows 1651.
91   setling] ; seling 1651.
100 in *Genesis*; iu *Genesis* 1651.
103 lukewarmness] ; lukewarness 1651.
116 diverse] ; dverse 1651.
120 how can Fire] ; how can Fre 1651. Periods after the
      aphorism numbers stop at 120.
140 intense cold]; intense heat 1651. (Latin *frigus*.
      Corrected by hand in NLM copy.)
146 *Macrocosm*] ; *Microcosm* 1651. (Latin *Macrocosmi*.)
156 art & nature.] ; art & nature 1651.
165 irrational]; irration 1651. (Latin *irrationalis*.)
166 divine]; diviue 1651.
180 sufficiently evinced, by] 1651. (Missing word added
      by hand in NLM copy.)
181 pre-ordination]; pre ordination 1651.

192	understood]; under stood 1651.
	found by sense.] ; found by sense 1651.
197	by its rays] ; by it rays 1651.
198	universal Receptacle]; nniversal Receptacle 1651.
214	in which it is.]; in which it is, 1651.
216	partly of a watrie] ; parly of a watrie 1651.
219	authough]; although 1651.
228	conservation]; conversation 1651. (Latin *conservationi*. Corrected by hand in NLM copy.)
230	extrinsecal] ; intrinsecal 1651. (Latin *extrinsecam*. Corrected by hand in NLM copy.)
233	so that it wheels] ; so that wheels 1651. (Latin *verset*.)
237	orders .] ; orders, 1651.

Arcanum

Canons

11	betraied.]; betraied 1650.
12	then by words]; then by worps 1650.
27	Wedlock.]; Wedlock 1651.
29	they are dyed]; the are dyed 1650.
38	acknowledged a threefold]; acknowledged athreefold 1650.
42	*noto.*]; *nota* 1650.
	on high]; *an high* 1650.
71	favourable]; fovourable 1650.
84	greatest modertaion.]; greatestmoderation 1650.
86	With this]; with this 1650.
90	parts of the body.]; parts of the body 1650.
91	doe compleat]; idoe 1650.
	circulation]; circulaton 1650.
99	homogeneous]; homonogeneons 1650.
103	example)]; example 1650.
111	solutary for]; solutary of 1650.
135	the Elixir]; the Elixr 1650.

Commentary

Enchrydion Physicæ Restitutæ

The Authors Epistle. D'Espagnet states his reason for studying the occult. He does not want to be blamed for deserting the life of public service and regards his studies as a service to all mankind.

¶1. *dangerous attendants.* D'Espagnet's modern French translator, J. Lefebvre-Desagues, thinks that he may have been forced to leave office during the decade of difficulty between 1614, when the Hugenots tried to establish a separate state, and 1624, when Richilieu restored order. Lefebvre-Desagues notes that there is a pun on *curia*, used to describe both the dangers and the duties that the author has left behind. See *EPR* (1972), 19–20; also see the note below on *AHP*, §61.

Here is the Freedom the Soul gains. Ovid, *Amores*, 3.11.3. See the more lively and more literal translation of Guy Lee: "I've slipped my shackles, Yes, I'm now a free man"; *Amores* (New York, 1968), 165.

the Studie of the Occult. D'Espagnet uses the word "occult" in its literal sense of hidden, concealed, and therefore secret. See *EPR*, §2.

¶3. *the Light began so to rise.* Probably an echo of *Corpus Hermeticum*, 1.4. See the useful translation with facing text in Walter Scott, trans. and ed., *Hermetica*, 4 vols. (Oxford, 1924–36), and the more accurate translation in Brian Copenhaver, *Hermetica* (Cambridge, 1992). D'Espagnet also alludes to "the light of Nature" (*lumen naturæ*), which the Bible calls "the candle of the Lord" (Proverbs 20:27).

¶4. *Errours of the Ancients.* Swift ridiculed such criticism of the ancients in *A Tale of a Tub* (London, 1704) and borrowed D'Espagnet's view of philosophy as fashion clothing, mentioned in ¶9 of the Epistle.

¶6.   *nominal, though seemingly real.* D'Espagnet alludes to the philosophical traditions of nominalism and realism. The first maintains that the phenomena are only names; the second holds that they are images of higher realities.

¶7.   *Advancement of Learning.* The translation alludes to *The Tvvoo Bookes of Francis Bacon of the Proficience and Advancement of Learning, Divine and Humane* (London, 1605), as if to suggest that D'Espagnet's book is the sort that Bacon hoped to see. For the divisions among Baconians in the mid-seventeenth century, see Charles Webster, *The Great Instauration* (London, 1975).

¶10.   *a buckler against the delusions of Sophisters.* The sophister is the person who "sophisticates" knowledge in the sense of diluting or debasing it—a reference ultimately to Plato's opinion of the Sophists. Everard's phrasing has a deliberately Biblical overtone; see Psalms 18:2 and Isaiah 59:17.

Epigram. Omitted from the English translation of 1651. The last line, which alludes to the birth of Athena, is best glossed in *EPR*, §2. Also see Michael Maier, *Atalanta Fugiens*, 2nd ed. (Oppenheim, 1618), emblem 23, which shows the birth of Venus in a shower of gold.

The First Rule. D'Espagnet arranges his work as a set of numbered aphorisms or *canones*. Everard translates this word as "rules"; Ashmole translates it as "canons." Compare, for example, Bernardus Penotus, *Canones seu RegulæDecem, de Lapido Philosophico* in *Theatrum Chemicum*, 6 vols. (Strasbourg, 1659–61), 4:414–16; hereafter abbreviated as *TC*.

1.   DEVS [God]. Glosses in capitals are from the original Latin edition of 1623. Translations in square brackets are mine.

   abyss. See Dionysius Areopagiticus, *De Mystica Theologia* on the darkness surrounding God at Mt. Sinai; esp. book 1, chapter 3, in *Patrologia Græca*, 3:1002.

2.   MVNDVS [The World]. IN PIMANDRO [In *Pymander*]. See *Corpus Hermeticum*, 1.4.

   A book rowld up. See Isaiah 34:4: "and the heavens shall be rolled together as a scroll" and Revelation 6:14: "And the heaven departed as a scroll when it is rolled together." D'Espagnet projects back to a time before the scroll was first unrolled. On the world-as-book trope see Ernst Robert Curtius, *European Literature and the Latin Middle Ages*, trans. Willard Trask (New York, 1953), chapter 16. Also see Thomas Willard, "Rosicrucian Sign-Lore and the Origin of Language," in Joachim Gessinger and Wolfert von Rahden, eds., *Theoriem vom Ursprung der Sprache* (Berlin, 1989), 1:131–57.

The Ancients. See D'Espagnet's poetic epigram.

3. IN TABVLA SMARAGDINA (i.e., SMAGARDINA) [in the *Emerald Tablet*].

Hermes. See *Tabula Smagardina*, §1: "Quod est inferius, est sicut id quod est superius," quoted with commentary in Gerard Dorn, *Physica Trismegisti; TC*, 1:362. This famous axiom stands behind the terminology of Renaissance analogy, introduced here: "bond," "coherence," "likeness," "medium." For a useful introduction to the terminology see Michel Foucault, *The Order of Things*, trans. Alan Sheridan (New York, 1970), chapter 2.

The second edition of *The Divine Pymander of Hermes Mercurius Trismegistus*, trans. John Everard (London, 1657) included a prefatory note, by J.F. (probably John French): "The Description of this great Treasure, is said to be found ingraved upon a *Smagardine* Table, in the Valley of *Ebron*, after the Flood" (sigs. A4v–A5r). For the ultimate source of this legend, see the literal translation in *The Egyptian Book of the Dead: The Papyrus of Ani*, trans. E.A. Wallis Budge (London, 1895), 13: "To be said over a scarab of green stone . . . placed upon upon the dead person at his neck. Was found . . . in Hermopolis under the feet of the majesty of god. . . . " For a medieval memory, see Damimigeron (attrib.) on the emerald scarab; *De Virtutibus Lapidum: The Virtues of Stones*, ed. Joel Radcliffe, trans. Patricia Tahil (Seattle, 1989), 13–14.

4. NATVRA [Nature].

Chaos. "The Unformed Matter, and the Confused First State of all Things. According to Theophrastus [Paracelsus], it is Air"; Martinus Rulandus, *A Lexicon of Alchemy*, English trans., ed. Arthur E. Waite (London, 1893), 98; cited hereafter as Ru-

landus. The word "gas" is derived from "chaos." D'Espagnet
identifies the "first waters" as those in Genesis 1.
5. *Soul of the world.* In Neoplatonism, the world spirit (*spiritus mundi*) is the creative counterpart of the world soul (*anima mundi*), and the world soul is the closest we come to a concept of
nature. See George D. Economou, *The Goddess Natura in Medieval Literature* (Cambridge, MA, 1972), chapter 1. D'Espagnet
turns the world soul into the Holy Spirit and treats nature, in
the next aphorism, as the secondary soul.

Ignaro. Ignoramus. See Spenser, *Faerie Queene* 1.8.31.
6. *i.* "The earlier equivalent of *i.e.=id est* (Lat.) that is to say"
(*OED* 'i' III). Translator's interpolation, also made in §92.

Natura naturans . . . Natura naturata. The creating and
created (i.e., active and passive) aspects of nature. The terms
date back to the twelfth century, and the distinction is older yet.
See George Boas, "Nature," *Dictionary of the History of Ideas*,
ed. Philip P. Wiener (New York, 1968–74), 3:351.
7. *Zoroaster.* D'Espagnet refers to Fragment 10 of the *Chaldaic Oracles*: "All things are born from a single fire." D'Espagnet
may have known the allegorizing commentary of Michael Psellus
(*Patrologia Latina*, 122:1145): "All beings are, in fact, intelligible and sensible and only receive their essence from God: those
which are only essential, those which are essential and live vitally,
and those which are essential, live vitally, and think intellectually. Thus all are born from one being, and to one all beings
return." Like Psellus, D'Espagnet allegorizes the fire; hence his
distinction in §15 between the "true" fire and the actual fire at
the end of a match. For a modern edition of the Zoroastrian
logoi, see *Oracles Chaldaïques*, ed. Édouard des Places, S.J.
(Paris, 1971).

Heraclit. Fragment 29. See Fragments 30–35 in Philip Wheelwright, ed, *The Presocratics* (New York, 1966), 71–72. The
fullest classical summary of his natural philosophy was in Diogenes Laertius, book 9, chapters 8–11; see Wheelwright, 82–83.
9. MVNDVS [The world].

Links of the chain. The notion of the chain of being was
traced back to the boast of Zeus in Homer's *Iliad* 8.19–26:

Let down our golden everlasting chain,
Whose strong embrace holds heaven, and earth, and main:
Strive all, of mortal and immortal birth,
To drag, by this, the Thunderer down to earth:
Ye strive in vain! if I but stretch this hand,
I heave the gods, the ocean, and the land;
I fix the chain to great Olympus' height,
And the vast world hangs trembling in my sight!
(Alexander Pope's translation)

10. *three-fold Region.* In the Renaissance occult sciences, the region below the moon was the sphere of alchemy, the region below the *primum mobile* the sphere of astrology, and the higher region the sphere of cabala or angelogy. In §20, D'Espagnet refers to the last two regions as "Material" and "Intellectual" heavens.

12. IN PIMANDRO [in *Pymander*]. See *Corpus Hermeticum*, 1.24. Also see *Æsclepius*, 3.27–28 (Scott, 5:367–69; Copenhaver, 83–84) for an account of the soul going to the chief daimon for judgment. Especially for these *loci classici*, the *commentaria* by Marsilio Ficino are especially valuable; see his *Opera Omnia*, 2 vols., continuous pagination (Basel, 1576), 1817–19, 1859–60.

LVCRET. LIB. 2 [Lucretius, book 2]. The quotation is from *De rerum natura* 1.215–16.

13. MATERIA PRIMA [The First Matter]. Some authors say the first matter is where the radical moisture is concentrated; see *Rosarium Philosophorum* (Frankfurt, 1550), (sigs. K4v–L1r); hereafter cited as *Rosarium*. Also see §89.

14. CAP. 5. LI. 1. DE ORTV & INTER., CA. 1 & 2 LIB. 2 DE ORTV & INTER. The reference is to *De ortu et intertiu*, better known in Latin as *De generatione et corruptione*. See 329A and *Aristoteles Latinus*, vol. 9, ed. Joanna Judyck (Leiden, 1986), 53. Here Aristotle discusses Plato's theory of *materia prima* as articulated in *Timaeus* 52, but without admitting that it exists independently of nature.

D'Espagnet alludes further to Aristotle's *De caelo*, the first book of which states that heaven neither came into being nor will be destroyed; it suggests that heaven is eternal and includes the infinity of man.

15. *The Philosopher*. D'Espagnet corrects Aristotle's assumption, cited in §14, that the first matter contains the element in warring states. D'Espagnet distinguishes the "true Elements," which are invisible, from the "mixt bodies" that we see. In §21, he explains how "Reason" requires that the true water and fire work. It was common to say that the four qualities and four elements of Aristotle provided the rationale (*ratio*) for alchemy; indeed, it was said in a treatise widely attributed to Aristotle, *De Perfecto Magistero; TC*, 3:82–83.

16. DE VARIIS PHILOSOPH. OPINIONIBVS [On various opinions of the philosophers]. The English translation has the garbled note "*De* Sariis Philo's *Opinion*." See Philo of Alexandria, *On the Sown Fields*.

1. GENES [Genesis 1].

Thales. See Aristotle, *De caelo* 294A. The teaching was frequently repeated—for example, in Cicero, *De natura deorum* 1.25. Alchemists cited Thales as an authority; see *TC*, 5:245.

Heraclitus. According to Aristotle (*Metaphysica* 984A), Herclitus called fire (not water) the first principle.

Hesiodus. *Works and Days* 42–50. Hesiod calls fire the means (*hekousi*) of life, hidden by Zeus so that people will not become lazy, then stolen for them by Prometheus.

Genesis. Alchemists never ceased to explore the testimony that, in the beginning, "the Spirit of God moved upon the face of the waters" (Genesis 1:2). Paracelsians were especially fond of interpreting the creation of the world as a chemical separation.

18. MVNDI CREATIO [The creation of the world].

the Rabbines. In the *Zohar*, the primal mass is called *ein soph*. See *Zohar: The Book of Splendor*, ed. Gershom G. Scholem (New York, 1963), 27. For alchemical commentary influenced by the *Zohar*, see Blaise Vigenère, *De Igne et Sale* (*TC*, 6:1–139), esp. chapters 2, 10, and 26.

Hyle. The Homeric word for timber came to mean any building material or simply matter.

this depth of darkness. The Latin text reads "Orcus," a reference to the god of the underworld.

19. *the Scripture*. Genesis 1:2, 6.

20. MATERIA ET FORMA SVNT ANTIQVIS SIMA RERVM
PRINCIPIA [Matter and form are the first principles of things].
It follows, for D'Espagnet, that everything in the material world
corresponds to something in the world of forms. Quotations in
the text are from Genesis 1.
21. *the artifex of the world.* Artificer; here God, the creator of
the world.
23. *the twinkling of the eye.* See 1 Corinthians 15:52 (Authorized Version). The Latin *in ictu oculi* echoes the Vulgate.
24. *subjacent dark Mass.* Latin *massa tenebrosa subjacentâ*,
literally, the underlying shadowy mass.
25. *two Principles.* D'Espagnet's version of the Aristotelian
doctrine of generation and corruption as the forces of light and
dark, spiritual and material, active and passive, and, inevitably,
male and female.
28. SOLIS CREATIO [The creation of the sun].
29. *the Philosopher.* Probably Aristotle; see *De generatione
animalium* 716A, and *De generatione et corruptione* 333A.
30. *some Philosophers.* In Plato's *Leges* 898D–E, the Athenian
maintains that the sun has a soul. In Plato's *Theaetetus* 153D,
Socrates interprets Homer's chain as the sun, on which all else
depends (see §9). Eratosthenes made the most famous ancient
case for heliocentrism.
32. LVX EST FORMA VNIVERSALIS [Light is universal form].
D'Espagnet finds the original light of the universe in the soul
spark.
33. *homogeneous bodies.* The fire and water D'Espagnet describes here are close to what Aristotle calls "unmixed bodies."
35. *Vicegerent.* Deputy. The view of the sun as a trinity, giving
off heat, light, and motion, was a Renaissance commonplace; see
George Herbert, "The Starre," ll. 17–18, and Henry Vaughan,
"The Tempest," ll. 31–32, and compare Sendivogius' remark:
"In the microcosm of man's nature the soul is the deputy or
Viceroy of the Creator." The last remark appears in *The Hermetic Museum Restored and Enlarged*, English trans., ed. A.E.
Waite (London, 1893), 2:139; hereafter abbreviated as *HM*.
37. HOMINIS CREATIO [The creation of man].
     a thousand years with God. See 2 Peter 3:8 and Psalms 90:4.

141

D'Espagnet allows the possibility that creation took place over a period of six thousand years, rather than six days.

39. *that sacred Philosopher.* Moses, the traditional author of Genesis.

40. INFORMATIONIS MATERIÆ PRIMÆ RATIO TRIPLEX [The triple reason informing the first matter]. The first matter has a spiritual, heavenly, and earthly quality, corresponding to the three regions (§10).

43. CORRVPTIO A QVALITATVM CONTRARIETATE NON PROCEDIT [Corruption does not proceed from the quality of contrareity]. Alchemical treatises discuss the Tree of Life as an elixir. *The Glory of the World,* a Paracelsist treatise, says that Seth brought fruit from the tree to help Adam prolong his life (*HM,* 1:188). The orthodox explanation is that Adam had to be expelled from Eden after eating the fruit of the Tree of Knowledge so that he would not live forever in a state of sin.

45. *Privation.* Privation (*steresis*) is one of Aristotle's basic categories, the opposite of possession. See *Categoriae* 12A.

47. HARMONIA VNIVERSI [The harmony of the universe].
Hermes. See the note to §3.

49. *drie water.* The water that "wets not the hand" is a recurrent feature in alchemy, dating back to the Byzantine period. Sendivogius treated it in his "Ænigma" (*TC,* 4:444–47; *HM,* 2:110–15). Thomas Vaughan cites this aphorism in his introduction to *The Chymists Key* (London, 1657), sig. A4r, to help explain what he calls "a *Water and no Water.*"

50. ELEMENTA [The Elements]. Again, D'Espagnet asserts that the real elements are invisible. What we see are the "shadows and figures" mentioned in §51.

51. LVCRET. LIB. 2. See Lucretius, *De rerum natura* 2.866–67.
mixtion. Mixture.

52. *Micro-cosme.* Literally, the little world; understood to be man, in the first place, and the alchemical body in the second. Rulandus explains that man is the little world because he is placed between heaven and earth and participates in both. "Whatsoever is actually and visibly contained in them [the elements] is in like manner spiritually and potentially held in man"

(232). See §124 and note. Blaise Vigenère writes, "Man is therefore the image of the great world, and is called the little world or microcosm, just as the world made from the archetype, by similitude, and composed of the four elements, is called the great man" (*TC*, 6:3).

57. *three elements.* D'Espagnet shares the doubt whether fire should be called an element; here he is close to the view of Empedocles as recorded in Aristotle, *De generatione et corruptione* 330B and to the view of Sendivogius (*HM*, 2:137–40); he notes in §81 that Genesis does not refer to fire.

Jupiter. D'Espagnet assigns fire to Jupiter, air to Juno, water to Neptune, and earth to Pluto; this may again recall Empedocles, who assigned fire to Zeus, air to Hera, water to the sea god Nestis, and earth Hades (see Wheelwright, 150).

59. TERRA [Earth]. D'Espagnet's account of the earth and the growth of metals follows Sendivogius and *The Glory of the World* (*HM*, 1:194–98).

62. *putrefaction.* Literally, putrefying, making putrid; the alchemical process of decay, essential to the *nigredo* or first stage of the alchemical work. Rulandus calls it the "Dissolution of a Composite Substance by Purification in Heated Moisture." He adds, "It is the key to the most brilliant alchemical operations" (265).

magnetick love. A strong "sympathy" or "affinity," of which the attraction of the iron to the lodestone and to the north is an example. The entire earth is a magnet, attracting all the elements; and a sponge, absorbing what it attracts. Thus everything above can also be found below.

64. AQVA [Water]. Because it can freeze or vaporize water is the most changeable element. Any other liquid is, in this sense, watery.

65. *Mercurie.* Continuing the mythological line (begun in §57) D'Espagnet attributes the roles of Mercury to the chemist's quicksilver: Mercury is the patron of merchants, the messenger of the gods, the watcher at borders, the go-between. A feminist reader may pause over images like "the bosom of Nature" (§167).

66. *rarity and levity.* Thinness and lightness, the opposites of the "density and gravity" mentioned later. Heaven is thus dis-

tinguished from earth as they emerge from the original "Chaos" (the "Abyss" of §67). D'Espagnet applies the Aristotelian qualities to the Biblical story of creation, so that the hot, dry breath of God moves upon the cold, moist abyss.

69. *menstruum.* A liquid medium or solvent. The *OED* explains: "in alchemy the base metal undergoing transmutation into gold was compared to the seed within the womb, undergoing development by the agency of the menstrual blood." D'Espagnet uses "matrix" in the etymological sense of "womb."

clay. Latin *limum.* See Genesis 2:7: "And the LORD God formed man of the dust of the ground" (Vulgate *de limo terrae*). A comparable "clay" is made from the male *semen* and female *menstrum* of each species. The great question of alchemy, "that Philosophical Secret," is how to find the "clay" produced by a proper mixture of male sulphur and female mercury.

70. *Aqua fortis.* A corrosive liquid. Rulandus (34) identifies it as a purified form of nitric acid (HNO_3).

71. *divided in two.* See Genesis 1:6.

72. *Caroach.* Variant spelling of "caroche," a stately coach or carriage.

Bars of the Heaven. The translation alludes to Job 38:10.

77. *Nature's sieve.* This term for air, the third element under consideration, seems original with D'Espagnet. Thomas Vaughan thought it a witty phrase; see *Anthroposphia Theomagica,* 14.

Tracts. See Sendivogius on "Elementary Air" in *HM*, 2:136–37. See also *The Golden Tract,* which draws the analogy between the trinity of sulphur, salt, and mercury and the trinity of body, soul, and spirit (*HM*, 1:11–41).

78. *cohobation.* Latin *cohobando.* Redistillation. See Ben Jonson, *The Alchemist,* 2.5.26–28, where the word is considered especially obscure:

Subtle. What's cohobation?
Face. 'Tis the pouring on
Your *aqua regis*,
and then drawing him off . . . .

79. *sulphureous exhalations.* On the theory of aerial niter, propounded by Sendivogius, see Allen G. Debus, "The Paracelsian

Aerial Niter," *Isis* 55 (1964): 43–61, and Zbigniew Szydlo, "The Alchemy of Michael Sendivogius: His Central Nitre Theory," *Ambix* 40 (1993): 129–46.

80. *the Schools.* A reference to the Scholastic philosophy, which dominated debate in universities. The sphere of fire, which official physics still maintained, was a ring about the cosmos, beyond the *primum mobile*—a concept preserved in the word "empyrean."

81. IGNIS [Fire].

83. CA. 11 PRIOR. TESTE. *Testamentum Magistri Raymundi Lulli, & primum de Theorica* (*TC*, 4:1–134). The passage that D'Espagnet cites corresponds most closely to chapter 28 (445–47); however, the work of "pseudo-Lull" appeared in numerous editions. Lullist alchemy appealed to D'Espagnet because it aspired to the systematic approach of the real Lull's mnemonics. See Michela Pereira, *The Alchemical Corpus Attributed to Raymond Lull*, Warburg Institute Surveys and Texts, 18 (London, 1989), esp. 6–8.

84. *unition.* Conjunction (*OED*).

85. IGNIS NATVRÆ EST IN SOLE [The fire of nature is in the sun]. D'Espagnet's last sentence says just this.

86. *most Philosophers.* Especially Neoplatonists, taking their lead from Plato, *Leges* 589E.

87. *some Ancients.* Perhaps a reference to Plato's play on words in *Respublica* 509D, which the Loeb translation treats as a play on eyeball and "sky-ball." Anaxagoras taught that the sun was a god and the source of all vision; see Plato, *Apologia* 26D and *Respublica* 509A; also see Theophrastus, *De sensu* 1.27, quoted in Wheelwright, 173.

88. *elementated.* Composed by the elements, "impregnated with an element" (*OED*). Alchemists sometimes made the distinctions between the elements (*elementa*) and their first compounds, the physical elements (*elementata*). See §15 and compare *Rosarium*, sig. G2v.

Antiperistasis. Resistance, literally "standing against."

89. *radical moisture.* The sap of life. Rulandus calls it "HUMOR VITÆ—Vital Moisture, which prevents all living things from becoming dry, the Radical Humour, the Food and Nour-

ishment of the Natural Heat" (175).

Prince of nature. Man is the sun's deputy, as the sun is God's.

91. *vivifical.* Life-giving.

92. *i.* See §6.

94. AMOR NATVRÆ GENIVS [Love is the genius of nature].

Plato. See *Symposium* 178A. This is the thesis of Phaedrus' speech.

96. CONTRARIETAS ABEST AB ELEMENTIS [Contrareity goes away from the elements].

avaunt. Beware.

97. CA. 9. LIB. 1. DE NAT. D'Espagnet wishes that followers of Plato, the Academicians, would respond to Aristotle's remark, at the end of his first book on nature, that matter desires form as the female desires the male; see *Physica* 192A. D'Espagnet also asks how love can arise from strife, as Hesiod suggested (see §16). Indeed, he echoes the questions Plato's Aristophanes puts to Erymimachus in *Symposium* 189A–B.

98. *their School.* The Peripatetics or followers of Aristotle, whose doctrine was mentioned in §97.

99. *'Twixt moist and drie.* Ovid *Metamorphoses* 1.19.

100. *Genesis.* See Genesis 1:4. Further reason for D'Espagnet to think of the dark, receptive, and symbolically female as "not good."

101. *temperament.* The proper mixture, each element in due proportion; every "mixed body" has its temperament. In §229, D'Espagnet extends the discussion to mental and musical temperament.

102. *Drougth.* Variant spelling of "drought" (*OED*).

103. CONTRARIETAS AB INTENSIONE QVALITATVM PROCEDIT [Contrareity proceeds from the intensity of the quality].

intension. Intensity or stretching. The temperament of a body requires that the elements be present as means, not extremes. D'Espagnet resists the notion of warring elements, emphasizing their cooperation.

104. ELEMENTORVM QVALITATES SVNT REMISSÆ [The qualities of the elements are remitted]. Extremes are relaxed,

tempered.

106. adust Choller. Black bile; Latin *atra bile*. Black bile was associated with earth; hence the suggestion that it is choler (Hippocrates' word for bile) which has been calcinated (see *OED*, "adust"). D'Espagnet's understanding of temperament makes him doubt that the four bodily humors of Galenic medicine are intense opposites: fiery choler and watery phlegm, earthy melancholy and airy blood.

107. *ÆNEID*. 6. See Virgil, Æneid 6.728–29.

108. *in-born*. Innate. Latin *innatas*. The elements are the four consituents of Nature, whose operations will be described in the next aphorisms.

109. *a Potters trade*. See Maier, *Atalanta Fugiens*, emblem 15, and the caption "May the potter's work, consisting in dry and moist, teach you"; trans. Joscelyn Godwin, Magnum Opus Hermetic Sourceworks, 22 (Grand Rapids, MI, 1989).

112. QVINTEM ELEMENTVM [The fifth element]. The quintessence is necessitated as a way of reconciling elements that are at war with one another. D'Espagnet's theory does not require the "fifth heavenly and tempering Nature" mentioned in §113.

114. *the name of the salt Nature*. Although the term *sal naturæ* does not appear there, the concepts in the "Epilogue" of Sendivogius correspond closely to what D'Espagnet describes; see esp. *TC*, 4:440, and *HM*, 2:106–7. The *Rosarium* distinguishes common salt from the salt of metals, equating the latter with the philosophers' stone, and that with quicksilver (sig. A3v).

115. PRIMA CONTRARIETAS INTER LVCEM ET TENEBRAS FVIT [The original contrariety was between light and darkness]. See Genesis 1:1.

117. PSAL. 18. See Psalms 18:10–11.

Rain-bow. Genesis 9:13.

118. MVNDI PARTES NEQVE ELEMENTA SVNT NEQVE INTER SE CONVERTVNTVR [The parts of the world are neither elements nor to be converted into one another]. D'Espagnet denies what Aristotle affirms in *De generatione et corruptione* 331B, and sees any attempt to unite extremes as abortive.

120. TERRA ET IGNIS NON CONVERTVNTVR [Earth and fire are not convertible.] This proposition follows from §118.

121.　*Aristotle.* See the note to §118.

122.　*unctious.* A variant of "unctuous," a soft, oily, quality. "Extrinsecally" and "outwardly" are synonymous.

124.　*The fire of nature is double.* The universal heat warms the world from without, while the particular heat warms the body from within. D'Espagnet reasons that because common kitchen fire would burn a man (the microcosm), a different sort of fire must therefore heat the universe (the macrocosm).

125.　TERRA ET AQVA NON CONVERTVNTVR [Earth and water are not convertible]. Again, D'Espagnet differs with Aristotle; see note to §118.

126.　*centre of the World.* Although D'Espagnet has mentioned heliocentrism in §30, he inclines toward the Ptolemaic view. "World" is used here to mean "universe."

127.　AQVA ET AER NON CONVERTVNTVR [Water and air are not convertible]. See note to §118. Mersenne's editors note that D'Espagnet defended the corpuscular theory of Pierre Gorlée, *Exercitationes Philosophicæ* (Lugd. Bat. [Leiden], 1620); see de Waard, Tanery, and Pintard, 1:148.

128.　*legerdemain of sence.* The deception of the senses. Latin *sensus fallaciâ*, by the fallacy of sensory experience.

129.　AQVA SOLA CIRCVLATVR [Water alone is circulated]. The late Walter Pagel cited this aphorism with §133 as evidence of D'Espagnet's interest in "circulation as the common instrument by which nutrition and generation are sustained in the world"; see *The Smiling Spleen* (Basel, 1984), 21. Pagel classed D'Espagnet as a "supporter" of Paracelsus rather than a "critic" or "moderator."

130.　*exuberation.* State of agitation, abundance. See Norton's "Compound of Alchymie":

> of our Menstrue by labour exuberate
> And wyth hyt may be made *Sulphure* of nature
> If itt be well and kyndly acuate;
> And cyrculate into a Spirit pure.

(*Theatrum Chemicum Britannicum*, ed. Elias Ashmole, 126).

134.　LIB. 1. DE DIÆTA. *De diaeta,* also known as *De salu-*

bri victus ratione, was attributed to Hippocrates by Polybius and other ancient authors, and was joined to Hippocrates' *De natura hominis* in ancient manuscripts. See Alberto Lodispoto, trans., *Del regime salutare* (Roma, 1961). On the other hand, Hippocrates says in *The Nature of Man*: "I am not going to explain man as air or fire or water or earth, nor as anything else that is not clearly descriptive of him" (Wheelwright, 267).

131. *Woman.* D'Espagnet's symbolic distinction between light and dark (see §25, 100) inevitably leads to misogyny. Despite D'Espagnet's respect for Nature, this attitude led to what Carolyn Merchant has called *The Death of Nature* (San Francisco, 1979).

Nemeses. Nemesis, especially in Roman mythology, the goddess who swiftly punishes excesses.

135. TRES CIRCVLATIONIS ROTÆ SIVE CIRCVLI [Of the three rotations of the wheel or circle]. D'Espagnet names three stages in the water-cycle: evaporation ("Sublimation"), precipitation ("Demission" or "Refusion"), and absorption back into the earth ("Decoction"). These three "operations" are defined in §136–41). Sublimation is, technically, the passage from a solid state to a vapor.

136. PRIMVS CIRCVLVS [The first rotation]. D'Espagnet explains the benefits of sublimation. The impure is made more pure as the dregs settle out and the rest is cleansed or mundified. The vaporized water gains virtue, and the earth's pores are opened.

138. SECVNDVS CIRCVLVS [The second rotation]. The benefits of rain are explained in §139.

139. *number, weight, and measure.* Wisdom 11:20. The Latin *in pondere, numero & mensurâ* echoes Sapientia 11:21.

141. TERTIVS CIRCVLVS [The third rotation].

143. *Sovereign Moderatour.* The sun presides over the cycle of water through the dry and wet seasons, the fallow and fruitful years.

castling. Aborted.

144. *the order.* D'Espagnet casts his lot with the uniformitarians rather than the catastrophists, looking for the rule that the exception can only prove.

145. CIRCVLATIO HVMORIS IN MIXTIS [The circulation of the humour in mixtures]. Drawing the analogy between the macrocosm and the microcosm, D'Espagnet likens evaporation to food, precipitation to drink, and decoction to sleep.
146. *infinite worlds.* Here D'Espagnet is most revolutionary, pointing out that his definition of the microcosm can extend to a worm as well as a man. As he allows here for an infinity of worlds under the microscope, he allows later for infinite worlds glimpsed through the telescope.
147. AQVÆ FERMENTATIO [The fermentation of water]. The ferment worked on metals as yeast worked on dough; its effects could include coloring (*Rosarium*, sigs. E2r, F4v). D'Espagnet uses "ferment" in the broad sense that includes not only "to leaven" but, more generally, "to boil" (Latin *fervere*).
148. ELEMENTORVM PER AQVAM FERMENTATIO [The fermentation of the elements by water].
149. *not by bread alone.* See Matthew 4:4, which echoes Deuteronomy 8:3.
150. TRIA ELEMENTA SECVNDA [According to the three elements]. Having discussed earth, water, and air, under the influence of fire, D'Espagnet turns to the Paracelsist *tria prima*: sulphur, mercury, and salt.
153. *Democritus.* The "atomism" of Democritus is treated in Aristotle's *Physica*, its consequences for the soul in Aristotle's *De anima*; see Wheelwright, 186–92. Philosophical atomism was widely considered heretical because it questioned the stability of the created world; however, it was consistent with D'Espagnet's doctrine of the infinity of worlds under the microscope and formed the basis for the thought of his younger contemporaries Descartes and Gassendi.
154. TRIA SVMMA MIXTORVM GENERA [The three main types of mixtures].
155. MINERALIA [Mineral].
156. *in-set fire.* Hence the flint was commonly said to contain a spark of fire; see Sendivogius in *HM*, 2:138. Alchemists could free this spirit through their art.
157. VEGETABILIA [Vegetable].
159. ANIMALIA [Animal].

Symbole of the Trinity. Here the holy family of mother, father, and child.

160. HOMO MICROCOSMVS [Man the microcosm]. Democritus was the first to call man a little cosmos; see Wheelwright, 184.

161. QVODLIBET MIXTVM EST MICROCOSMVS [Whether the microcosm is varied]. See §146.

162. MIXTA VIVENTIA CORPORE, SPIRITV, ET ANIMA CONSTANT. CORPVS [Body, spirit, and soul stand together in the living. Body.]

163. SPIRITVS [Spirit].

165. *natural mediums.* Intermediaries in nature.

166. FORMÆ [Forms]. The "character" imprinted on the creature is akin to the signature, mentioned in §150.

170. *their father is the sun.* See the third maxim in the *Emerald Tablet* (*TC*, 6:715).

174. *Limbeck.* Alembic, an alchemical vessell; see §213 and note.

Philosophical Fire. A gentle fire, as opposed to common kitchen fire.

that noble son of the Sun. Alchemical gold. See §170 and note.

177. A FORMA VIRTVS MVLTIPLICATIVA DEELVIT [The reproductive power flows from the form].

a third light. Man has not only sensation and imagination (that is, the ability to hold an image in the mind) but also understanding. This third faculty sets man over the animals.

178. LVX ET TENEBRÆVITE ET MORTIS SVNT PRINCIPIA [Light and shadows are the principles of life and death].

life is light. See, for example, Psalm 36:9: "For with thee is the fountain of life: in thy light shall we see light."

loose their life, loose their light. Lose (Latin *priratur*); variant spelling (*OED*).

179. ANIMALIVM ET VEGETABILIVM FORMÆ SVNT RATIONALES [The forms of animals and vegetables are rational]. In Biblical terms, these forms proceed from the Word and are words (Greek *logoi*, Latin *rationes*).

182. RERVM ORTVS ET INTERITVS [The origin and de-

struction of things].

Tenet of Transanimation. The transmigration of souls, expounded in Ovid's *Metamorphoses* 15.60–479.

183. CORRVPTIO [Corruption].

184. GENERATIO [Generation].

186. RERVM SEMINA [The seeds of things]. The physical seed encloses the radical moisture, which in turn contains the spirit, described in §214 as the spark.

187. VITA ET MORS [Life and death].

188. SPIRITVALES NATVRÆ [Spiritual natures].

through corporal and sensible resemblances. See Romans 1:20.

190. DVPLEX ALIMENTVM CORPOREVM ET SPIRITVALE [The dual food of the body and spirit].

CA. 33. DEUTER. See Deuteronomy 33:13–15; also see *AHP*, §49 and note.

mystical speech. Enigmatic language, pregnant with meaning. See the note on language in the supplement to Rulandus, 381–82; the note is drawn from Antoine-Joseph Pernety, *Dictionnaire mytho-hermetique* (Paris, 1787).

191. *spiritual Diet.* Nourishment for the spirit. D'Espagnet explains that the lungs bring heavenly refreshment to the heart and body.

192. *intelligencies.* Angels, devils, and other incorporeal messengers. These are not the only "spiritual Natures," D'Espagnet says; airy material, invisible to the eye, is also spiritual. The "spiritual" need not be incorporeal, just too refined to be perceived by the five senses.

193. IGNIS NATVRÆ EST SPIRITVALIS [The fire of nature is spiritual]. This aphorism follows from §192. The "Fire of Nature" is the internal heat, not the "common Fire" of the kitchen, discussed in §194.

194. IGNIS COMMVNIS EST INTER SPIRITVALIA [The common fire is amongst the spiritual things].

195. LVX INTER SPIRITVALIA [Light is amongst the spiritual things].

198. *spiritual Fountain.* See, for example, Psalm 36:9, quoted in the note to §178.

199. SPIRITVS VNIVERSI [The spirit of the universe]. The spirit is conveyed into the seed by sunlight but comes from God.

204. CORPVS DIAPHANVM [The diaphanous body]. The discussion of transparency continues through the next two aphorisms.

206. *Homers Juno.* See Homer, *Iliad* 15.18–22.

207. *Jacob.* Genesis 28:11–15. Like Homer's golden chain, Jacob's ladder was commonly allegorized as a description of the *scala* (scale or ladder) of nature.

Messenger of the Gods. Both Homeric hymns to Hermes call him "the messenger of the undying gods" (*aggelon athanton*) in the third line.

208. PRINCIPIA ACTIVA SVNT SPIRITVALIA Spirits are the active principles]. Conversely, materials are the passive principles.

210. QVALITATES SVNT INSTRVMENTA NON CAVSÆ ACTIONVM [The qualities are the instruments of action, not the causes].

efficient causes. What makes things as they are; a scholastic term. See *OED*, "efficient" B1.

211. *tinctures.* Agents of color. "Tincture is a Specific Arcanum, having a certain essence, qualities, and forms, and also a colour, which it can impart, and so, as it were, infuse its own appearance into a substance" (supplement to Rulandus, 318).

accidents. Accidental as opposed to essential qualities; another scholastic term.

212. RAREFACTIO ET CONDENSATIO SVNT NATVRÆ INSTRVMENTA [Rarefaction and condensation are instruments of nature]. The alchemists' procedures of distillation and precipitation have a basis in the workings of nature, discussed earlier with reference to the water-cycle.

213. HVMIDIVM RADICALE [The radical moisture]. See the note to §89.

Alembicks. Alchemical vessels placed over retorts to collect vapors. Rulandus writes: "The Alembic is of two kinds, beaked or curved, and without beak. The first transmits the resolved vapours by a channel or neck to the receiving vessel. The second, which is without a beak or conduit, is used in sublimations, and in some cases is pierced at the top for the passage of the rising vapours" (21).

215. HVMOR RADICALIS EST IMMORTALIS [The humor, or nature, of the radical is immortal]. On the theory advanced in §215–16, "natural philosophers" of D'Espagnet's day attempted the resurrection or palingensis of a rose from its ashes.

216. HVMOR DVPLEX IN MIXTIS [The humor is twofold in mixtures].

217. VIRTVM FIT EX HVMIDO RADICALI [Glass made from the radical moisture].

218. HVMIDVM RADICALE CINERI INHÆRET [The radical moisture inheres in ashes]. Pagel cited this aphorism and the next in a discussion of "The Cosmic Monarchy of Salt"; *The Smiling Spleen*, 38.

219. *Balsame.* Another term for moisture or ferment.

220. HVMIDVM RADICALE EST RADIX MVNDI MATERI-ALIS [The radical humidity is the root of the material world].

Axle-tree. The world tree, a symbol of the center of things.

221. *insects.* A reference to the theory of spontaneous genera-tion, most famously the generation of maggots by rotting meat. In §222, there are further examples of such "bastard births."

223. HVMIDVM RADICALE EST MATERIÆ ET FORMÆ VINCVLVM [The radical material is the bond of matter and form]. By "bond," D'Espagnet suggests a link in the chain of being.

224. CALIDVM IN NATVM ET HVMIDVM RADICALE [Nat-ural heat and the radical humidity]. These are contained one in the other, the heat here being like the spirit described in §186.

Vulcan's Shop. As the smith god in classical mythology, Vulcan is the prototypical chemist and became an allegorical figure for the chemical processes in nature.

225. *Catholical Balsam.* Universal moisture.

Elixar of Nature. The elixir, panacea. The *Rosarium* says the elixir nourishess each thing according to its needs (sig. M1v).

Treasure. The goal of alchemical medicine is to find the fluid that gives life to each creature; the way to this goal, D'Espagnet suggests, is the birth process. Thomas Vaughan cites this apho-rism for its description of "what thou has attained to"; see *The*

Chymists Key, sig. A5r.
226. PRIMA ET SECVNDA RERVM EXEMPLARIA [The first
and second copies of things]. The world-book analogy is continued in the second sentence.
    things below depend on things above. See §3 and note.
227. VNIVERSI HARMONIA [The harmony of the universe].
The universe is a single body, alive and human but androgynous.
231. QVATVOR QVALITATES SVNT HARMONIA NATVRÆ
TONI [The four qualities produced the harmony of nature]. "Natures musick" is something like the song of the cosmos, heard by
those who are in tune with the world; lost, when the world is out
of tune. This was a Renaissance commonplace; see, for example,
Ulysses' speech in Shakespeare's *Troilus and Cressida*, 1.3.85–
110. It was based, however, on Pythagoreanism, discussed in
S.K. Henninger, *Touches of Sweet Harmony: Pythagorean Cosmology and Renaissance Poetics* (San Marino, CA, 1974).
232. *a motion.* The action in putrefaction was a commonplace.
See Donne's "Second Anniversarie," 22: "For there is motion in
corruption."
    NATVRÆ MOTVS [The movement of nature]. Specifically,
D'Espagnet discusses the movement of the universe.
235. *inflection.* Bending, specifically of light (*OED*). Newton
used the word in the *Opticks.*
237. CŒLVM VNIVERSVM CONTINVVM EST [The sky a
universal continuum]. D'Espagnet draws the line at the possibility of "many Heavens," which would deny the unity of God's
design in the creation.
    a fancied Astrologie. D'Espagnet rejects judicial astrology
as an affront to the divine hierarchy, where the stars rule the
world below, rather than God, and where men who read the
stars control events.
238. *that first mover.* D'Espagnet sees no use for Aristotle's
concept of the prime mover, discussed in *Physica* 256A and elsewhere. His views on space, and on movement by the agency of
intelligences, may be compared to those in *Corpus Hermeticum*,
book 2.
239. *the Archetype.* Here used in the sense of God's original
design. Sendivogius speaks similarly of the "celestial archetype"

(*HM*, 2:138). Also see the diagram of the *mundus archetypus* in *HM*, 2:9, and Thomas Willard, "Archetypes of the Imagination," *The Legacy of Northrop Frye*, ed. Alvin A. Lee and Robert D. Denham (Toronto, 1995), 15–27.

240. INTELLIGENTIÆ [Of intelligences]. See §192 and note.

Herculean bond. Perhaps a reference to the grip Hercules put on Cerebus in order to complete his twelfth and most difficult labor: fetching the dog from Hades. The labors of Hercules were allegorized into chemical quests, for example, in Michael Maier, *Arcana Arcanissima* (London, 1614), book 5; see the summary in J.B. Craven, *Count Michael Maier* (Kirkwall, 1910), 44–48.

ternarie. The threefold state; compare "binary" and "quaternary." Thought to have special power in magic. See Dorn, *Physica Trithemii* (*TC*, 1:388–96).

241. MVNDI PLVRES IN VNIVERSO [Many worlds in the universe]. D'Espagnet defends the possibility of many worlds, containing many suns and planets, within a single universe. The doctrine of infinite worlds was associated with the poet Lucretius, whom D'Espagnet quotes in other contexts; see *De rerum natura* 1.951–1007. It was a dangerous doctrine. Giordano Bruno, who maintained it stoutly and even wrote a long poem on the subject in the style of Lucretius, was burnt at the stake in 1600; see Frances A. Yates, *Giordano Bruno and the Hermetic Philosophy* (Chicago, 1964), 318. For a classic study of this development in the history of ideas, see Alexandre Koyré, *From the Closed World to the Infinite Universe* (Baltimore, 1957).

242. TERRÆGLOBVS INTER ASTRA [The globe of earth amongst the stars]. D'Espagnet sees no reason why the earth could not move along with the heavenly bodies, though he is not sure such movement is necessary. He is ready to imagine life on the moon.

poured out himself upon the creatures. Perhaps an echo of Joel 2:28. Latin *effunderit*.

Law for Multiplication Genesis 1:28. The memorable "increase and multiply" is from the Douay translation (1609).

244. *the Cherub.* Posted to guard Eden with a flaming sword in Genesis 3:24, and traditionally identified with the covering cherub of Ezekiel 28:16, the cherub helps to explains man's lim-

ited knowledge in the fallen world. To those who would argue that the Bible says nothing about other worlds, D'Espagnet replies that it speaks of them in an allegorical ("mystical") way. He refers to the Augustinian "doctrine of accomodation," by which God accomodates his message to our limited human faculties.

245. *Understanding and Will.* D'Espagnet draws a traditional distinction between intellectual virtues, or powers, specifically knowledge and wisdom, and moral virtues, including goodness, mercy, and justice. Humans also have a measure of the divine understanding and will. D'Espagnet again alludes to Wisdom 11:21 (Vulgate); see §121 and note.

Arcanum

Title. The *arcanum* or secret is the *je ne sais quoi* of alchemy, which one can only learn by experience. Rulandus says, "It is the interior virtue of any substance which can achieve a thousand more wonders than the thing itself. The unrevealed principle, undying essence" (36). And just as there is the inner nature of a metal, there is the inner work that allows the adept to reveal it. The *Rosarium*, which D'Espagnet recommends to readers, says the *arcanum* is knowing how to destroy the outer quality of a metal without destroying the inner essence (sig. E1v). The *Rosarium* is especially concerned with the first work of alchemy, or putrefaction; D'Espagnet, however, uses *opus* to describe the whole work of alchemy.

In the Prolegomena to his famous *Theatrum Chemicum Britannicum*, Ashmole writes of "sacred *and* Serious Mysteries *and* Arcana," saying, "I know enough to hold my *Tongue*, but not enough to speake" [London, 1652], sig. A4r).

Preface: "To the Students"

HERMETICK Philosophy. The true alchemy, as D'Espagnet understands it.

Labyrinths. The myth of Ariadne laying a thread in the Cretan labyrinth, so that Perseus could find his way out, was a favorite of alchemical writers. See the author's epistle in *AHP* and the preface in Appendix I. Also see *Artephius His Secret Book*: "Know assuredly, (I am no whit envious as others are) he that takes the words of the other Philosophers, according to the ordinary signification and sound of them, hee doeth already, having lost *Ariadnes* thread, wander in the middest of the *Laberinth,*

158

and hath as good as appointed his money to perdition"in Laurinda Dixon, ed., *Nicholas Flamel: His Exposition* (New York, 1994), 70.

Michael Maier's *Viatorum* (Oppenheim, 1618) also uses the story of Ariadne; see the summaries in Frances A. Yates, *The Rosicrucian Enlightenment*, 116, and J.B. Craven, *Count Michael Maier*, 104. On the psychological and alchemical dimensions of the labyrinth, see C.A. Maier, *Soul and Body: Essays on the Theories of C.G. Jung* (San Francisco, 1986), chapter 1.

unlesse it be illuminated. Cf. §5 and Thomas Vaughan's remark that the Biblical "void" is hopelessly obscure "except a man were illuminated with the same *Light* that this *Chaos* was at first" (*Anthroposophia*, 11).

health and fortunes. See Aristotle, *Rhetorica*, 1060B, trans. W. Rhys Roberts: "We may define happiness as prosperity combined with virtue . . . or as a good condition of body, together with the power of guarding one's property and body and making use of them."

a Tower impregnable. This may be a reference to Gerard Dorn's *inexpugnablie Castrum* (*TC*, 1:238). The more distant reference is to the Lord as a rock and fortress in Psalm 18.

The study of hiding this Art. The practice (Latin *studium*).

Golden Fleece. See §32, 138. The legend of Jason and the Argonauts was popularly associated with the alchemical quest. Thus Ben Jonson's would-be adept Sir Epicure Mammon claims: "I have a piece of Jasons fleece too, / Which was no other than a book of alchemy, / Writ in large sheepskin, a good fat ramvellum" (*The Alchemist*, 2.1. 89–91). Ashmole assumed that it was "Orpheus, *who writ that admirable Allegory of the* Golden Fleece, *and was the first of all the Grecians that brought the* Chemick Learning (*with other* Sciences) *out of* Ægypt"; see *Theatrum Chemicum Britannicum*, sig. B3r. William Mennens of Antwerp wrote a long alchemical commentary entitled *Three books on the Golden Fleece* (*Aurei Velleris Libri Tres* in *TC*, 5:240–428). D'Espagnet preferred to liken false alchemists to the "Plunderers" of the fleece. Antoine Faivre treats what he considers this especially French concern in *The Golden Fleece and Alchemy* (Albany, 1993).

Oedipus. On Oedipus as solver of riddles, and thus a model for the alchemist, see Maier, *Symbola,* 202. Also see Maier, *Atalanta Fugiens,* emblem 39.

Palmer-worms. "Name for various hairy caterpillars destructive to vegetation" (*OED*).

Tripod. "Any oracular seat" (*OED,* sb. 2). Originally, the seat of the priestess at the Delphic oracle.

an itching style. See 2 Timothy 4:3.

my crime. D'Espagnet refers to the ancient oaths of secrecy surrounding alchemy. He hopes that his crime against alchemy may counteract the greater crimes of ignorance.

1. PARÆNESIS (*Admonition*). Glosses in capitals are from the original Latin edition of 1623. Translations in parentheses are Ashmole's and retain his italics. Translations in square brackets are mine.

Gods fear. Proverbs 9.10: "The fear of God is the beginning of wisdom."

endowing religious entertainment. Literally, "temples and shrines." Nicholas Flamel is said to have provided funds for St. Innocents' Church in Paris. See Laurinda Dixon's edition of Flamel's *Exposition of the Hieroglyphicall Figures* (New York, 1994).

2. *The gift of God.* Latin *donum Dei.* A common theme in alchemy. See, for example, the engraving prefixed to Norton's *Ordinall of Alchimy* in Ashmole's *Theatrum,* 12. The words of the alchemical master to his student begin: *Accipe donum Dei* (Accept the gift of God). See §6 on the need for a teacher.

3. *analysis.* "The resolution or breaking up of anything complex into its various simple elements; the opposite process to *synthesis*" (*OED*).

catholick Medicine. D'Espagnet takes the panacea or elixir to work equally on men and metals, while others say the *elixir vitae* is a further stage of preparation. See *EPR,* §225.

4. *of no value.* The study of philosophy is like the search for the kingdom of God as described in the parables of Jesus; see Matthew 14: 44–46.

6. *Operations.* The various procedures are discussed by Rulan-

dus; however, D'Espagnet suggests they are unnecessarily confusing. Note also that he distinguishes the Hermetic philosophers from the overly subtle alchemists.

Lybian quicksands. Latin *Syrtes.* Notoriously treacherous sandbars off the coast of Africa, near Carthage; mentioned in Virgil, *Æneid* 1.111 and elsewhere. These quicksands are the "dangerous attendants" (*syrtibus*) mentioned at the start of the "Epistle" to *EPR.*

7. *Tyro.* Tiro; a beginner.

9. *mystical Names.* See *EPR* §190, 244 and notes.

truth lies hid in obscurity. This is typical of alchemical rhetoric. See Thomas Vaughan's motto on the title page of the English translation of *The Fame and Confession* (London, 1652), *Veritas in profundo* (Truth in the depths). Compare §17.

10. *Morienus Romanus.* See *A Testament of Alchemy, Being the Revelations of Morienus, Ancient Adept and Hermit of Jerusalem to Khalid ibn Uazid ibn Muawiyya, King of the Arbas of the Divine Secrets of the Magisterium and Accomplishment of the Alchemical Art,* trans. Lee Stavenhagen (Hanover, NH, 1974). Also see the *Liber Trium Verborum Kalid Regis Acutissimi* in *TC,* 5:186–90.

Count Trevisanus. See *De Alchemia* in *TC,* 5:683–709.

Lullius. See *Testamentum Magistri Raymundi Lulli, & primum de Theorica* in *TC,* 4:1–134; *Practica Magistri* in *TC,* 4:135–70; and Compendium in *TC,* 4:171–94. Also see *EPR,* §83.

11. *A noble Polonian.* Michael Sendivogius, on whose "double Anagram" see Introduction, xxiii.

12. *Seniors Table.* See figure 7 and the *Tabula Chimica* of Senior in *TC,* 3:191–239. Also see §108.

Rosarius. See the facsimile of *Rosarium Philosophorum: Ein alchemisches Florilegium des Sptmittelalters* 2 vols. (Weinheim, 1992) with the scholarly commentary of Joachim Telle. Also see the extended commentary of C.G. Jung in *The Psychology of the Transference,* trans. R.F.C. Hull in *The Practice of Psychotherapy,* 2nd ed. (Princeton, 1966).

Maierus. See *Symbola* and the translation of *Atalanta Fugiens* by Joscelyn Godwin (Grand Rapids, MI, 1989).

14. DE MATERIA LAPIDIS (*Of the Matter of the Stone*).

disagreeing in Words . . . consent in the Thing. The distinction between *verba* and *res* was a leading theme of seventeenth-century science.

15. ÆNEID. 6.

equivocall words. The very context adds equivocation to the poetry inasmuch as the historical Virgil knew nothing of alchemy.

Quem tegit. Virgil, *Æneid* 6.138–39. D'Espagnet substitutes *quem* for *tunc.*

Maternas. Virgil, *Æneid* 6.193, 190–91. The golden bough was widely associated with alchemy. See Maier's comment on *Æneid* 6.138ff. in *Symbola*, 179–81. For D'Espagnet's comments on the doves of Venus see §42 and note.

18. AVGVREL. CHRYSOP. book 1. Joannes Aurellius Augurellius, *Chrysopœia*, book 1, in *TC*, 3:211. This long didactic poem was recognized as belonging to the same school of alchemy as D'Espagnet, and was reprinted with *EPR* and *AHP* in 1653.

19. *salt mingled with the other two.* The reference is to the *tria prima* of Paracelsus: mercury, sulphur, and salt; see *EPR*, §150. However, D'Espagnet goes on to say that he is concerned only with gold and silver (§20). In the discussion that follows he observes the strict distinction between male and female begun in *EPR*, §25, 100. The sun is masculine and active, governing sulphur and the tincture of redness; the moon is feminine and passive, governing mercury and the tincture of whiteness. Sun and moon become brother and sister in the allegory of §23.

20. *copulation.* Conjunction, union.

23. *unnaturall.* There was a tradition of male birth, for which see the possibly spurious Paracelsian *Liber de Animalibus ex Sodomia Natis* in Karl Sudhof, ed. *Sämtliche Werke*, 14 (Berlin, 1933), 379–88.

Gabertius to Beia. These are alchemical names for sulphur and mercury (Arabi *kibrit* and *al-baida*, respectively). The names appear in the *Ænigmata ex visione Arislei* in the *Rosarium* (sigs. F3v–F4v) and are derived from the *Turba Philosophorum*, §5–10 (*TC*, 5:5–8). According to Maier, Gabritus is the son of Isis and Osiris, and Beia is Isis herself; Gabritus dies soon after their marriage (*Symbola*, 515–18). Pernety sees "Beza" and "Gabertin" as the volatile and fixed parts of the alchemical *materia*, and notes: "The author of the *Secret Work of Hermetical Philosophy* says that without sacrificing her virginity, she contracts a spiritual union before she is joined in wedlock with her brother Gabritus" (supplement to Rulandus, 364, 437). Also see Hannemann's remarks on D'Espagnet's hermaphrodite (*Instructissima*, 27). For an account of Beia, who prostitutes herself before marriage, see Jung, *Mysterium Coniunctionis*, 60; *Psychology and Alchemy*, 329n, 331; and *Alchemical Studies*, 93.

24. CAP. 63 PRIORIS TESTAM. *Testamentum Magistri Raymundi Lulli, & primum de Theorica* in *TC*, 4: 93: "You cannot perform what you desire without Mercury and the Moon for silver, and Mercury and Sun for gold." Ashmole refers the reader, probably by mistake, to "Cap. 62 *Priois Testam.*"

29. *Arsenick.* Rulandus writes: "According to Geber, it is Sulphur's companion. It is the soul, the hermaphrodite, the means whereby Sulphur and Mercury are united" (49). D'Espagnet probably refers to yellow arsenic or orpiment (AS_2S_3) rather than red arsenic or realgar (AsS), but he does not specify.

30. *Usury.* Interest (Latin *faenore*).

31. *Spes tandem Agricolas.* Unidentified. Lefebvre-Desauges says the passage is borrowed from Virgil's *Georgics* (*EPR* [1972], 129n1). But though similar to 1.145–46, it says the opposite and probably comes from a poem in the manner of Virgil.

33. *Cum labor.* Unidentified. Lefebvre-Desauges takes this to be a versified proverb (*EPR* [1972], 131). However, the line seems to continue the passage quoted in §31.

Saturne. See Waite's supplement to Rulandus, 422: "Though according to vulgar chemists this term signifies Lead only, the Hermetic Philosophers apply it to a number of things. In the first place, it is the Black Colour, or the Matter when it has arrived thereat under the operation of dissolution and of putrefaction; it is again the Adrop of the Sages, or the Azoqueated Vitriol of Raymund Lully. . . . "

34. OZEA. CA.7. Hosea 7:9. D'Espagnet substitutes *meus* for *eius*.

Phrygians. A people of Asia Minor; perhaps an allusion to Acts 16:6–7.

36. MERCVRIVS PHILOSOPHORVM (*The Philo.   Merc.*). The philosophers' mercury, as opposed to common mercury.

Scilla and Charybdis. The twin monsters about which Circe warns Odysseus in Homer's *Odyssey* 12.101–10. Mentioned frequently in antiquity—for example, in Virgil, *Æneid* 3.420—they were equivalent to "a rock and a hard place" in the American expression: a bad place to get caught. Compare Eirenaeus Philalethes on the "straight course between Scylla and Charybdis" in the black work (*HM*, 2:189).

38. *threefold Mercury*. A distinction between common mercury, prerpared mercury, and sublimated mercury.

39. *Rebis*. From *res bis*, two things. The alchemical androgyne. Rulandus defines it as "Man and Wife, body and soul, the first stage of the operation" (275). See the illustration in Maier, *Atalanta Fugiens*, emblem 38. An older contemporary of D'Espagnet, Gaston Dulco, complained that it was a "barbarous" term for the union of gold and silver (*TC*, 4:400).

40. ÆNEID. 6. Virgil, *Æneid* 6.129-30.

41. *Proteus*. The mythical figure of Proteus was applied to the changeable nature of matter.

42. PHILOSOPHICA MERCVRII SVBLIMATIO (*The Philosophical sublimation of Mercury*). Jung quotes this aphorism and discusses this "Herculean labor" in *Mysterium Coniunctionis*, 157, n. 329, and 163.

AVGVR. CHRYSOP. LIB.2. Joannes Aurellius Augurellius, *Chrysopœia*, in *TC*, 3: 221.

Diana. Pernety writes: "This is properly the Matter when it has attained the White Colour, which appears previously to the red in the Work. The red colour is called Apollo. Then is Diana wholly unveiled. When the Philosophers apply the name of the Moon, they understand their Mercurial Water. D'Espagnet says that the yoke of Diana is alone capable of containing the ferocity of the philosophical Dragon. Philalethes calls this yoke the Doves of Diana" (supplement to Rulandus, 356).

43. GEORG. 1. Virgil, *Georgics* 1.44.

Tunc Zephyro. Virgil, *Georgics* 1.64–65. The original reads *et* instead of *tunc*.

44. CA.4, PARTIS 1. LIB.2. PERFECTI MAGISTER. The

marginal reference in 1623 is to Geber's *Summa Perfectionis*, 2.1.4: "*Of the Nature of* Marchasite, Magnesia, *and* Tutia." Geber explains, "*Marchasite* hath in its *Creation* a two-fold *Substance, viz.* of *Argentvive* mortified and approaching to *Fixation*, and of burning *Sulphur*"; see *The Works of Geber Englished by Richard Russell, 1678*, ed. E.J. Holmyard (London, 1928), 128. Argent vive or quicksilver is closely related to gold, as he explains in the following chapter: "*Sol* is created of the most subtle *Substance* of *Argentvive*, and of most clear *Fixture*; and of a small *Substance* of *Sulphur* clean, and of pure *Redness*, fixed, clear, and changed from its own *Nature*, tinging that" (130). (Ashmole's marginal note incorrectly cites book 1.)

Geber has earlier offered the following definition: "*Argentvive*, which also is called *Mercury* by the *Ancients*, is a viscous *Water* in the *Bowels* of the *Earth*, by most temperate *Heat* united, in a total *Union* through its least parts, with the substance of white subtile *Earth*, until the *Humid* be contempered by the *Dry*, and the *Dry* by the *Humid*, equally. . . . without it, none of the *Metals* can be gilded" (61–62; 1.3.6). "Geber" was an author who wrote in Latin and cursed alchemists who propounded errors (44; 1.1.4). His English translator, who had also translated Croll, remarked that Geber "used no *Tautologies, Circumlocutions*, or fruitless *Ambrages*; but (like a good *Master*, intending to inform, not to perplex the *Minds* of his *Disciples*) so succinctly speaks of all *Things*, as is rarely seen in any other *Author*" (xxxvii). D'Espagnet seems to have shared this opinion, though others accused Geber of being a great misleader. If Lull emphasized quicksilver (see *Clavicula*, chapter 1, in *TC*, 3:296), D'Espagnet was not going to ignore Geber's instructions on working with it.

46. Jung discusses this aphorism in *Mysterium Coniunctionis*, 302.

48. *glasse is extracted.* See *EPR*, §217. Jung discusses this aphorism in *Psychology and Alchemy*, 338n52, noting the similarity to digestion "in a belly."

49. GENES. CA.1. DEVTER. CA.33. [Genesis 1, Deuteronomy 33]. Ashmole follows the Authorized Translation for the first passage (33:13) and translates the Vulgate for the second

(33:15). His marginal note indicates that the Geneva Bible or "old transla." gives "sweetness" in vs. 13, whereas the Authorized Version or "new transl." gives "precious things." The Hebrew "meged," which Ashmole gives in the Hebrew alphabet, is translated by the Latin "pomum," which can designate any kind of fruit but which resembles the French "pomme" and so suggests the English "apple." The passage had alchemical overtones for D'Espagnet, who also cited it in *EPR*, §190 and *AHP*, §74, 119. Modern readers will recall "The Song of the Wandering Aengus," by W.B. Yeats, which ends: "The silver apples of the moon, / The golden apples of the sun."

50. *intercutal water*. Dropsical fluid (*OED*).

leprosie. "Terrestrial Impurities, which Metals contract in the mine, and which the mere Powder of Projection is incapable of curing" (supplement to Rulandus, 383). He adds that impure sulphur can cause the imperfections in lead and tin (Saturn and Jupiter) that D'Espagnet describes in §51.

51. *Iupiters purple star*. The star regulus of antimony. See Rulandus, 32.

Virgins milk. "Mercurial Water, the Dragon's Tail; it washes and coagulates without any manual labour; it is the Mercury of the Philosophers, Lunar and Solar Sap, out of catholic earth and water" (Rulandus, 188). Pernety identifies it with Beia, as D'Espagnet discusses her in §23, noting that she is mercury "purified from the unclean and Arsenical Sulphurs with which it has been combined in the mines" (supplement to Rulandus, 437). The *Rosarium* identifies it as white arsenic (sig. F2r).

the first gate. Compare the five gates of Beatus in *TC*, 4: 501–2.

52. *the Hesperian Dragon*. The dragon guarding the tree in the western garden; the eleventh labor of Hercules was to get the apples from this tree. For classical references see Michel de Marolles, *Tableaux du Temple des Muses* (Paris, 1655), 329–30. Maier combines this labor with the quest of the Golden Fleece; see *Arcana Arcanissima*, book 2, and Craven's summary: "Hercules is the labourer, artificer who from his labours evolves the golden medicine. What is the dragon? The same as Cerberus, the Sphinx, the Chimaera; the tree, vegetable life in general"

(38). Maier identifies the apples of the Hesperides with the universal medicine in *Symbola*, 577.

Rulandus writes: "DRACO is Mercury, also the Black Raven, or the Black on the Floor. It devours the tail, drinks the mercury. It is called Salt and Sulphur of the Dragon. It is Earth and the body of the Sun" (128).

53. *Amaranthus*. Not the common amaranth but a purple flower that never wilts. See John Milton, *Paradise Lost*, 3.353–56:

Immortal Amarant, a Flour which once
In Paradise, fast by the Tree of Life
Began to bloom, but soon for mans offence
To Heav'n removed where first it grew . . .

54. *their Sea*. See *The Book of Lambspring*, figure 1, in *HM*, 1:277.

55. *oldest mountains*. See Maier, *Atalanta Fugiens*, emblem 12.

58. PRAXIS (*Practice*).

gradivated. Made pregnant.

59. PRAXIS (*Practice*). An allegorical description of the *opus*. The eagle and lion, representing volatile (sublimated) white mercury and fixed red sulphur, are placed together in a glass vessell; the mercury consumes the sulphur, becomes dropsical, and metamorphoses into the black crow, the putrid matter that is reborn when it evaporates (flies up) and becomes the white swan (the *terra foliata* of §64).

60. LAPIDIS MEDIA ET EXTREMA (*The middle and extreames of the Stone*).

the Ape of Nature. The ape as mimic, associated with Thoth, the Egyptian Hermes. The second tract of Robert Fludd's *magnum opus* was entitled *De Natura Simia*; see Fludd, *Utriusque Cosmi Historia*, 2nd ed. (Frankfurt, 1624), part 1, tract 2, and Joscelyn Godwin, *Robert Fludd: Hermetic Philosopher and Surveyor of Two Worlds* (London, 1979), 76.

62. MEDIA MATERIALIA (*Materiall means*). The chemical substances required for the *opus*.

63. MEDIA OPERATIVA (*Operative means*). The stages the matter must be put through in the first work: liquefaction ("the

Liquefying of a Mineral Body"), ablution ("washing away the impure refuse, and reducing the matter to a pure state"), reduction (a return to the metallic form), and fixation ("an operation upon a volatile subject, after which it is no longer volatile, but remains permanent in the fire, to which it is gradually accustomed"); definitions are from Rulandus, 2, 147, 207.

decocteth. "Decoction" is "the Action of Digestion, the Circulation of the Matter in the Vessel, without the addition of any foreign matter whatever" (supplement to Rulandus, 334).

64. MEDIA DEMONSTRATIVA (*The demonstrative meanes*). The colors associated with completion of the different stages: black, white, and red. D'Espagnet adds orange between the traditional white and red. He notes in §65 that other colors are produced, but only in passing.

white and foliated. Rulandus writes of *terra foliata*, "Leaves, Mercurial Water, wherein Gold is sown ... the crown of victory— spiritual water extracted from ashes of other bodies" (314). See Maier, *Atalanta Fugiens*, emblem 6: "Sow your gold in white foliated earth."

67. DIGESTIONES LAPIDIS QVATVOR (*Foure Digestions of the Stone*). Rulandus defines digestion as "simple Maturation, by which an uncooked matter is digested in a digestive heat. True digestion," he adds, "is after the pattern of that process to which food is made subject in the stomach, a corresponding warmth which restores dissipated energy" (126). The four digestions correspond to the four operations described in §63.

68. PRIMA (*First*).

69. SECVNDA (*Second*). GEORG. 1. Virgil, *Georgics* 1.70. D'Espagnet substitutes *humor arenam* for *umor harenam*. In celebrating the rebirth of putrefied matter, he also alludes to Biblical passages.

the spirit of the Lord walketh. The words combine Genesis 1.2 and Matthew 14:25.

a new Heaven and new Earth. Isaiah 65:17, echoed in Revelation 21:1.

Weight and Measure. Wisdom 11:21.

70. Ashmole notes, "*Third*" digestion.

71. GEORG. Virgil, *Georgics* 1.47-48. Ashmole notes, "*Fourth*"

digestion.

72. *nothing but Solution and Congelation.* Hence the motto *solve et coagula*, dissolve and coagulate. The *Rosarium* defines *congelatio* as the return to "solid substance" (sig. Z1v).

73. Jung discusses this aphorism in *Psychology and Alchemy*, 390, n.138.

74. *blessed them.* Genesis 1:28.

Terra Adamica. The red earth from which man was made, sometimes called earth of Damascus and equated with "Mercury of the Sages, Sulphur, Soul, Fire of Nature" (supplement to Rulandus, 333).

Dew of Heaven. Deuteronomy 33:13.

75. CIRCVLATIO ELEMENTORVM [The circulation of the elements].

humidum and siccum. Humid and dry, Aristotelian qualities. They are described in the cycle of water, from earth through air and back, under the influence of fire; the water-cycle is therefore a "figure" of the work, as D'Espagnet says in §76.

77. *Saturne.* Lead, the eldest of the metals, followed by tin (Jupiter), iron (Mars), copper (Venus), and quicksilver (Mercury).

81. *Externall Fire.* Kitchen fire, which regulates the internal body heat, elsewhere called the fire of nature. The alchemist's work is to regulate the internal fire by use of the external.

82. *the Earth is its Nurse, and being carried in the wombe of the wind.* From par. 3 of the *Emerald Tablet* in *TC*, 1:362.

83. ROTA DVPLEX MAIOR ET MINOR, CIRCVLI (*The twofold Wheel, the great and the less*). CIRCVLI TRES (*3 Circles*). Compare the four wheels in Nicholas Barnaud, *Quadrigiæ Auriferæ* (*TC*, 3:833).

the Physicall Tract. Enchyridion Physicæ Restitutæ, §135–41. What D'Espagnet has described in the world is now described in the alchemical retort.

85. CIRCVLVS PRIMVS (*First Circle*). "Evacuation" clenses the substance as evaporation cleanses the earth. This evacuation must be done in moderation (§86). Pernety cites D'Espagnet on evaporation of the sulphurous humidity as a repair of original sin (supplemt to Rulandus, 359–60).

169

87. CIRCVLVS SECVNDVS (*Second Circle*). "Restauration," or restoration, corresponds to condensation the return of vapour in rain. This too must be done in moderation (§88).

    potter like. See *EPR*, §109 and note.

89. *colligation.* Conjunction, binding together (*OED*).

    assation. "Roasting or baking" (*OED*). Related to *assatio*, "A species of hard and dry Ash" (Rulandus, 51).

90. CIRCVLVS TERTIVS (*Third circle*). Digestion corresponds in the retort to the absorption of water by the earth and all that it supports.

    Inhumation. "Humectation in a Dung-bath" (Rulandus, 184). The substance is kept warm by the heat of putrefying excrement, usually horse dung.

92. IGNIS NATVRÆ TVM ETIAM ARTIS (*The Fire of Nature and Art*).

    Ixion. Bound to a fiery wheel by Hermes, in punishment for an attempt to seduce Hera, Ixion thought he could deceive Zeus, but only deceived himself. D'Espagnet suggests the uninformed alchemist is in a similar position, bound to endless repetitions. The allusion is especially apt in that Hera speaks of Ixion's fate as the gods discuss Jason's quest for the Golden Fleece in Apollonius Rhodius, *Argonautica* 3.62.

93. *Metonymically.* By metonymy; in this instance, substitution of cause (fire) for effect (heat).

94. IGNIS LAPIDIS TRIPLEX (*Threefold Fire of the Stone*). NATVRALIS (*Naturall*). INNATVRALIS (*Unnaturall*). CONTRA NATVRAM (*Against Nature*).

    Compositum. Composite, chemical compound.

97. AQVA LAPIDIS EST IGNIS (*The Water of the Stone is Fire*).

98. IGNIS DVPLEX INTRINSECVS ET EXTERNVS (*Fire is twofold, intrinsicall and extrinsicall*).

102. IGNIS GRADVS QVATVOR (*Foure degrees of Fire*).

103. *Optetick.* Visible; Latin *opteticus*, a variant of late Latin *opticus*.

104. IGNIS PVNCTA (*The point of Fire*).

106. ELEMENTA LAPIDIS QVATVOR (*Four Elements of the Stone*).

107. *Lullius.* See *Theorica*, chapter 23 (*TC*, 4:45–47) "on the diverse action of fire" and chapter 67 (*TC*, 4:100–3) "on the effect of fire."

108. PROPORTIO (*Proportion*).

Lullius. See his *Practica*, chapter 18, in *TC*, 4:150–51, for the seven distillations needed to complete the white work, though Lullius does not use the symbolism of eagles here.

Senior. See Senior's "Explanation of the Table" (*Explanatio Tabulæ*) in *TC*, 5:202. Senior explains that there are ten colors of the eagle (whence the ten eagles shown in figure 7), but that there are six parts of the eagle and that the work is done with nine eagles, that is, nine distillations.

109. VASA NATVRÆ ET ARTIS (*The Vessels of Nature and Art*).

Femella. Young woman (Latin).

110. *Bolts head.* A long-necked flask used in distillation, symbolically identified as an ostrich; sometimes written "bolt head."

113. *cucurbit.* Rulandus defines this as "a vessel shaped for the most part like an inverted cone." He notes, "One form is globe-shaped at the bottom; another is flat" (120). D'Espagnet calls for the first kind, and adds that it must be hermetically sealed at the top. See figure 8 for a reader's attempt to visualize the vessels.

114. *Trevisanus.* The reference is to the "parable" at the end of Bernard of Trevisan's *De Alchemia* and offers a solution to the parable. Bernard sees "the clearest fountain, of the most beautiful stone, placed in the hollowed trunk of an oak" (*TC*, 1:706). A venerable sacredote tells him that it belongs to a king and that it can rejuvenate the king in eight days. Pernety noted the parallel in a comment quoted in Faivre, *The Golden Fleece and Alchemy*, 50.

116. FVRNVS ATHANOR (*The Furnace*). D'Espagnet's description of the furnace in §117–18 may be compared with Rulandus' detailed description of his own "oven" (52–53).

119. PRAXIS [S]VLFVRIS (*The practice of Sulphur*). The marginal note is corrected in an old hand in the NLM copy. The epigram has been expanded by Chymeriastes to summarize the allegory of the "first Work." On Chymeriastes see the

171

Introduction and Appendix I.

dew of Heaven. Deuteronomy 33:13.

120. *the Red.* The second work or *rubedo.*

the occult begin to be made manifest. I.e., the invisible be made visible.

123. *Lullius.* See *Practica,* chapter 23 (*TC,* 4:157–60) "on the multiplication of our second sulphur."

124. ELIXIRIS COMPOSITIO (*Composition of the elixir*). Ashmole attaches this note to §125.

125. *fusile.* Meltable, molten.

129. TRES LAPIDIS HVMORES (*Three humours in the Stone*).

130. *flow forth without smoke.* A "signe" that the substance is fully oxydized.

131. PRAXIS ELIXIRIS [The practice of the elixir].

like Butter. Thomas Vaughan makes the same comparison in his Introduction to *The Chymists Key,* sig. A3v. He cites D'Espagnet shortly afterward.

133. ELIXIRIS MVLTIPLICATIO (*Multiplication of the Elixir*). The *Rosarium* describes this as an increase of the elixir's goodness, an increase in potency as well as quantity (sig. V3v).

the Prince of Luminaries. The sun, from whence flows all life and increase of life.

134. PRAXIS MVLTIPLICATIONIS (*The Practice of Multiplication*). Ashmole attaches this note to §135.

Lamell. Lamella; a layer, in this instance, of stone.

136. *Writings of Arnoldus . . . Lullius.* For Arnold's comments on the elixir, see *Liber Perfecti Magisterii* in *TC,* 3: 141–42 and *Rosarium Philosophorum* as quoted in Maier, *Symbola,* 325–26. For Lull's comments, see *Practica,* chapter 22 ("on the fourth operation, by which the elixir is made") and chapter 28 ("on the composition of the red elixir") in *TC,* 4:153–56, 166; also see his *Clavicula,* chapter 11 ("reduction of the white medicine in the red elixir") in *TC,* 3:301.

137. TEMPORA LAPI[DES] (*The Times of the Stone*). Expanded by I.C. Chymeriastes, who added a chart and commentary under the same title. See Appendix II for Chymeriastes' interpretation. Jung discusses this aphorism in *Mysterium Coniunctionis,* noting "the fixed, symbolical times" (154n319) and

"the coincidence of the apotheosis of the king with the birth of Christ" (356n380).

    Sic in se sua. Virgil, *Georgics* 2.402. D'Espagnet substitutes *sic* for *atque.*

138.   Quoted as an epigraph in Umberto Eco, *Foucault's Pendulum*, chapter 61. Eco emphasizes the secret tradition attached to the Golden Fleece. According to Rulandus, the three-tailed dragon symbolizes "Mercury when animated, for then it contains the three chemical principles—Salt, Sulphur, and Mercury" (357).

APPENDIX I
I. C. CHYMERIASTES' POSTFACE

Ashmole translates the preface by D'Espagnet's first Latin editor, which holds special interest in that it tries to reconcile the Hermetic philosophy and the Christian religion. In the French translation of 1651, Bachou identifies "Chymeriastes" as "an amateur in chemistry," using *amateur* in the positive sense of a lover of the art (366).

> *To the Lovers* of Hermetick
> Philosophy *I. C. Chymierastes*
> *wisheth prosperity.*

SUch is the difference between the Hermeticks living Philosophy, and the dead Philosophy of the Ethnicks; that the former hath been Divinely inspired into the first masters of Chymistry [the Queen of all Sciences,] and therefore may challenge the Holy Spirit of Truth for its onely Author; who by breathing where he listeth, doth infuse the true Light of Nature into their minds; by virtue whereof, all the darknesse of errours is straight-wayes chased away from thence and utterly expelled: but the latter may ascribe its Invention unto Pagans, who having left, or rather neglected the pure Fountains of Learning, have introduced false Principles and causes, (proceeding from their own brain) for true ones, to the great dammage of the Republique of Learning. And indeed what good were they able to do, upon whom the Day-Star of Truth, the Eternall Wisedome of God, the Fountaine of all Knowledge and Understanding *Christ Iesus* hath never risen? We cannot wonder therefore, that they have onely proposed old wives Fables, and foolish toyes, that they have introduced pure dotages, and innumerable inventions of lyes, whereby they have so bedawbed holy Philosophy, that we can find nothing of Native beauty in it.

But you will object that *Hermes* himself the Prince of Vitall Philosophy was an Heathen also, yea and lived before other Authors many ages, by whose decrees Philosophy in every place entertained, with greatest applause of almost all men, now flourisheth. But granting that, what followeth? This *Hermes Trismegistus* indeed was borne in an Heathen Country, yet by a peculiar priviledge from God he was one, who worshipped the true God in his life, manners and Religion especially; who freely confessed God the Father, and that he was the Creator of Man, and made no other partaker of Divinity with him: He acknowledged the Son of God the Father, by whom all things which are existent, were made; whose name because it was wonderfull and ineffable, was unknowne to Men, and even to Angels themselves, who admire with astonishment his generation. What more? He was our *Hermes* who by the singular indulgence and revelation of the most great and gracious God, foreknew that the same Son should come in the Flesh, and that in the last ages, to the end he might blesse the Godly for ever. He it was who so clearly taught, that the mystery of the most Holy Trinity ought to be adored, as well in the Plurality of Persons, as in the Unity of Divine Essence, in three Hypostases, (as any quick-sighted and intelligent man may gather from that which followes;) as that it can scarcely be found any where more clearly and plainly: for thus he: *There was an Intelligent Light before the Intelligent Light, and there was alwayes a cleare Mind of the Mind: and the Truth hereof, and the Spirit containing all things, was no other thing: Besides this God is not, nor Angell, nor any other Essence; for he is Lord of all, both Father, and God, all things are under him, and in him. I beseech thee O Heaven, and the wise worke of the great God; I beseech thee thou voice of the Father, which he first spake, when he formed the whole world: I beseech thee by the onely begotten Word, and Father containing all things, be propitious unto me.*

Now yee sons of *Hermes*, turne over and over againe, both night and day the Volumes of Heathen Philosophers, and inquire with what diligence you possibly can, whether you are able to find such Holy, such Godly and Catholick things in them.

Our *Hermes* was an Heathen, I confesse, yet such an Heathen as knew the power and greatnesse of God, by other creatures and also by himselfe, and glorified God, as God: I shal not spare to ad, that he far excelled in godlinesse most Christians now a dayes in name onely; and gave immortall thanks unto him as the Fountaine of all good things, with a deep submission of mind for his benefits received. Hear I pray, yee sonnes of Learning, whether God was as much conversant, and wrought as equally in the Heathen Nation, as amongst his own people, when he saith: *From the rising of the Sun unto the going downe thereof his name is great amongst the Gentiles; and in every place a pure oblation is sacrificed and offered unto my name, because my name is great amongst the Nations, saith the Lord of Hosts by his Prophet.*

Rub up your memory, I intreat you, and speake plainly; were not the *Magi* Heathens, which came from the East by the guidance of a Star, that they might worship Christ, whom neverthelesse the unbeleeving people hanged upon a Tree. Lastly consider well I beseech you, yee faithfull favourers of true Wisdome onely; from what Fountaine other Heathens besides *Hermes* have taken the Principles of their Learning. Weare and better weare out their Volumes with diligence, that yee may discerne them to refer their wisdome not unto God, but to attribute it, as gotten by their owne Industry. On the contrary cast your eyes upon the beginning of the admirable Tractate having seven Chapters of your Father *Hermes* concerning the Secret of the *Physical Stone,* and observe how holily he thinketh of God the bestower of this Secret Science: for *Hermes* saith: *In so great an Age I have not ceased to try experiments, nor have I spared my Soul from labour: I had this Art and Science by the Inspiration of the Living God only, who hath vouchsafed to open it to me his servant. Tis true, he hath given power of judging to rational creatures, but hath not left unto any an occasion of sinning. But I, unlesse I feared the day of Doom, or the souls damnation for the concealing of this Science; I would make known nothing of this Science, nor prophetize to any. But I have been will-*

ing to render to the Faithfull their due, as the Author of Faith hath been pleased to bestow upon me. Thus *Hermes*: then which nothing could have even bin said more wise, or more agreable to Christian Religion. And hence it is, that so many as are or have been of a more sublime wit and manly judgement, have imbraced the Living, Holy, and Divine Philosophy of *Hermes,* with all their Soul and Strength (rejecting that dead, prophane, and humane Philosophie of the *Ethnicks*) and have commended and illustrated it in divers of their Writings and Watchings. Of all which, that I may confesse ingenuously, seeing that I could never read unto this day any Writer more true, neat, and clear, then the Author of this Tractate, *Anonymous* indeed, yet one that truly deserves the name of an Adepted Philosopher; I have thought it worth my pains, and have deemed hereby to confer not the least favour upon the sons of *Hermes,* if I shall againe publish the hidden Work of *Hermetick Philosophy,* with the *Philosophers Signifer,* according to the intention of this most wise Author.

Farewell.

Notes

the Holy Spirit of Truth. 1 John 4:6.

where he listeth. John 3:8.

by whom all things were made. An echo of the Nicene Creed.

the Day-Star of Truth. 2 Peter 1:19.

There was an Intelligent Light. The Latin text appears in Maier's defense of Hermes; see *Symbola,* 11–12. Maier names Suidas, the Greek lexicographer, as his source; see the entry on "Hermes, ho Trismegistos" in *SuidæLexikon,* ed. Ada Adler, 5 vols. (1928–38; rpt. Stuttgart, 1967–71), 2:413–14.. The passage is not included in modern collections of Hermetic texts and fragments, but it recalls, e.g., *Hermetica* 1.31 and 13.9–10. Marsilio Ficino's commentaries on these two passages are explicitly Christian; see *Opera Omnia* (Basel, 1576), 1839, 1856. Scott regards the second passage as the only passage in the *Hermetica* that shows a possible Christian influence; see *Hermetica,* ed. Walter Scott, 4 vols. (Oxford, 1924–26), 1:12, and compare *Hermetica,* ed. Brian P. Copenhaver (Cambridge, 1992), 189. Garth Fowden notes the existence of a still more Christianized version of *Hermetica* 13, preserved in Syriac; see *The Egyptian Hermes: A Historical Approach to the Late Pagan Mind,* rev. ed. (Princeton, 1993), 34.

From the rising of the Sun. Malachi 1:11.

the Magi. The "wise men" of Matthew 2 (Greek *magoi;* Latin *Magi*).

In so great an Age. The opening sentences of *Hermes Trismegistus Tractatus Aureus de Lapidis Physici Secreto,* printed with anonymous *scholia* in *TC,* 4:592, 604, 605.The long *scholium* after the first sentence is devoted to showing that Hermes was a good Christian without knowing it. For an English translation of with commentary see Mary Anne Atwood, *A Suggestive Inquiry into the Hermetic Mystery,* 2nd ed. (Belfast, 1920), 105–6.

the Philosophers Signifer. See Appendix II.

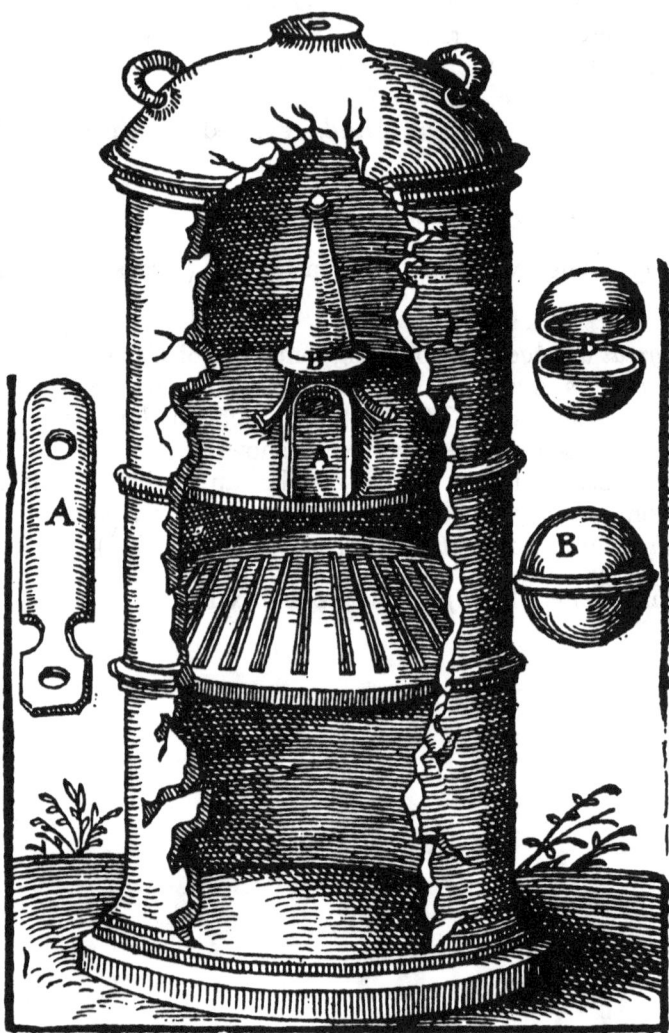

Figure 9.   Cut-away view of an athanor from *Theatrum Chemicum*, vol. 3 (1659).

252

The Signifer of Philofophers with the Houfes of the Planets.

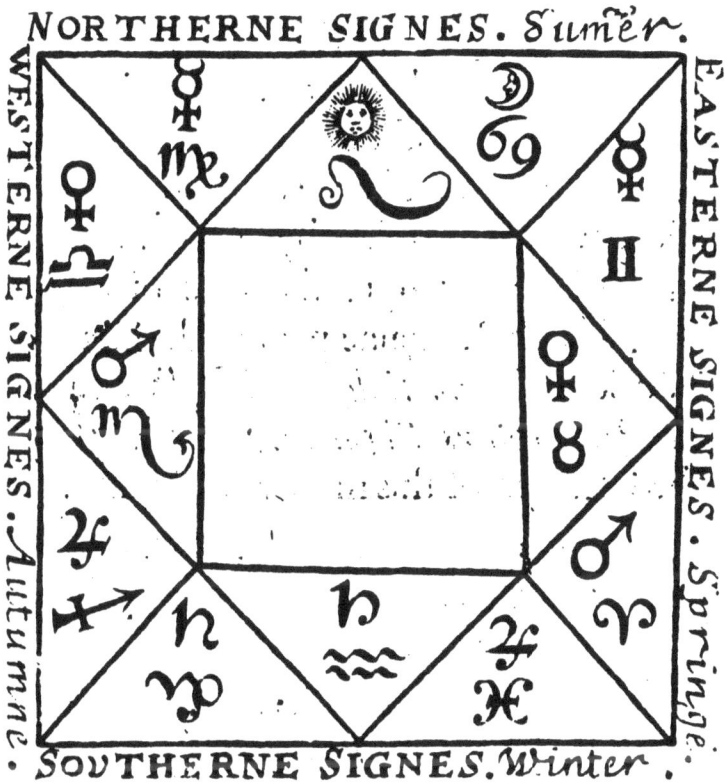

Figure 10. "The Signifer of the Philosophers" appended to *Arcanum* (1650).

APPENDIX II
THE TIMES OF THE STONE

"Chymeriastes"includes a timetable of the alchemical operation, based on the widespread association of the planets and metals, and thus of astrology and alchemy, the "superior" and "inferior" works of God. The table is mentioned in aphorism §137 and takes the form of an astrological chart (figure 10); it may be compared to Ashmole's own horoscope, which appears in lieu of his face on the frontispiece (figure 5). Ashmole's marginal gloss describes it as *"The Interpretation of the Philosophers Scheme."*

THE TIMES OF THE
STONE.

The Figure described is the Philosophers *Signifer.* To every Planet a double House is assigned by the Ancients, *Sol* and *Luna* excepted; whereof every one borroweth one House onely, both of them adjoyning. In the said Figure every Planet possesseth its proper Houses. Philosophers in handling their Philosophical work, begin their yeare in Winter, to wit, the Sun being in *Capricorne,* which is the former House of *Saturne,* and so come towards the right hand. In the Second place the other house of *Saturn* is found in *Aquarius,* at which time *Saturne i.e.* the Blacknesse of the Dominary work begins after the 45 or 50. day. *Sol* coming into *Pisces* the worke is black, blacker then black, and the head of the Crow begins to appear. The third month being ended, and *Sol* entring into *Aries,* the sublimation or separation of the Elements begins. Those which follow unto *Cancer* make the Worke White. *Cancer* addeth the greatest whitenesse and splendour, and doth perfectly fill up all the dayes of the Stone or white Sulphur, or the Lunar worke of Sulphur, *Luna* sitting and reigning gloriously in her House. In *Leo* the Regal Mansion of the Sun, the Solar work begins, which in *Libra* is terminated into a Rubie-Stone, or perfect Sulphur. The two Signes *Scorpius* and *Sagitarius* which remaine, are indebted to the compleating of the Elixir. And thus the Philosophers admirable young taketh its beginning in the Reigne of *Saturne,* and its end and perfection in the Dominion of *Jupiter.*

FINIS

Notes

Signifer. A signifier or, here, a system of signs. The "Figure" is an astrological chart (figure 10). As the commentary suggests, there is an appropriate time for each stage in the alchemical *opus.* The first work or *nigredo* is performed in the winter, the second work or *albedo* is completed in the spring or early summer, and the third work or *rubedo* is completed in the fall. Traditionally, the seven planets correspond to the seven metals, and they in turn to houses of the zodiac. If we remember the order of the planetary spheres, we can see that the scheme calls for the adept to descend through the spheres and then ascend:

sphere	planet	metal	signs	stage
seventh	Saturn	lead	Capricorn, Aquarius	black
sixth	Jupiter	tin	Pisces, Sagittarius	
fifth	Mars	iron	Ares, Scorpio	
fourth	Sun	gold	Leo	red
third	Venus	copper	Taurus, Libra	
second	Mercury	quicksilver	Gemini, Virgo	
first	Moon	silver	Cancer	white

If we visualize the constellations in a square with the spring constellations at the right, the summer constellations at the top, the
autumn constellations at the left, and the winter constellations
at the bottom, we can see a pattern of movement from Saturn in
Capricorn (the beginning of the black work) around through the
Moon in Cancer (the beginning of the white work) and the Sun
in Leo (the beginning of the red work). This chart is a synthesis of several rules of thumb in alchemy; see, for example, Titus
Burckhardt's chapter on "Planets and Metals" in *Alchemy: Science of the Cosmos, Science of the Soul,* trans. William Stoddart
(London, 1967; Baltimore, 1971), 76–91.

The chart should not be taken to mean that the planets are
necessarily in conjunction with the sun when it passes through
the houses they govern. Saturn passes from Capricorn into
Aquarius only once every twelve years, and Jupiter never passes
through both Pisces and Sagattarius in the same year. However,
alchemists seized on planetary conjunctions and oppositions as
opportune moments.

The chart is meant to be in the Lullist tradition, and a
marginal note on the "head of the Crow" refers the reader to
the account of the sublimation of mercury in chapter 49 of Lull's
Theorica (*TC*, 4:74–75). Ashmole changes the reference to chapter 39 (*TC*, 4:60), probably in error. There is a lesser known work
of pseudo-Lull on the light of mercury, which Maier discusses in
Symbola, 416; see item I.47 in Michela Pereira, *The Alchemical
Corpus Attributed to Raymond Lull* (London, 1989), 79.

the Philosophers. . . young. Latin *foetus.* See Ashmole's "Corollary" and his remark: *"Seek therefore the Philosophick Embryon
in its due place, and mature immaturity, and you shall know (as
Rosarius saith) our Stone is found created of Nature,"* in *Fasciculus Chemicus* (London, 1650), 14. He refers to the discussion
of the *tempus fœti humani* (time of the human foetus) in the
Rosarium Philosophorum (Frankfurt, 1650), sig. c4r.

APPENDIX III
ELIAS ASHMOLE'S POSTSCRIPT

Elias Ashmole explained his decision to append a translation of the *Arcanum* to his translation of Arthur Dee's *Fasciculus Chemicus*. The postscript (sig. A8r) follows his "Prolegomena," dated 1 March 1650.

POSTSCRIPT.

*A*Fter *I had writ this* Preface, *and committed it to the Press, I happily met with the following* Arcanum, *and perceiving it to suit so punctually with these* Chymical Collections, *for the solidity, likeness, and bravery of the* Matter *and* Form, *and to confirm some of those Directions, Cautions, and Admonitions I had laid down in the* Prolegomena; *and withal, finding it a piece of very* Eminent Learning *and* Regard, *I adventured to translate it likewise, and perswaded the* Printer *to joyn them into one* Book *which I hope will not dislike the* Reader, *nor overcharge the* Buyer: *And though in the* Translation *thereof, I have used the same solemnity and reservation, as in the former, and such as befits so venerable and transcendent a* Secret: *Yet I hope, that those who (favored with a propitious* Birth) *search into the Sacred Remains of* Ancient Learning, *admire the rare and disguised effects of* Nature, *and through their* Piety *and* Honesty, *become worthy of it, may finde* Ariadnes *thred to conduct them through the delusive windings of this intricate* Labyrinth.

1. *April*, 1650.

James Hasolle.

Notes

James Hassolle. An anagram of Elias Ashmole.

Prolegomena. Ashmole's brilliant introduction to Dee's *Fasciculus* is included in the English Renaissance Hermeticism series, volume 6.

Ariadnes *thred.* The labyrinthine imagery recurs frequently in alchemical texts. See the author's epistle in *AHP* and the note on labyrinths.

APPENDIX IV
INSTRUCTIO DE ARBORE SOLARI

The *Theatrum Chemicum* includes an *Instruction on the Tree of the Sun* (6:163–94). The tract offers "The Most Faithful and Pleasant Instruction Taken from the Manuscript of an Anonymous French Philosopher, in which the father declares to his son everything that is necessary for the composition and preparation of the great stone of the wise, contained in ten chapters." The Latin translation by Dr. Johann Jacob Heilmann is placed immediately before *The Elucidation of the Art of the Transmutation of Metals,* by Christopher of Paris, the second book of which concerns "The Practice of Science of the Philosophical Tree" (228). Christopher is described as "an imitator of the old philosopher Raymond Lull" (195), and the *Instructio* is also in the Lullist tradition. Christopher's appendix is dated 1545 (288), though the work has been dated as late as 1580.

The *Instructio* is sometimes attributed to D'Espagnet, and is cited under his name in C.G. Jung's *Psychology and Alchemy,* trans. R.F.C. Hull, 2nd ed. (Princeton, 1968), 502; the attribution is uncertain, as Jung's editors note on 255. Jung returned to the *Instructio* at the end of his career, for he was struck by the tree imagery; see *Aion,* trans. R.F.C. Hull (Princeton, 1959), 154. Although it seems a parallel work to D'Espagnet's rather than a work of his, it is sufficiently interesting to warrant a brief summary.The section headings are as follows:

Preface. Of what things these instructions treat.
I. Of the divine and natural differences between the great work of the wise and the damnable vulgar art of the alchemists.

II. Of the planting of the golden tree.
III. Of the virgin earth of the philosophers.
IV. Of the water of the wise, which irrigates the philosophers' tree.
V. Of the differences between mercury of the wise and of the vulgar.
VI. Of the extraction of the precious seeds of metals.
VII. Of the natural calcination.
VIII. Of the coction of the philosophical earth.
IX. Of the coction or maturation of the seed of gold and mercury, and of the living fire of the philosophers.
X. Exhortation of the true use and the excellence of the great work of the philosophers.

The author tells his son that, after many days of deliberation, he has decided to reveal the mystery of nature and to do so without parable or a false copiousness. In his old age, he will write for his son only, what his son should not communicate to his Cabalistic friends: how the water of fire or fire of water produces an *oleum auream,* which, truly, is the ancient *aurum potabile.* Our work is simple, and therein lies the difference between the true and the false alchemy. As God made everything out of nothing, the false alchemists make nothing out of everything.

True alchemy is the hidden part of philosophy and the most necessary part of physics (or the investigation of nature) and so is called the flower of wisdom *(flos sapientiæ).* The work of alchemy is that of planting and transplanting the solar and lunar trees (chapter 1). If one observes a grain of wheat, giving off heat as it putrefies, one has a good analogy for the work of alchemy. For the alchemist farms *terram nostram* (chapter 2; see *Psychology and Alchemy,* 255). He finds the virgin earth everywhere, in valleys and meadows, in caves and mountains: a natural niter, the rose of heaven, the *viscosa materia ex qua Adam fuit factus*—briefly put, the virgin earth whose father is the sun and whose mother is the moon. In a passage that Jung studied closely, the adept compares the mercury of the wise to the little fish known as the remora, which swims in the sea yet attaches itself to the object of its desire (chapter 3; see *Aion*, 140–42, 154–55). Turning to the water itself, he quotes Virgil and Ostanes (chapter 4). Then he comes to the center of his attention, the nature of argent vive. This was a crucial point for Lullist alchemy, and for D'Espagnet's *EPH*, 44, 45). The living silver is derived from "our" mercury, not that of the "vulgar," and the living gold *(aurum vivum)* from "our" sulphur. "Our" mercury is the opposite of the vulgar substance, not cold and moist on the outside, but hot and dry (chapter 5). "Our" sulphur impregnates it, after which the *aqua vitae* of "our" heaven waters the seed (chapter 6). This sulphur is the prime matter of metals and the living gold. A salt of nature is produced from this sulphur, "which is the metallic seed, the generating spirit, or the first matter of all things of nature" (chapter 7) as well as the "heavenly water of life" (chapter 8). The tract closes with comments on the final union of sulphur and mercury (chapter 9) and the "mystery of the universal medicine" (chapter 10).

It seems unlikely that D'Espagnet wrote the tract, but if he did, we may be able to guess about his relations with his son. When the Danish alchemist Olaf Borch interviewed Étienne D'Espagnet, he found that the son shared the father's passion for Lullist alchemy, but could not leran whether he had learned the father's secrets. *De Abore Solari* offers a tempting possibility; for it shows the father's satisfaction in having passed on the secret to his son and his concern that the son use the *donum Dei* wisely (chapter 10).

There are several important parallels, in addition to Christopher's work on the "Science of the Philosophical Tree." A tract "On the Secret of All Things," written by an anonymous Frenchman in 1447 and printed in Nicolas Barnaud's *Triga Chemica* (*TC*, 3:774–83) includes a sort of genealogical tree of metals. Maier worked out the details in his *Symbola*, 343–46, and noted mythological associations with Isis and Osiris and with Beya and Gabritus. Like the philosophical tree of Christopher of Paris, the design that Maier used is based loosely on the Lullist memory system. Flamel's *Philosophical Summary* has an even longer account of the alchemical tree (*HM*, 1:143–45). Sendivogius' "Parabola seu Ænigma," appended to the *New Chemical Light,* likens the alchemical tree further to the golden boughs in Virgil's underworld and says its fruit is "living, sweet" (*TC*, 4:458–90). The "Parable or Enigma" offers a time frame for the alchemical work under the reign of Saturn, and thus resembles the "Times of the Stone" appended to later editions of the *Enchyridion* (see Appendix II).D'Espagnet knew the books of Maier, Flamel, and Sendivogius. The tradition continued with a treatise "Of the Tree of Life or the Solar Tree," by an author born in 1651; see Sylvain Matton, ed., *"De l'arbre de vie ou de l'arbre solaire* par Jean Vauquelin des Yveteaux," *Chrysopoeia* 1 (1987): 209–84.

GLOSSARY

The *lematta* here do not include allegorical terms like crow, eagle, and swan, which are discussed in the commentary.

ablution: Washing, most often with water; cleansing, purifying.

alembic: A still, specifically the upper part, seated on the **curcurbit**: Sometimes written "limbec," it derives from the Arabic word for the Greek "ambix."

amalgam: An alloy, combining mercury and another metal, usually gold.

analysis: Breaking up into constituent parts.

aqua fortis: "Strong water"; a corrosive liquid such as nitric acid, a powerful solvent.

archaeus: The healing virtue hidden in all things and peculiar to each; a Paracelsian term.

archetype: The idea on which the creation is based, the prototype.

argent vive: Quicksilver or "living silver"; mercury.

athanor. The furnace used to keep a substance at a steady temperature for a long period.

balsam: The sustaining moisture, also called the radical humidity; thought to be present in all living things though associated most often with the resin from trees. "Catholical balsam" is the moisture sustaining all life.

bath: A warming place of water, sand, or ash.

bolt's head: A long-necked flask used in distillation.

calcination: Reducing a substance to ashes or powder; purifying by fire, burning.

chaos: The unformed matter from which the elements were made; also called "hyle."

choler: Bile, thought to cause anger; a hot and dry bodily humor.

circulation: Continuous distillation, causing a liquid to evaporate and condense repeatedly.

cohobation: Redistillation. Reuniting the distilled liquid with its dregs in preparation for further distillation.

condensation: Conversion from vapor to liquid.

congelation: Solidification, freezing.

copulation: The act conjunction, union, bond.

corruption: Decomposition, putrefaction.

curcurbit: A vessel curved at the bottom and hermetically sealed at the top; so called because it resembles a gourd.

decoction: Digestion, effected through repeated distillation and condensation; extraction of the essence.

demission: Making a substance less pure, as in the "degradation" of gold.

digestion: Breaking down a substance by heat or solvent to purify it, as an animal processes food; separating the pure from the impure, the nutrients from the faeces.

distillation: Purifying a liquid in a proces of evaporation and condensation, effected by heating and cooling in a still.

dragon: The sulphur or salt that attacks impure mercury.

drye water: A viscous fluid; mercury.

eagle: Vapor, often produced during distillation. The number of eagles in a flock indicates the number of times a substance must be distilled.

earth: One of the four elements, characterized as cold, dry, and solid; a metallic substance worked on to form the philosophers' stone, for example, the red "Adamic" earth.

egg: The vessel containing the philosophers' stone; by metonymy, the stone itself.

elements: The four elements (fire, air, water, earth) from which all other substances are created and into which they can be broken.

elixir: A medicine, an agent of transmutation; in alchemy, the medicine of long life, the agent for turning metals to silver or gold.

evacuation: Release of impurities, emptying; removal of contents.

extraction: Removal of a substance by means of heat or a solvent.

exuberation: State of agitation, abundance; literally, overflow.

ferment: A substance that works on metals as yeast works on flour; an agent of change, leading the work into the next stage; in modern parlance, an enzyme, a catalyst.

first matter: The first formed matter, produced by light entering the dark chaos; hyle.

fixation: Turning a spirit into a body, a vapour or liquid into a solid; making it non-volatile.

homogeneal water: A homogenous fluid, having the same consistency throughout; a solution.

hyle: The first matter; the Greek word for "timber," generalized to include any matter, especially building material.

inceration: "The combination of moisture with a dry matter to the consistence of soft wax by gradual blending" (Rulandus).

inhumation: "Burying in earth"; placement in a warm substance, often horse dung, in order to provide a gentle heat or "natural fire" for distillation.

Jupiter: Tin.

leprosye: Impurity in metals, especially evident on the surface.

liquefaction: Converting to a liquid, by use of heat or a solvent.

macrocosm: The "great world," the universe; corresponding on the large scale to the microcosm on the small scale.

medium: A middle quality or degree between two extremes.

menstrum: A liquid medium or solvent; so called on the analogy of the menses as they were thought to feed the foetus.

Mercury: Quicksilver; the counterpart of sulphur, symbolically female.

microcosm: The world in miniature, especially as the world in summarized in man.

Moon: Silver.

multiplication: Increasing the quantity of a metal.

phlegm: A cold and damp bodily humour, opposite choler. The watery residue from distillation. philosophers' stone: The ferment or agent of change *par excellence*, used to change

193

common metals into silver or gold.

projection: Casting the philosophers' stone onto a substance; the final step in transmuting base metals to gold.

putrefaction: Dissolution, decomposition; symbolic death.

quintessence: A fifth substance, in addition to the four elements; thought to be concentrated in the heavens, but present in all things.

radical moisture: The sap of life, present in all living things. Also called the radical humour or balsam.

rarefaction: Making less dense; causing to evaporate.

rebis: "Two things"; the alchemical androgyne, the union of male and female, sulphur and mercury; a puzzle, but not a "rebus."

reduction: The process of returning a substance to a simpler form, often through deoxidation.

salt: With mercury and sulphur, one of the basic substances; thought to give body, permanence; not necessarily sea salt (NaCl)

salt nature: The quintessence, which helps to bind the elements together.

Saturn: Lead.

seed: The part of a vegetable or animal that may be sown in the proper soil in order to reproduce it; Latin "semen."

separation: Removal of the pure substance from impurities.

solution. Dissolving, dissolution; any dissolved matter, a liquid; also called a "homogeneal water."

Soul of the World: The connection between the world's body and spirit, similar to the concept of Mother Nature; the principle of order.

spirit: The portion of a substance that escapes the flames, as the spirit of sulphur or the spirit of mercury.

stone, philosophers': The wondrous substance that will transmute base metals to gold; it can purify and rejuvenate all that comes into contact with it.

sublimation: Vaporizing a solid substance by heating it.

sulphur: The counterpart of mercury, symbolically male; also spelled as "sulfur."

sublimation: The art of converting a solid to a gas; the converted substance.

Sun: Gold.

temperament: The proper mixture of elements; the condition that results from the blend.

ternary: The threefold state; composed of three elements.

tincture: A coloring agent, usually liquid; a pigment.

Venus: Copper.

virgin's milk: The water of mercury, purified and separated from the sulphur of the mines, used as a solvent.

vitriol: A caustic liquid prepared with sulphur, now known as sulphuric acid (H_2SO_4); a conjunction of sulphur with another metal, now known as a sulphate.

INDEX OF BIBLICAL, CLASSICAL, AND HERMETIC REFERENCES

All citations are to commentary on the numbered aphorisms.

Biblical References

Classical References

INDEX

209

Index

Sécret, Franqis xvn1, liv1
secret, philosophers 94, 97
seed 11, 36, 65-66, 75, 98-99, 122, 152, 193
Sendivogius, Michael xxiii, xxiv, xxviii-xxx, xlv, xlix, liv, 97, 141, 142, 143, 144, 150, 156, 161, 189
Senior xlvi, 97, 122, 123, 161, 171
separation 15, 120, 130
Sercy, N. de xlii
Shakespeare, William 155
signatures 75, 151
signs 110
Silberer, Herbert xxxiii, liv
sky 155
Socrates 141
solution 95, 109, 111-12, 119, 122, 169, 193
son, philosophers' 100
Sorel, Charles xxvii-xxviii, xlix
soul 5-6, 58-59, 139; world 11-12, 18, 35, 138, 193
Spenser, Edmund 138
sperm 110
spirit xxxv, 33, 95, 129, 151, 153, 192; world 11-12, 15-17, 71
Starkey, George liv
stars 27, 31, 82-84, 107, 156
Stavenhagen, Lee xlviii-xlix, 161
stone, philosophers' 97, 99, 103, 107-13, 120, 127, 130, 170, 175
Styx 9
sublimation xxxv, 33, 49, 51-52, 95, 103-4, 106, 122, 127, 149, 193
Suidas 176
sulphur xxxv, 30, 55-57, 79, 99-101, 103, 105, 107-10, 122, 126-28, 144, 162, 163, 165, 166, 167, 169, 171, 172, 181, 188
sun (sol, gold) xxxvii, 17-20, 31, 35-36, 51, 55, 60, 69-72, 84-85, 99-102, 107, 110-12, 114, 117-18, 121, 128, 130, 162, 165, 172, 181, 192; *see also* gold
swan 108, 126, 167
Swift, Jonathan xxviii-xxix, xlix, 135-36
Szydlo, Zbignew lv, 145
Tagus xiii-xiv
Telesio, Bernardino xxii
Telle, Joachim xxxix, 161
temperament 146, 193
ternary 156, 192
terra adamica 113, 169
Thales 14, 140
Theatrum Chemicum xxxiii, xlv-xlvi, 136, 185
Theophrastus 145
Thomason, George xxv

For Product Safety Concerns and Information please contact our EU
representative GPSR@taylorandfrancis.com
Taylor & Francis Verlag GmbH, Kaufingerstraße 24, 80331 München, Germany